EXPLODING CINEMA

1991 - 1999

Exploding Cinema 1991 – 1999

artists collectives becoming knowledge

Stefan Szczelkun

Originally a doctoral thesis at the RCA completed in 2002 with the subtitle: 'culture and democracy'

Routine Art Co 2021

ISBN 978-1-870736-04-6

Acknowledgements

Thanks firstly to the members of Exploding Cinema who feature on these pages and who helped in so many ways. I hope that this simplification of their work is a still validation of what they have achieved, and they will forgive me for many omissions.

Thanks to my supervisors A.L.Rees and Jeremy Aynsley for their interest, feedback and respect. And to my examiners Theo van Leeuwen and David Curtis for their close reading and incisive criticism of my text.

Thanks to Professor Jerry Palmer at London Guildhall University for help with my interpretation of Jurgen Habermas' Theory of Communicative Action.

Thanks to Vanda Playford and Emmanuelle Waeckerle for setting up the RCA research students group.

Thanks to friends and family for their help or encouragement during the research period 1997 - 2002. These people include Chloe Bowles, Chris Saunders, Mathew Fuller, Simon Ford, Micheline Mason and the Monday group, Emilyn Claid and Howard Slater.

Thanks to my colleagues at CARTE, University of Westminster for their encouragement in the last nine months of writing up, especially Helen Coxall.

The Tomato Bursary paid for my first two years of tuition costs at the RCA. Other help for material expenses and fees came directly from the School of Communications at the RCA. Thanks for this to Professor Dan Fern, Head of Department.

A grant towards the cost of books was given at an early stage from the London Guildhall University staff development fund. A grant towards finishing expenses was awarded by CARTE, University of Westminster.

The doctorate thesis was bound in an edition of six A4 copies. The printing and binding costs were sponsored by CARTE, Centre of Art Research, Technology and Education, University of Westminster. (no longer in existence) One copy given to the British Library.

An additional single sided copy was bound by the Royal College of Art library.

CONTENTS

ABSTRACT

Using several research methodologies I try to capture a rich body of information about this open artists collective from different angles. The idea is to record the cultural and political value of this groups activities. Artists collectives are barely represented in mainstream knowledge so I saw this work as being of use in the future study of such complex groups. There is a focus on the distinction between oral and literary or mainstream culture.

My assumption was that collectives offer a platform to all those excluded from the establishment's cultural platforms.

New Introduction 2021

My 1993 book *The Conspiracy of Good Taste* revealed to me the profound extent of the repression of the newly formed urban working class culture in the UK,with particular focus on the first half of the C20th. It suggested some principles by which culture is used as a component of class oppression. Part of the picture formed by this study was that working class culture has been relatively invisible as Knowledge. That is from the literary world's publications and in archives that tend to reflect the interests of the dominant classes. This contributes to the low status of many working class cultural formations.

My next written work (1996) was to extend *The Conspiracy of Good Taste* into an examination of why this was so, using the work and testimony of Herbert Gans, Richard Shusterman, Diane Reay, Valerie Walkerdine, Simon Evans, Georgina Boyes, Duncan Reekie and Emmanuel Cooper. This was unpublished but is now available from the Internet Archive. https://archive.org/details/WcCulture1996

Within the broad idea of working class culture I saw the open artists collectives, that had been a part of my life, as a particularly valuable formation that contradicted the individualism, exclusivity and elitism of high culture. They had not been documented in Thames & Hudson art books. In fact, they were barely even studied or adequately archived. I felt that I might be able to take on this task with a single example and in that way explore the problematics of representing such collectives and look at some possible remedies. Apart form their ideological exclusion they do present generic problems to adequate representation due to their dynamism and complexity.

The Exploding Cinema, was a short-film showing collective with many characteristics of the working-class habitus. I decided to make an intensive study this artists collective as a participant observer in the framework of a doctoral study.

The work was also intended to provide a model study to fuel and validate future studies of open artists collectives. With this in mind I thought it important to be transparent about my research methodologies, although some readers might find this a little technical. These research methods were intended to go beyond the limitations of the subjective viewpoint of a single eye-witness account and to go deeper than the bare information afforded by surviving archival records.

One reason I didn't pursue the publication of my 2002 PhD at the time was because a book can contribute to a symbolic termination and Exploding Cinema was a going concern. As I write this twenty years later Exploding Cinema is still a going concern and with a largely new collective. So this study does not represent what happened in the last 20 years or so.

Chapter 3, which is mainly a chronological account of venues, is a bit pedantic in the later stages. It is, in effect, a collection of archive record cards which might not be the most exciting read for those not involved. For instance, I list every single major venue even when some of them left very trace. So this part of the book is what it is, an archival record. I suppose the point is to show the huge diversity of spaces that were used as cinemas in this period.

My original theoretical considerations, linking this specific site of cultural dissemination with ideas about the part cultural works play in democracy, is reduced here to a short appendix. The theory chapters included in the 2002 thesis can be consulted in the original or found on my Blog.

So this book has a slightly split personality in trying to be a detailed archival record as well as being a polemical book. It records the first decade of Exploding Cinema but it also aims to point towards future possibilities of art production within the context of an emerging democratic culture led by working class artists.

As I made the book I included more and more reproductions from the many programmes from the shows that I had attended. These are there for visual stimulus but it occurred to me that the texts provide a contrasting prose style that is more true to Exploding culture, than my written attempt to have the subject 'taken seriously'. I should also point out that these illustrations extend beyond the 1991 - 97 period of the original research.

Stefan Szczelkun 2021

Chapter 1

Introduction (2002)

In the packed back-room of a pub the place is dark, except for a crossfire of light coming from a multitude of projectors. The crowd of two to three hundred are yabbering furiously at the back, swigging beer, checking out the book and zine stalls from the 121 and 56a bookshops and the nutsoid offerings of mail art superstar Mark Pawson. Down at the front the people are attentive to the main film. It could be a short documentary someone's made on their pet hamsters; a paranoid sci-fi horror about the underground trains in London really being giant flesh eating worms; or some cataclysmic animation, with unnamable debris seething into chaotic life. There is undoubtedly some compere berating or coaxing the crowd between each film.

Mathew Fuller 1995

The Exploding Cinema can be described as a hybrid fusion of projection, performance and social space. It began in South London in late 1991.

Architectural spaces, transformed with the use of slides and loop film projections are used as an environmental context for a programme of short films and video. A 'master of ceremonies' sets up a dialogue with the audience and introduces the films. He or she encourages filmmakers who are present to speak or be questioned. The audience are even encouraged to make films themselves and invited to show them at future Exploding events with a promise that nothing will be rejected. By thoughtful programming this inclusive process of soliciting material, along with a printed programme and the work of members of the group who provide slides and film loops to decorate the space, results in a varied and lively programme which regularly attracted lively audiences of 100 - 300.

In its first nine years it put on more that 100 events and showed the work of over 1000 filmmakers. It was unfunded, and supported itself entirely from low admission prices of £3 - 4.

Previously I had played a central or active role in other similarly inclusive groups. These included: Portsmouth Artsworkshop (1969-71), The Scratch Orchestra (1971-73), New Dance Magazine Collective (1977-79), The International Mail Art Network (1981-1986), Brixton Artist's Collective (1983-87), Bigos, Artists of Polish Origin (1986-92), Working Press: books by and about working class artists (1987-97). It is my involvement with these artists groups that have led to this thesis.

My foundational assumption was that democracy, in the sense of people inclusively participating in evaluation and decision making, is intimately connected to the processes of culture. I understood culture as the processes by which we evaluate, think and adapt to changing circumstances using all of our senses and the cultural expressions of those senses.

My central research questions were: Did these open groups of cultural producers, which often flourish on the margins of society, play an important role in cultural processes of adaptation and re-evaluation? Why are they, for various reasons, under represented within our accepted body of knowledge? Of course, there have been movements, networks and groups throughout Art history, which have been well documented. We think of Dada, Fluxus and Situationism as large and important collective sites of cultural production which have been widely influential. However, it was my perception that there were problems in the historicisation of the groups I had been part of and that, as a whole, our perception of art is an activity by a gifted individual rather than as a process which is often much more social. When I visited the Tate Library around 1996, looking in their catalogue for 'artists collectives', the only thing I could find was a study of the St Ives Group initiated by the Tate itself.

To begin to remedy this lack I wanted to sketch a historical account of one such artists collective, Exploding Cinema. And to do this using well thought out methodologies which should allow this account to be legitimated by the accepted practices of communications studies and social science.

My core research method was to be of 'participant observer'. To this end I joined the group in 1997 and made my research from this insider position. The Exploding Cinema did leaves traces of its history in written and published materials, as well as on video and audiotape. This allowed me to construct a conventional historical account through the summary and analysis of these materials referenced to the primary source documents, which I hoped to archive with the British Film Institute. Additionally I used content analysis and semiotics as methodologies with which to further analyse this material. The existing archival material has been augmented from 1997 from my own participant observation logbooks and a set of focused oral history interviews. From the sum of these materials I have narrated an open-ended and multi-layered historical account of this group's activity.

I will begin with a chapter that examines the interwoven historical film provenances that preceded Exploding Cinema. I start off by looking at early cinema. Exploding Cinema has empathy with the music-hall background of early film and with the oral nature of its discourse. I take this line further by discussing amateur film, as a cinematic expression of oral culture and then go on to outline some specific influences of amateur film on the US underground of the late Fifties and early Sixties. The US underground films were shown in Britain in the mid-Sixties and inspired the formation of the London Filmmakers Co-op. Politicised film workshops also appeared as autonomous production companies. Finally, I make a case study of a film club started by a later London Film-makers Co-op member that immediately preceded Exploding Cinema and has some of the same characteristics - David Leister's *Kino Club*.

Next I give an account based on the archived materials. This translates a mass of raw data into a readable account without rendering a banal simplification. As I have said, I joined the group in 1997. At this point the style of the narrative changes from a straight transcription of archive materials to being enriched from my own notes and observations. I also made occasional use of the oral history transcripts to supplement the information given by the archive records.

This section is not intended to be a history of British collective film endeavours. Notable amongst the omissions are the Workers Film groups of the Thirties, and the Film Society movement, which started in 1925 but was almost a mass movement in the Fifties. Members of the Exploding collective knew about all these precedents.

My theoretical considerations, with a preliminary discussion of the meanings of the key terms culture and democracy, has now been moved to an appendix. A particular understanding of culture as a process of 'total qualitative assessment' is taken as central to understanding of Exploding Cinema. Culture is then described as the agreements reached through the fundamental expressions of human sense media along with the meta-code of verbal language. The main argument here is that culture is fundamentally about reaching agreements and it is such agreements, based on ongoing qualitative assessments, that provide the ground of any formal democratic discourse. This assumes an understanding of the permeability between the categories of culture and politics.

Having considered the historical provenances I now move into the core of the study with five chapters on the different methodologies of data collection and interpretation I have used.

The Exploding Cinema keeps its own records simply within the domestic environs of its members. To use these records for the production of knowledge they need to be gathered together, ordered and brought into the public realm, so they can be referred to by future researchers who would undoubtedly bring their own interpretations to the primary source material.

Once these materials were collected, I analysed them using two methodologies. First, simple Content Analysis was used to measure attendances at meetings as recorded in minute books, and these numbers were used to chart the ebb and flow of participants. A similar approach of measuring the regularity of involvement of filmmakers was taken from the information supplied by the collected programmes. A semiotic analysis was then applied to begin to understand the complex use of imagery in the programmes and how this conveys a group ethos.

The next two chapters deal with the two methodologies I used to collect new data. A reflexive consideration of Participant Observation uses my observer notes, written up in logbooks, to discuss three key aspects of the group. These key aspects were: open access, independence and its financial base, and questions of group identity. Finally a chapter using the transcripts of individual interviews are used to show how the value and practices of Exploding Cinema can be seen reflected in the biographies of the participants.

Unlike the London Filmmakers Coop of the Seventies the films shown at Exploding Cinema were not archived or made available for distribution. I did not study the films directly for two main reasons. Firstly, because for the diverse films shown at Exploding Cinema to constitute an entity by the context that the Exploding Cinema has given to them, it would be necessary to have this context mapped out before setting out to understand the films. This thesis does this contextual work and should provide strong grounds to argue for the need to collect, archive and analyse this body of work. Secondly, before this study could occur there is considerable recovery and archiving work required. Within this milieu there are rarely multiple film prints and in the early period the 'show copy' may be a spliced edit of the actual film shot. A film print being too expensive. There are similar problems with video. The material shown has often been projected from VHS copies, which were considered unsuitable as archive material by the BFI, at that time. Obtaining a satisfactory archive copy of the edit master tape is often a complex and expensive process both technically and administratively. With up to one thousand films to archive, this was a project well beyond my resources.

Chapter 2

Historical background

I want to trace the cinematic precedents of Exploding cinema, but at the same time problematise any attempt to understand Exploding Cinema through the framework provided by normative film histories. Some readers will know this stuff and are invited to hop, skip and jump.

Exploding Cinema relates closely to a history of 'underground film', which must itself be understood in relation to wider counter-cultural traditions. Even then, we need to further extend the frame of reference beyond literary discourses. Exploding Cinema seems to relate to fields of 'amateur' and 'oral' culture more than some of its precedents in underground film.

An Underground is by definition outside and in opposition to a mainstream or dominant culture. This mainstream is briefly defined before I look more closely at the resonance of early film to the Exploding Cinema events. I then move on to the Post WWII underground film culture in the USA describing the relevant features and indicating how this counter culture crossed the Atlantic to Britain in the mid-Sixties. The effects of this counterculture, which persisted through the Eighties, are sketched. This leads on to an immediate precursor of Exploding Cinema: David Leister's Kino Club, which forms a short case study. The field of amateur film is then considered and related to the US underground and to Exploding Cinema.

Early Cinema to Exploding Cinema

Contemporary mainstream cinema tends to be defined by its basis in a scripted drama and an industrial mode of production. Its power is inevitably related to the way it concentrates a massive amount of resources on the production of a sequence of images.

On the other hand film and video production isn't inherently expensive and films that are made outside of this commercial system will often have a different form, content and aesthetics to the mainstream. The huge capital investment into mainstream film inevitably guides the overall content within the realm of its own (financial) interests, interests which are admittedly dynamic, heterogeneous and in contention with each other. The apparent diversity of the mainstream is all contained by a form which is based on the entertainment of a passive and atomized audience.

In spite of the heterodox content, the general effect of feature films inevitably protects the ideology of the financial backers. Films made outside this system are able to articulate ideas, which are either of no interest to the mainstream or are critical of the mainstream, in ways that are not possible within that system. Not all ideas of relevance to the human condition are commercial or entertaining. Most people would probably agree that the interests of capital could never be congruent with the totality of human interests.

It is worth noting that the industrial mode of cinema did not appear fully-fledged. The early days of cinema shared much in common with those areas which are now outside the mainstream. Magic lantern shows preceded the invention of film by three hundred years. It was popular in those places of entertainment without fixed seating that preceded the purpose-built music halls of the latter nineteenth century. The sense of variety, the Master of Ceremonies, the magic lantern slide projections, the drinking audience, the raucous atmosphere, even the occasional technical chaos, seem to be reflected in a typical Exploding Cinema show.

Film found a popular audience from its

earliest days in the late 1890s. Films were made by entertainers and showmen and shown in empty shops, local halls, amusement arcades, itinerant peepshows, circuses and particularly fairs and music-halls.

> In that shuttered shop there was a miracle to be seen for a penny, but only twenty-four could enter at a time; there wasn't room for more.
>
> Low & Manvell 1973 p36

The Empire in Leicester Square was one of the first three music hall venues to show films in 1896. After a while the fad for simple cinematic illusion wore thin in the Music halls but stayed firmly established in the fairgrounds.

> Films spread quickly through the fairs as they did through music halls. They first reached Hull Fair, for example, in October 1896, brought there by one of the original fairground showmen of the cinema, Randall Williams.
>
> Michael Chanan 1996 p140

At the peak of fairground popularity there were six cinemas at The Goose Fair in Nottingham. It was the fairgrounds that bridged the gap to the respectable picture palaces of the 1920s with their increasingly sophisticated narrative product.

As a low-art form of entertainment with a popular audience, cinema had a set of aesthetic values somewhat at variance with those of high art and more in line with those of other working class cultural traditions. These were values that highlighted comedy, spectacle, improvisation and spontaneity, a somewhat explicit sexuality, satire, 'irony in the face of establishment homilies' and a general vulgarity.

> Pantomime had given rise to a certain type of theatrical clowning which was later carried to a very high level of perfection in the cinema by such artists as Chaplin, while acrobatic clowning like Buster Keaton's evolved rather more from circus traditions.
>
> Michael Chanan 1996 p130

The Middle classes had, however, already realised the power that cinema had to inculcate the values of respectability into the working man and 'rationalise' his entertainment.

> Calls for the best writers often accompanied demands for the uplift of the industry. The trade press urged the motion-picture industry to legitimate itself by producing scenarios penned by well-known writers of fiction and drama. In 1908, for example, the *New York Dramatic Mirror* ran an article by a 'moving picture enthusiast' who strenuously advocated 'a higher class of authorship in the construction of plots or stories' as opposed to the 'crudest kind of drama' and 'the lowest kind of slapstick comedy'. Which had hitherto dominated, stories produced by higher-class authors would appeal to the 'more intelligent class of spectators'.
>
> Uricchio & Pearson 1993 p46

It was not until 1904 that the first purpose-built 'electric palaces' made their appearance. Movie production rapidly expanded in the early 1910s. By 1925 the USA had nearly a thousand opulent 'picture palaces' - no longer simple halls but buildings of spectacular opulence which rivalled the best theatres. By this time the total cinema audience in the USA had reached 50 million a week with the industry increasingly centred on Hollywood.

> As a form of popular mass entertainment, cinema-going did not generally find favour among the middle class until the advent of sound systems heralded the era of art deco picture palaces in the 1930's.
>
> Maryanne Gomes 1998

The inception of sound and the increasingly large sums of money to be made also brought the mass-market film firmly under the control of the capitalist class. They imported their own literary culture by way of the script and the aesthetics of good taste. The Charlie Chaplin films of the 1920's can be seen as a bridge to this period. His influences from working class culture and music hall met a Hollywood system which had an ethos of respectability and taste, and a literary heritage and articulation. Commercial cinema continued to evolve through the 1930's and 1940s with an increasing reliance on scripted dramatic narratives. The content was respectable and sentimental. The illusion of narrative continuity was smooth. There was a sheen of perfection which created an increasing gulf from the self-generated activity of artists and amateurs. This dominance was maintained until there was a resurgence of the vulgar in the form of B-Movie horror, rock and sex genres in the consumer explosion of the 1950's.

Through the 1920s and 1930s, as the Hollywood Star/glamour system was evolving, there was a lot of experimental activity in Europe, from the agit-prop cinema trains of the Soviets to the abstract film experiments of artists, to the worker film groups in England. From the time of the Futurists, artists quickly saw film as a new medium of experimentation. The inventiveness of this experimentation supplied a stream of innovation to the commercial mainstream.

The North American Underground

The rise of Nazi fascism made many of the leading European artists and film makers flee to the USA. Following this, the centre of cultural gravity shifted decisively from Paris and Europe to New York and the USA. This was not just an effect of the World War, the size of the unified North American free market economy made it a magnet of irresistible force.

The west coast of America was as energised as the east. Hans Richter was organising his 'Art in Cinema' screenings in San Francisco in 1946. These brought together the "avant garde classics together with new films by the US'ers Maya Deren... and Kenneth Anger" (Rees, 1999, p.55). Deren and Anger together with a recent Lithuanian immigrant, Jonas Mekas, were soon to be the leading lights, both writing and shooting a *New American Cinema*. This was to merge with the literary Beat Movement of the late 1950s and find an extraordinary moment of radical popularity with the youth led counterculture of the 1960s and early 1970s.

> I saw the best minds of my generation destroyed by madness, starving hysterical naked,
>
> dragging themselves through the negro streets at dawn looking for an angry fix,
>
> angel-headed hipsters burning for the ancient heavenly connection to the starry dynamo in the machinery of night.
>
> Allen Ginsberg, Howl, 1956

A key moment for the underground filmmaking community followed a general outrage at the rejection of the Stan Brackage film *Anticipation of Night* by one of the key art cinemas in 1960 (see David Curtis in James 1992 p256). The gathering of filmmakers at the funeral of Maya Deren then led directly to the founding of the Film Makers Co-op, led by Jonas Mekas, in 1961. This was an autonomous artist-run library and distribution centre for experimental film. Mekas's *Film Maker's Co-op* had a policy of no selection and it was this powerful egalitarian gesture that was copied by the London Filmmakers Coop of the late Sixties and Seventies and echoed in a new form by the Exploding Cinema of the 1990s.

Jonas's co-op was unlike any that had preceded it in its unique undertaking to distribute all works submitted to it, and not engage in individual promotion. The 1989 catalogue is remarkably matter-of-fact about this: 'Film-Makers Cooperative is a film-rental library open to any film-maker wishing to place a print on deposit for a rental fee set by its owner. Films are accepted without any viewing or evaluation by the Cooperative' (Film-Makers Cooperative Catalogue 1989). This is neither an invitation, nor a caution. The benefits of doing things this way are assumed to be self-evident.

David Curtis in (James 1992 p255)

Filmmakers also wrote their own catalogue notes and took the major part of any rental income. Mekas's reviews in *The Village Voice* were important. His fulsome encouragement catalysed a rapid growth and opening out of experimental filmmaking activity. There was no equivalent of either The Village Voice, or a champion critic like Mekas for the London underground filmmakers of the Nineties. And this difference may be crucial in their relative cultural impact.

In 1930 Hollywood had developed *The Motion Picture Production Code* (The Hayes Code) which controlled the decency of films and was meant to protect the American Public from its own base desires. Underground culture laid siege to this hypocritical middle-class morality. In the face of this activity and mounting consumer pressure the code was finally abandoned in 1968.

The counter culture which arose from the massive anti-Vietnam War movement of the 1960s embraced the Beats and became infused with a revolutionary anarchist ideology and an associated lifestyle - an ideology which was articulated in cultural terms rather than political. Left politics in the USA had been destroyed by *The House of un-American Activities* - when the repressed bounced back twenty years later it was in cultural rather than political form.

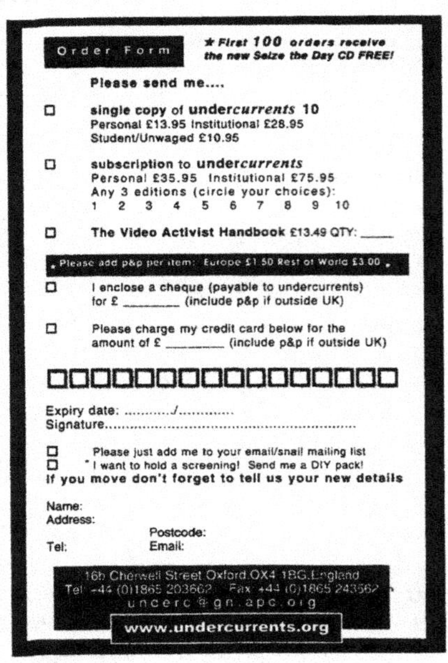

WHY NO SELECTION?

The process by which you the audience decides what you like or don't like in an open public forum is crucial for direct democracy.

Rather than film club impressarios and curators doing the selection beforehand on the basis of their own taste, which is inevitably not a live consensus. It means that the nth% of times that they are wrong and reject what the audience would recognise as of value, destroys the possiblity of innovation through open collective evaluation. These delicate morsels which are kept out by those arbiters of taste are likely to include the most unexpected viewpoints. As Foucault pointed out, change happens through breaks with accepted practice - often artist driven, non-professional, quirky obsessions which seem to head against the current.

This is argument enough — quite apart from no-rejection being an effective way of encouraging more filmmaking — and especially by the more vulnerable outsiders who will often give up if rejected on their first tentative outing. When their 2nd or 3rd film will often not only pay-off but probably say something new and valuable.

Policies of rejection are anti-creative, anti-outsider and anti-democratic. Boycott the filmgroups who want to play gatekeeper! Every filmmakers has a right to show their film in public.

Exploding Cinema calls on all underground filmmakers to picket the film festivals and expose their selectors to endless abuse.

British Counter Culture and Film (1960s-70s)

In Britain a post-war baby boom and economic growth fuelled a new phenomenon - youth cultures. The American myth of freedom, choice and opportunity already dazzled Europe through such icons as Hollywood stars, cars, Levis, Coke, Playboy and Elvis. American style was an integral part of the authenticating of this appeal. Preceded by jazz and blues, imported American underground films were first shown in London in Bob Cobbing's *Better Books* basement in 1966 (Rees 1999 p77)

> What was striking to us - an audience of artists, writers, journalists and filmmakers - was the assumption evident in all these films, that making cinema could be a first-person-singular affair, and that film language could be as complex and highly individual. In contrast, The films supported by the one source of public funding at the time, the *British Film Institute's Experimental Film Fund*, were very definitely cinema shorts, stepping-stones to cinema features.
>
> Curtis 1992 p258

From Better Books the screenings moved to *The Arts Lab* in Drury lane where they were programmed by David Curtis. This was where I saw many of my first underground films in 1968. The group that met through these screenings formed a London Filmmakers Co-op on the Mekas model.

British TV was also 'swinging'. Shows like Elkan Allan's '*Ready Steady Go!*' and Mike Hedges '*New Tempo*' art programme had already been reflecting the new energy with their camerawork and editing style as well as content. Progressive directors like Ken Loach were directing the '*Wednesday Play*', and others like Paul Schlesinger and Ken Russell experimented with the new medium of television. This is the home environment into which the members of the Exploding Cinema collective were raised.

By the end of the Sixties two types of film groups were emerging in England: the London Filmmakers Co-op offered access to production, distribution and exhibition resources with a large open membership; the other type, the 'film workshops', were collectively run film production companies and mostly overtly political.

The formation of *The London Filmmakers' Co-op*, in 1966, occurred in the context of a burgeoning counter culture in which communes and collectives were springing up everywhere. This was also close to the time of the Paris Uprising and the Workers' Control Movement. A central theme in British radical culture was the idea of 'getting control of the means of production'. If this could be achieved it was felt that liberation would follow. In the light of this general ethos it is not surprising that the LFMC quickly put a lot of effort into getting its own processing and printing equipment.

However 'avant garde' soon replaced 'underground' as the preferred label for Co-op output. Many of the filmmakers, who had come out of art rather than film schools, moved away from the ethos of underground film with the development of a formal 'structural materialism' in the Seventies. These were formal and abstract experiments with the material and technology of filmmaking - that fore-fronted film form as content in classic modernist fashion.

The move to 'Structuralism' was not seen at the time as quite the retreat into a safely disengaged abstraction that it can look like in retrospect. This was meant as a radical move to rethink things from the ground up. However, Structuralism institutionalised well. On the other hand the informal and politically abrasive underground style did not breathe easily in academic environments and in the UK did not find the discursive support that Jonas Mekas had provided for the US underground. The revolutionary moment of 1968 - 72 had perhaps simply passed.

In contrast to the co-op model the more political *Film Workshops* were focused on the collective production of films (although equipment was lent on an ad hoc basis). Examples of the workshops are *Cinema Action* (1968), with its mobile cinema and agit-prop productions, and *Amber* (also 1968), a community film outfit based in Newcastle. Before Margaret Dickinson's book *Rogue Reels* (1999) little had been published about these important political film groups whose members were mainly lower middle and working class.

> Cinema Action were making films and showing them on the hoof. The people who were making the films were presenting them. It was a very exciting thing. They'd put films on in factory canteens, in bus depots, in dock areas, in shipyard assembly areas, in locations where there were masses of workers. The UCS film was shown at Plessey's during the occupation there. It's very evocative when you've got films thrown as a huge projection against a big factory wall showing images of workers in struggle!
>
> Dave Douglas interviewed by Dickinson 1999 p273

Before being absorbed by institutions like Channel Four TV, the film workshops had challenged the lack of discourse amongst the conventional cinema audience. Many of the workshops put a high priority on film as a catalyst for discussion and debate. This comes up at least seven times in the interviews which make up the last third of *Rogue Reels*, but this is not analysed by Dickinson.

The live film event in which tens of people meet, collectively witness a film, and then talk, tends to be valued by most filmmakers as less important than glamorous mass media exposure in which hundreds of thousands of people are addressed as individuals or family groups in domestic isolation. But this assumption should be challenged. The value of live fora in the democratic regeneration of culture may be key.

Dickinson's attention and arguments in the first two sections of her book concern the relation of 'independent' filmmaking to the state. It seems like a sad history of recuperation in a period that was full of high idealism and grassroots cultural activity. According to Dickinson the lively radical scene was gradually institutionalised during the late Seventies and Eighties. The filmmakers' own organisation, the *Independent Filmmakers Association* (IFA) that formed in 1974, was sandwiched between the BFI and the workplace demands of the ACCT, the union of the film industry. This process of institutionalisation of independent film production was completed by the formation of *Channel Four* television.

> By 1984 many IFA activists were working for, or funded by, the new Channel Four... Within ten years the IFA and nearly all the other structures which promoted oppositional filmmaking were gone.
>
> Margaret Dickinson 1999 p62

Al Rees took a more positive view of its influence:

> The IFA was ... a fragile and temporary union, strung together by partisans for a 'free cinema' from the many different and contradictory if overlapping directions: Cinema Action, the Co-op, disaffected media workers, parts of Screen, film students, documentarists and artists in loose alliance. Astonishingly its impact lingers on. Many of its members were to spread out into the wider mainstream, transmitting its key values into documentary television: John Ellis, Anne Cottringer, Simon Hartog, Keith

Griffiths, Rod Stoneman.

AL Rees 1999 p92

The demand for access to a 'TV channel of their own', however much it seemed a radical democratic demand (and utopian dream even!), seems to have been a major factor in the decimation of oppositional filmmaking. The process of institutionalisation may have started with the BFI's funding of the IFA in 1977; or earlier when *The First International Underground Film Festival* was held at The National Film Theatre in 1970. An anonymous article in *Cinematics 3,* July 1970, describes this festival as an 'establishment take-over bid, disguised as an open screening.'

Margaret Dickinson gives a brief but detailed analysis of how the professional practices of television undermined the collectivist spirit. It is within the details of such professional demands that hegemony reasserts itself. As an example of these mechanisms Dickinson points to the extra research and editing time required by experimental production which was excised by the fiscal control of schedules demanded by television's professional practices. The result was that "most of those who started off with radical objectives found themselves drifting towards industry norms" Dickinson 1999 p.78

An Underground Cultural Resurgence: the Eighties

During the Eighties artists continued to experiment with video but these works were shown almost exclusively in galleries. There was also a waning community video movement which included the survivors of the Seventies workshop movement who had not been absorbed by TV. There were also some newcomers like *Despite TV* which was established in the East End of London in 1983 by Mark Saunders and others.

Cinema audiences had been falling with the saturation of colour TV ownership and had reached the nadir of their decline around 1984. The home video recorder, introduced in 1981, was owned by seventy percent of UK/US households by 1991. The introduction of the VHS video cassette, video rental shops and the growth of a diverse 'take away' food industry helped to revive an ailing feature film industry and launched a new commodity, the pop video.

At the same time a new underground youth culture arrived in the field of electronically generated music. This was the advent of the home studio. Sophisticated sounds could be created in a spare room or garage and the first forms of this music, known as 'Garage', emanating from Chicago, made an impact on the music scene. Britain soon developed her own strand known initially as *Techno*. By the end of the Eighties *Electronic Dance Music* had achieved world-wide dominance, leaving the major record companies standing. It bypassed the music industry with self-organised giant raves at which the 'tunes' would be played by highly skilled DJs direct to thousands of ravers. Co-ordinated on the day by mobile phone this potent DIY music culture inspired other art forms to revitalise themselves from the grass roots. *The Cooltan Arts* initiative in which Exploding Cinema began came about in this context.

As the Nineties unfolded the 'raves' were gradually institutionalised and brought to heel by a new licensed club scene. Some of these, like the *Ministry of Sound,* became big players in the global music business. But remarkably the music was only partly commercialised. The autonomous productive base of the home computer and the direct patterns of production and consumption established in the early stage, still support a mass of home-produced music.

The rave scene did support some cinematic activity. The need for optical stimulation at raves gave rise to a renewed interest in light shows. The 'VJ' would mix two video streams into a single projected image. Some clubs also showed cult movies and found footage and caused some of the younger audience to get interested in the by now mythic Underground Films of the Sixties. What home computers could do for sound by the mid to late Eighties (using Midi) they couldn't do for video and film until the late Nineties.

I face an epistemic problem here. The history of film tends to be told as a specialised and almost hermetic practice. This may be the reality on the industrial level, imposed by division of labour and the need for specialisation, but it is not true on the level of popular consumption/ production. The underground is, if anything, a holistic culture which caters for all the senses, each of which correspond and are often in flux.

In order to understand what happened to film in the Eighties we have to take a wider view of culture. At the same time that raves were sweeping the country there was a revival of live performance particularly in the area of stand-up comedy. This resurgence of live urban culture had a direct influence on the Exploding Cinema format. This can be traced through the activity of a single filmmaker and cinema organiser - David Leister.

David Leister's Armchair Cinema & Kino Club

US born filmmaker and performance artist David Leister came to live in London in 1979. In 1984 he joined the London FilmMakers Coop.

Leister has been collecting 'found' footage since he was 15. His archive comprises some 600 films, particularly 16mm educational and industrial training films dating back to the 1940's, which now have a kitsch/utilitarian aesthetic. Of course often these films are low-budget productions and share a 'production value' based empathy with underground productions so there is a sympathetic affection for these films alongside the comedy of bygone cultural mannerisms.

He had shown some of these found films 'for laughs', at *The Comedy Store* in 1984, for which he would splice up a 20 minute compilation reel. Around the same time he showed similar material at Tony Allen's comedy club *Hecklers Graveyard*, and at a similar cabaret show at the Notting Hill Tabernacle. The comic potential of these types of films has since become part of British mainstream comedy being used by Simon Day and David Baddiel, parodied by Harry Enfield and most recently by Harry Hill with whom Leister has worked.

The first of his own shows was around this time (1984) at an early experimental music venue which is still running weekly events in The Sussex Pub, London N1 called the *Klinker* or *Cooler* club. He then started *Armchair Cinema* which ran three or four evenings in the basement of a restaurant called *The Dining Room* in Borough Market near London Bridge. The Dining Room was run by the filmmaker William English and his partner Sandra. These shows were based on screening of the archive fortified with extracts of work by classic experimental filmmakers such as Joseph Cornell and Rene Clair. This programme was interspersed with his own 'works in progress'. I went along to two or three of these shows and enjoyed the congenial cafe atmosphere which was a welcome break from the often pretentious atmosphere at the Film Co-op showings in Camden. This relaxed cabaret context for showing short films had been influenced by the prior explosion of alternative comedy venues. It was here that the cutting edge of improvisation and spontaneity could be found in the early eighties. This was a context that cinema had lost sixty or seventy years before when it moved from the fairs and variety theatres to purpose-made cinemas with fixed seating.

The Kino Club, which Leister started in 1987, was based at the Two Eagles pub in Kennington. Improvising musicians such as Ian McLachlan, Dave Fowler, Parney Wallace, Aleks Kolkowski and Steve Noble were invited to collaborate live with experimental and found films. David Leister, who was the MC and projectionist, would interject live comments along with inevitable heckling from the audience. The show was live in every sense. These continued twice a month for two years and then continued monthly in the Two Eagles and other pub function rooms into the early Nineties.

A review in *What's On*, December 19th, 1990 by David McGillivray describes a typical Kino Club:

> Live music might be provided by an accordionist and violinist playing Argentinean Tangos. A telephone may ring on one of the candle-lit tables and whoever picks up the receiver may be asked to identify three Beatles songs played in the style of hotel lobby muzak; the prize for correct answers might be a pomegranate or a tin of processed peas. On the other hand there might be a slide show or a look-a-like contest.

A later review by Jonathan Romney in 1993 describes the Kino Club as 'a cross between Andy Warhol's Exploding Plastic Inevitable and Olde-Time Music Hall'. In the same article Leister is quoted as saying:

> I'm very much a member of the low-tech society. To me film is about the machinery and the clattering, the sound of the projector becomes an instrument.

> Jonathan Romney, New Statesman & Society
> 30-4-93

These shows recreated an aspect of the silent cinema era in which films would regularly be accompanied by live music.

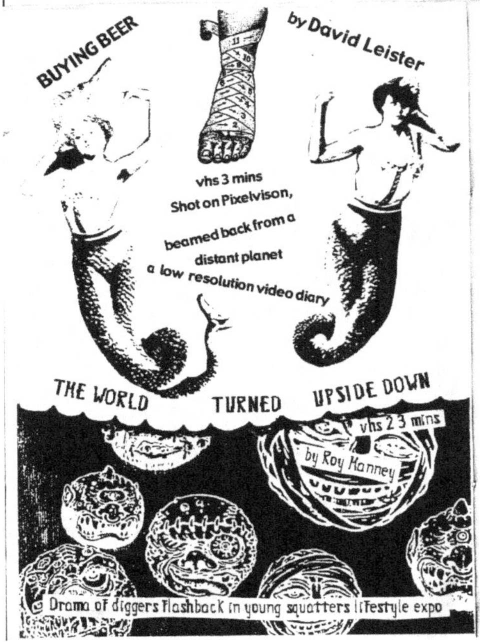

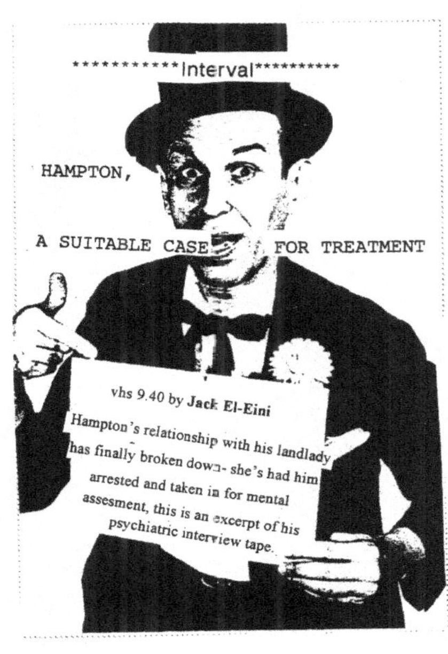

Leister also saw Kino Club as a meeting place for artists working in lens-based media, as well as an entertainment. At the time he was also taking part in other events and offering his extensive collection of projection equipment and technical expertise for low cost hire.

Specific similarities between Leister's events and the later Exploding Cinema are: the use of MC; live music/action with film; cabaret mix of film and performance; an emphasis on love of film technology rather than video; audience participation games; Cabaret audience layout; humour valued over a high art mind-set; use of found footage; the idea of it being the focus of a network; eating and drinking (and even talking) whilst consuming film; incomplete blackout; use of 'décor' slides.

Exploding Cinema was different in several important ways: Exploding espoused open access to filmmakers which changed the nature of the content; it was run by an open collective, which, amongst other things, allowed a higher level of energy, manifest in more intense décor; could fill larger venues with a more raucous energy; it produced a collectively made photocopied programme; didn't focus events on live music with film as a matter of course; had a more counter-cultural stance.

Although it is true that these differences give rise to completely different events, some key aspects of Leister's events are precedents to the form of Exploding Cinema and were probably an influence. According to Leister it seems that several of the key people who were to form Exploding Cinema had attended Kino Club events. Of course it is also likely that the people who formulated the Exploding model had also been to similar alternative comedy clubs to Leister and in a broader sense had been exposed to similar broad cultural influences. As I have pointed out underground culture tends to be a dynamic unity with trends flowing between media and people in unpredictable ways.

Leister can be seen as a minor second wave of influence from the USA which was quite different to the Sixties underground. What influences could he have brought from the US apart from a certain informality? One thing is the US institution of drive-in cinema. Here was a cinema in which you could eat, drink and talk with friends. The black-out was not complete so that immersion that is typical of mainstream cinema was not in place.

It should be pointed out that Leister was still, in 1999, listed as part of the crew of *Halloween Society* for their short film promotions at Notre Dames hall in Leicester Square. Halloween Society played a central part in the later Volcano! film festival. So Leister was still a part of that network. His collection of projection equipment was also an invaluable practical resource to a much wider field of short film culture.

Influences flow in both directions and Leister has shown regularly at the Exploding Cinema. Up to June 1998 Leister showed five films in Exploding Cinema Shows. Since then he has shown another one or two. For example: *Buying Beer* shot on Pixel Vision, a very low definition toy format, was shown on 27th August 1999.

He also continued to do his own shows. On Saturday 28th November 1998 I visited his Kino Club at *The Lux Cinema* in Hoxton which had the title *Sell Out*. This was a showing of commercial footage from his archive. Typically examples of these were an odd Seventies beer 'commercials' or a Forties film made to recruit retail assistants for a department store. They were introduced or followed, and very occasionally accompanied, by wry comments from Leister. Although this was ostensibly shown for laughs the material was droll at best. The museum atmosphere at the Lux, with its flat floor and hard upright chairs was hardly that of a comedy club of the Eighties. The audience was almost startlingly different from an Exploding Cinema audience. They all seemed rather well fed and nicely groomed, with no charity shop fashion in sight.

The US underground was fairly well documented at a time when Americana held Europe in thrall. If you rejected Disney, Coke and Levis you could still worship at the throne of the glamorous US rebels from James Dean to Kenneth Anger. My sense is that Exploding Cinema's attachment to this underground and its English version in the Sixties and early Seventies, is at least partly an attraction to beatnik negation. A negation that is glamorous and has a legitimate history. But another influence that is just as important, as you get to know the Exploding Cinema, and is quite the opposite of glamorous, is that of amateur film. If we use amateur in its best sense, the Exploding Cinema collective are amateurs in that they work without pay. They do it for love. And they follow other traits of lower class amateurism: they contradict good taste; they deny the importance of the professional standards; they are open access rather than selective.

Amateur film/ Home Movies - Underground film

Amateur work had not generated a great body of critical discourse at the time of my research. Archives were recent, crude and for the large part unstudied. I decided to describe the field of amateur film enough so we could see its influence on the underground in its US phase and in its later phase in London. Along with the evidence from my oral history interviews of the collective I hope to show that the cultural field of amateur film is important to a critical contextualisation of the Exploding Cinema.

So, very little analysis had been made of the home movies now in public archives.

I will sketch a history of amateur film before going on to discuss a selection of actual films. One of the few books devoted to the history of amateur film at the time was Patricia Zimmerman's *Reel Families, A Social History of Amateur Film* (1994), which deals exclusively with the USA and is mostly based on the study of contemporary discourses about what amateur film *should* be, rather than studies of the relevant primary materials to see what people actually made. I will first summarise some general aspects of her history that are relevant to my later examination of British amateur films.

> Amateurism... emerged between 1880 and 1920 as the cultural inversion of the development of economic professionalism.
>
> Patricia Zimmerman 1994 p7

Amateurism had connotations of spontaneity, anarchy, the whimsical, the personal and subjective. It stood for freedom, daring, mental agility and pioneering invention. In other words, it could be a positive label for all that was excluded by the corporate professional work structure. As leisure increased and became more widespread the meanings practically reversed and amateurism came to signify poverty of technique, lack of sophisticated aesthetic judgement and intellectual incoherence. But both meanings have continued to have currency and are evoked at different times for different purposes. Hand-held stills cameras had been introduced in 1888 and their use differentiated amateur from professional photographers. As picture making became available to all, for the first time, it was considered by many to be a democratic art form compared with the upper class associations that clung to painting.

The technical development of movie film from its early beginnings c1892 happened alongside the development of corporate industrialisation. Kodak had practically achieved a monopoly of

35mm film as early as 1910. This drove other film manufacturers to seek an amateur market but this did not take-off until the standardisation of the 16mm format in 1923. Amateur film making then took off in earnest through the Twenties. However, 16mm filmmaking was still a hobby for the relatively wealthy.

Within the broadened sphere of amateur production the positive significations of the films produced were: authenticity (being less mediated); an expression of nostalgia and emotion; the personal and intimate; spontaneity and immediacy; a direct relation with its subject (lack of illusion); an interaction with its subject; non-narrative (often using an unedited real-time chronology). These themes converged in a practice that, according to Zimmerman, typically occurred within the private domain of the bourgeois family. The idea of the 'home movie' was born in this context.

Following the consolidation of the 16mm standard in 1923, colour was introduced between 1928 and 1937, and the cheaper 8mm standard came out in 1932 boosting amateur camera sales. But the potential popularisation of cine culture afforded by the 8mm format was restricted by the effects of the depression.

In World War Two the military use and development of 16mm for mobile documentaries and surveillance, opened up methods of filming that had until then been derided as amateurish. These hand-held camera newsreels using only natural lighting were gradually incorporated by the mainstream film industry as a style that signified the real.

In the post-war period there was a dramatic rise in consumer wealth and a subsequent expansion of suburban living. In 1952 six percent of US families had movie cameras, but this was to rise rapidly throughout the Fifties and Sixties as cheaper 8mm foreign cameras flooded the market. These

cheaper imported cameras forced the mighty Bell and Howell out of amateur camera production in 1962.

Amateur film on 8mm was denigrated by film writers of the time as substandard, worthless and unwatchable. Amateur film-makers were at the same time constantly told to imitate Hollywood's narrative conventions. This advice was in practice, as Zimmerman notes, consistently ignored (1994 p74). Amateur 8mm film technique seemed to be typified by some of the following methods:

1. Shooting whatever takes your fancy within the constraints of a limited footage. (A reel is just under 4 minutes). This tends to make the filmic relation to perception transparent.

2. Flash panning and fire hosing. This means the camera follows eye movements. The effect achieved is anti-illusory fore-fronting the presence and spontaneous will of the camera operator.

3. Lack of planning. Having chronological rather narrative intentions. Recording 'experience' as an end in itself.

4. No editing; which gave a sense of an unmediated record or memory and made the production process transparent.

One of the values of home-movies is as an ethnographic record, with the crucial difference that they are unmediated self-representations. In this sense home movies can also be works of art in their own right. This was widely recognised by the US underground in the Fifties and Sixties.

In the early Thirties European experimental films, such as the works of Sergei Eisenstein and Dziga Vertov, had begun to circulate in the USA and their relevance to amateur practice had not gone unnoticed. Eisenstein's process of montage was closer to amateur practice than the script orientated professional Hollywood movie. The Second World War then left a deal of second-hand army-surplus 16mm equipment, that contributed to a flowering of independent cinema in the post-war years.

In this period many US artist filmmakers used amateur film language and there was an explicit cross-fertilisation between the two areas. The most important of the film artists in the Fifties was *Maya Deren*. She argued for the aesthetic values of amateur film and clearly saw her own practice as coming from this area even if her intentions were more formal. The American underground films of the Fifties and Sixties were widely circulated around the USA and imported to Britain in the late Sixties, as I have noted above. The prominent Lithuanian writer, organiser and film-maker *Jonas Mekas* took energetic leadership of this movement after Maya Deren died in 1961, articulating his support of the amateur aesthetic both in his own films and through his prolific writings.

> Mekas's home-movie aesthetic posits memory as the interpretive faculty of his films. Memory restores the possibility of community and inscribes the individual in history, reforming the ties that bind groups together.

Jeffrey K. Ruoff in, James 1992

Many other influential experimental U.S. filmmakers of the time, such as Bruce Conner, Stan Brakhage and Ken Jacobs, were also working in a home movie style. More recently in Britain David Larcher, Derek Jarman, Andrew Kotting, Paul Tarrago and Mark Saunders come to mind, although there has been no Maya Deren or Jonas Mekas to theorise their relation to amateur film practice.

Unfortunately, Patricia Zimmerman's pioneering book stops short in the early Sixties, before amateur filmmaking became most widely available. This period, which started with the first use of 8mm in the 1930s, reached a high point with the introduction of the superior quality 'Super 8' format in 1965. By this time many second-hand cameras were becoming available, so filmmaking had become accessible even to those on low incomes. By the early Eighties home movies were also being made with video camcorders and shown on television sets. Movie making on 8mm film with shows projected in the home were in decline, although Super 8 continued to be used by artists and enthusiasts.

The ritual of projection in the darkened living room within a familial gathering was an important part of the whole culture. Although this event had a sense of occasion, marked by its association with the cinema show, the audience was likely to be much more active providing a running commentary on the footage shown and reinforcing its communality through vocalised commentaries about what was depicted on screen.

What did 'ordinary' people record on film in this period? Material is being collected in the British Regional Film Archives but the study of this material is in its infancy.

> British Regional Film Archives value amateur footage highly - we have two thirds amateur and one third professional in our holdings.

Maryann Gomes, curator, N.W. Film Archive
(memo 21-6-99)

Archived home-movies in Britain are scattered between the Regional Film Archives, local history and oral history archives, folk custom archives and so on. Early amateur filmmaking was rarely affordable to working class people. Going by the holdings of the NorthWest Film Archives it was only in the 1950's that working class people could begin to afford to make home movies.

It is commonly assumed that home-movies consist solely of poorly framed images of children and animals in suburban domestic settings or sandcastles being washed away by the tide, intercut with over-exposed bodies. These subjects are common but there is much more besides.

The Home Front through Home Movies was a series of five 20 minute programmes made for Channel Four Learning and available as a video. 'It shows the ways in which ordinary people filmed everyday life in Britain and Germany during the years 1939 - 1945'. Thirty nine subjects are covered by the amateur footage, of which only three are the domestic, holiday or wedding footage that had been associated with 'home movies'. The rest are of public scenes of children's activity, the Blitz, resistance, work and recreation, victory celebrations and defeat. Apart from being a model of how home-movie footage can be used to construct history it also shows the diversity of material that was being filmed at this time.

As a detailed case-study of the later Super 8 period I went to a showing at *The Museum of the Moving Image* in London on 10th March 1999 entitled *Home Truths*. The films shown were mostly from the later 'democratic' period of 8mm filmmaking and included a few movies of families and holidays but also more diverse material. *Home Truths* was the seventh annual showing of home-movies at the Museum. Stephen Herbert had selected the programme from the archives of a network of amateur filmmakers and their descendants. He had decided to mainly show work made before 1975. The 8mm and Super 8 films shown at MOMI depicted important aspects of working class life and culture during this period.

The lack of critical discourse on amateur film means that many of the images can easily be dismissed as having little value once they had left the localised context in which they were made. The connections to their historical significance are difficult to draw spontaneously, even if a viewer is knowledgeable about the relevant history and regional culture.

My own brief study suggests not a poverty of aesthetics but of economic resource and of critical support for working class culture.

From the viewpoint of the professional film standards, home movies can seem discordant and stark. But they also evidence a truth and emotive insight which is unique to this genre. As Dan Snipe has pointed out the presentation of history on video as a documentary genre has the advantage of being closer to subject it represents. But it should be remembered that home movies can also be *an art form* in their own right, even if it has been a neglected one. They should not be seen simply as a convenient source of illustration to be plundered for clips. This would miss much of their value.

I have noted that home movies exist in public archives and that much more research needs to be done to explicate their significances and aesthetic value. It seems that they may not be just about the suburban nuclear family, as has been commonly assumed, but also contain a much wider range of subject matter. They still need to be made more easily accessible through digitisation. As this is done the area could be seen as a legitimate part of film history with unique significations and aesthetic values.

Exploding Cinema do not often show 'home movies' as such - it is just that the films shown could often be understood better as an extension of the amateur idiom as art form, rather than being compared with professional films. The references made to the amateur idiom in the programme images and the references in the oral history interviews make it clear that these connections are not simply being imposed by me. A typical Exploding Cinema programme will include both professional style films (eg 'calling card' films made by film students) and and more home-made varieties.

In short we can see that the Exploding Cinema is a product of Mekas' inclusive model of a film collective, but remodelled by the cultural and technological forces of the Eighties and Nineties alongside quite British traditions of 'underground' and live culture which can be traced back through music hall to the medieval fairs. The vector I have traced from the new comedy circuit through Leister's Kino clubs to Exploding Cinema is not meant to suggest a unicursal determination.

Cultural developments are complex and rhizomic.

The critical reframing of Exploding Cinema as relating to the field of amateur production, as much as to the literary, academic or professional definitions of film, will hopefully allow its value to be seen more clearly. The application of conventional 'film theory' would reveal little of such phenomena, which exist largely outside of such frames.

"The Rushes Soho Short Film Festival - a selective affair that exhibits a few dozen shorts out of the more than 700 films the organisers received this year...."

Evening Standard 27-7-2000.

Rushes Festival finished today, the 4th August. Exploding Cinema would like to show the 666, or so, films they rejected. For them short films are just calling cards in a race to make glampap. Let's have a film culture that comes out of home movies, and builds cultures of resistance. Film that is a common form of record and expression. A real democracy needs a democratic culture.

Reject the greed machine, join the collective, learn from our mistakes and then organise your own group. Our own megafest, Volcano! is just around the bend - in November. Start to organise your own show, your own culture, your own world, now.

To show your film or get involved telephone Jennet or Paul on 7732 8058 or Thomas on 8671 9422

The Reckoning, Nathan Hughes   VHS PAL   15mins

Duty Nickels, Richard Morbid & Jessica Kibel VHS NTSC 12min

So Macho, Kev Winser   VHS 1.45min

Ilford Ninja, Ben Slotover & Paul Eliott VHS 6min

20 minutes interval

Stretch of the Imagination, Rene Eyre VHS   6mins

Wrap Up, Sophie Critchlow VHS15mins

3x3, Initiation & Where's Judy?   Nichola Schauerman   VHS 2 + 2 + 3 mins

Little Voices that Speak from a box, A Montage of Memories,   Joanne Wallace VHS NTSC 16.5 mins

20 minutes interval

Maldoror trailer,   edited by Colette Rouhier 5mins or so

Kingdom Protista, Andrew Kotting VHS 5mins

10 Vincible Ninja   Dave Fanning   VHS   9 mins

London Underground trailer, David Charles Bailey 1.45

Scouts Honor, Steve Hall & Cathce Wilkins VHS NTSC 15mins

Chapter 3

A Narrative history of Exploding Cinema

Archival Methodology

This chapter uses a classic process of historicisation based mainly on paper archival documents. Exploding Cinema had three areas of archived records: minute books; programmes from each show; electronic documents and associated paper files. I typed a summary of key texts from the minute books, which was made available to collective members. The texts in paper and electronic format were copied and bound as an archived record. The programmes were laboriously scanned page by page [almost 700 scans] and copied as Tiff and Jpeg files to CDR discs. From the programmes a catalogue of all the filmmakers that had been listed in the programmes (with their name, work title, duration, format and date of show) was typed out and bound as a separate volume. From all this material I made a rough draft narrative and circulated copies amongst the collective.

Regular open access shows 1991 - 1998

Cooltan and the Cinema Cafe (1991)

Las Casas (1992)

Jugglers Arms (1993)

The Lido Show (August 1993)

Union Tavern (1993 - 1994)

The Collective split (1994 - 1996)

Venue Miscellany (1994 - 1996)

Three more venues - (1997 - 1998)

The Roof Shows (1997 & 1998)

Shows with selected programmes 1993 - 1998

3b Continental Touring (1993 - 1998)

3c Exploding Cinema presents The Ritzy Shows - (1995 - 1996)

3c Volcano! (1996 - 1998)

Cooltan and the Cinema Café: November 1991 to March 1992

Cooltan was the venue for a large open artists collective in South London that followed the pattern set by the *Brixton Artists Collective* in the mid-eighties. An open collective, called *Pullit*, started to put on large-scale open-to-all art exhibitions. The 'Cooltan' was an empty suntan oil factory in Effra Road in Brixton that had been empty and derelict for a number of years. It was squatted by the Pullit group from June 1991 to February 1992. The factory had approximately 800 square yards of space so the exhibitions could be impressively inclusive.

> A cinema was built into what was once a cold storage room with a sliding steel door. On the door in red wooden letters was spelt out THE REGAL. Around June Ken McDonald, filmmaker and impresario, moved his *Reel Love* show to the Regal. Reel Love was a regular screening of Super 8 films punctuated by technical breakdowns and serious drinking.

(e file: Origins of the EC)

Ken McDonald was something of an underground legend and had been doing his Reel Love shows since the Eighties. Ken still occasionally turned up at Exploding Cinema events. Here is an account of his appearance at the show in *Blue*, a club in a railway arch, on 27th August 1999: 'My highlight that night was finally seeing Ken McDonald, who did a long and rambling reading. He started with an easy going, shambolic introduction before launching into what Thomas Zagrosek described as a blood and sperm reading. It was accompanied by what appeared to be Super 8 'found' footage of some far away land with lots of luscious blurred shots of a tropical landscape. He asked three musicians present to improvise and they did a good job. Duncan was holding a torch aloft onto his manuscript which he hunched over swaying and turning away from the audience as he read, apparently lost in his text. Ken was an underground legend.' (Log3 p327)

Description of a *Reel Love* Show:

> That was really exciting, because here was a room full of people watching Super 8 films. And what I really noticed about the event was that everyone was drinking and smoking, and this, in a way, kind of totally changed the atmosphere of the event because you had a kind of social… It was a night out… It was no longer this incredible sort of sacred concentration upon the screen. And people were talking to each other and it was actually fun, you know, it was similar to going to a gig… or watching television.

Duncan Reekie interview 1996.

It is interesting to note the influence of television on Duncan and other collective members. This was the informal watching of television at home, except now it was an open social event in which you could meet people like you might at a party. This was a dramatic change from the passive closed off social space that mainstream cinema had become.

> The other exciting thing about what Ken was doing at *Reel Love* was that he was so inept. He was so incredibly inept. He would get the wrong films on, he would break the films in the middle, the machinery would break down for long periods. He would get incredibly stoned and talk over the films. It was just a complete fucking shambles. And whereas this irritated some people, to me this was amazing because you suddenly... It was revealed to you that you could do this. Anyone could do this. It was possible to do it!

DR 1996

Ken's 'lack' of professionalism was part of this enabling atmosphere. It had a direct relation to the Punk strategy of widening access and stimulating a general creativity by debunking professional standards, whilst promoting raw energy and enthusiasm. It was in *Reel Love* that Duncan Reekie met Stephen Houston and his girlfriend Cathy Gibbs who had already put up a notice about wanting to form a film group.

Duncan Reekie had previously joined the *London Filmmakers Coop* for a while at a time when it was in decline. He had been completely disillusioned by his experience of joining this group that had by then become thoroughly institutionalised. He describes it as being 'dead'. He left the Co-op aware that something completely new had to happen if underground filmmaking was to be revived. It is easy to see how enthusiastic he would have been about the meetings started by Stephen Houston and he attended them on a regular basis. Only about three people in this initial group actually made films, or had made a film. In other words they were refreshingly outside of, what Reekie saw as, the 'cut throat careerism' and incestuous politics of the independent film scene of the time.

Then, when Ken McDonald's *Reel Love* suddenly left the Cooltan in October of 1991, the Houston/ Gibbs group stepped into the breech. The core members of this group were:

> 'Stephen Houston, Cathy Gibbs, Jenny Marr, Danny Holman, Laura Hudson, Duncan Reekie, Suzanne Currid, Jennet Thomas, Anthony Kopiecki, Lorelei Lisowsky, Lepke B. and William Thomas. From the very beginning we decided to be totally open and democratic, anyone could show their work, anyone could join the group, all you had to do was come to a meeting and get involved. We drew up a loose constitution, the group was to be non-profit making, all work would be voluntary, no wages would be paid, all the money we made would be used to run our screenings and to buy collectively owned equipment.'

e file: Origin of the Exploding Cinema

The constitution was agreed in principle in a meeting on 20 October 1991. It was formally adopted in a meeting on 27 October. The first record of a show was on Sunday 10 November. They ran shows on Sundays at 3pm, preceded by an open meeting at 1pm.

But winter was coming on and the Regal was unheated and uncomfortably cold, so it was decided to move the screening to the Cooltan café, which was in one of the office spaces on a first floor to the front of the building. The room was only about twenty five foot square. The move to the cafe is described by Lorelie Lisowsky:

> The cafe was a big turning point and completely changed the way we viewed the films because there was food, drink and a casual atmosphere. It was warm. It also got the other co-opees involved more. Our first show in the café… I had programmed a line-up of films. We had spent a few days getting ready, making a screen by framing an old sheet/or canvas I had brought in, buying beer, posters, and food - It was always crepes at the beginning. The cinema was part of the art co-op activity that happened in the building. The cafe had been the focal point for Cooltan, in the middle stood a giant wooden cable holder for a table.

Lorelie Lisowsky email 26-6-2001

As Duncan points out the thing about the cafe was that the chairs were around tables so people were facing each other rather than being in rows. When people turned from watching the film they were facing each other.

The first café event seems to have been

on 10 December 1991 ('Subreal Film Presents') which was followed by another on the 18th of the same month. There were then shows on the 10th and 24th January, and then on the 7th and 21st of February.

> We made food... The kitchen itself was in the room with the films, so that all through the film, me and Stephen Houston - we'd both worked as chefs, so we did food. And there was like frying noises and saucepans being banged together and stuff like this. And there were smells as well, and that was one thing we always used to say was like, you got all your senses are catered for... So there we are, we're showing Super 8 films and home videos. I mean, we were different from *Reel Love* in that we'd got a monitor and started showing video. (DR)

Most of what characterised the Exploding Cinema for the next eight years seems to have evolved in the Cooltan Cafe. Some people had bought a couple of cheap projectors at a jumble sale and they discussed what could be done with them. An older improvising musician called Lepke B was quick to experiment with whatever was at hand. He would do things like put up mirrors and project off of them. Fairly early on it was decided that someone had to introduce the films:

> We had to have someone to introduce the films, so... they would introduce the filmmakers and get the filmmakers to come up and talk about their films. Then... the projectors would be constantly breaking down and everything would be breaking down the whole time, so it would help if the MC would do something entertaining. So you either had to improvise, like just talk to the audience for long periods. There was a girl, Jenny Marr, who used to be in the group and she would sing unaccompanied. And we

would say to the audience, is there anybody in the audience who can sing or can play the guitar or whatever? (DR)

So, there was this freewheeling atmosphere in which nobody was imposing their own will on the proceedings. The meetings were also almost laughably egalitarian and would go on for hours so everyone could say what they needed to. They were open meetings and sometimes they had to put up with people who weren't entirely focused or even 'completely deranged'.

The 5th Cinema Cafe programme. The first illustrated programme for a show on 21st February 1992 is the earliest surviving programme. The back cover declares 'an evening of film video, food and frolic'. Jennet Thomas, Duncan Reekie, Susanne Currid, Kathy Gibbs and Lorelei Hawkins are given as contact names. Films and videos are shown by Jennet Thomas, Lepke B, Marion Galton, Nick G. Smith, Dominique, Duncan Reekie (with spoken text), Ian Haley, Jenny Marr, Susanne Currid, Anthony Kopieki and others. Ten of these were, mostly Super 8, films and five or six were videos. There was a video from Victoria Mapplebeck listed and then scratched out.

The style of this programme was a crude collage of images and hand-written information in a doodling fanzine style. It was photocopied black onto white paper with self-cover, A6 size.

It included a menu: 'Coffee, tea, juice and sweet and savoury pancakes... Head Cook - Stephen Houston'. Host and compere was Sarah Adout and songs were sung by Jenny Marr.

There seems to have been regular meetings on Sundays at 2pm in which a move to a new venue in Electric Avenue was discussed but seems to have come to nothing. There were one or two more shows in the café at Cooltan in March but by the 9th of April the Exploding

Cinema, as it was now called, had moved to a restaurant in Clapham High Street.

So, much of the format was evolved around these early showings in the Cooltan cafe but it was the next stage that showed just how popular and powerful this format could be.

Las Casas: June 1992 to December 1992

Las Casas was a working restaurant at 153 Clapham High Street. The first show seems to have been on the 9th April 1992. A further thirteen to sixteen shows were put on at fortnightly intervals. Jennet Thomas remembers Stephen Houston finding the venue when they were evicted from the Cooltan. It was a vegetarian restaurant run in a friendly non-commercial way. The sort of place you could sit around nursing a cup of coffee without being hassled. It was used as a gallery for local artists so it already had a kind of arts centre feel to it.

> It was a long, thin, narrow space, trendily decorated - it didn't have the sense of a chain, or a style bar about it. It was like it had been decorated by the people that ran it, with a sense of joie-de-vivre. It didn't seat that many people; they crammed quite a lot of tables in, and when it was functioning as a venue, most of the time we were really jam-packed. We couldn't really take more than about 70 people, even that wasn't comfortable, but sometimes we would get 150 people turning up.
>
> Jenet Thomas interview

The over-crowding was solved by having standing room all the way back to the door. There was a convenient place to put projectors for loops and slides on a wooden construction over the stairwell that led down to the toilets. The projectionists had to crawl around in this space as it only had a few feet of headroom. There was no video projector at that time just a big TV as a monitor. This was mounted on a swing and attached to the ceiling with four chains.

> Steven Houston… constructed this wooden stage, I suppose about the size of this carpet here. Sort of 6 foot x 10… a wooden stage. He worked out a system for how it was assembled with sort of pins, and holes, and nuts and bolts, and each one had a number. You had to do it in a specific order. It was numbered and so it was almost like a puzzle, every time we did a show there, we had to get all these wooden bits out, and complete this wooden puzzle. (JT)

The effort put into having a raised stage shows the importance of live performance to the Exploding Cinema ethos.

The first show at Las Casas that I found any archived trace of was on the General Election night of 9th April 1992. There is no surviving programme but there is a poster and the minute book records a show in which TV screens were covered with red, blue and green gels. Shane Collins, the Green Party candidate who had connections with the Exploding network, was present. The next show at Las Casas was on 27th April (no surviving programme). A meeting, minuted only as being in May, notes Duncan as Chairperson with Jenny, Anthony, Cathy, Suzanne, Debbie and Donal attending. Each person is recorded as taking responsibility for a clear role in the plans for the next show: Donal Ruane is recorded as doing the programming, the projecting and putting together the printed programme; Duncan is the MC; Anthony is in charge of video and sound; Cathy is on the door and Jenny is doing 'stage' (floor manager) and transport. There is mention of surplus income being generated and plans to buy group equipment. The accumulated profit of c£300 was, at the time, kept in Duncan's Enterprise

Allowance business account. A separate group account was not started until October 1992.

The first show at Las Casas for which a programme survives was on June 4th 1992. The programme has a pale, peach-coloured, paper cover and entries were typed. The layout is neat with a separation of graphics and text. Every one of the sixteen pages has an image, one of which is an Exploding Cinema logo. The tidy design style would seem to imply that Donal Ruane, a skilled graphic designer, was making the programmes during this period.

There are short reviews by 'Captain Pat Porteus' (aka Duncan Reekie) from the show two weeks previously. Half of the reviews are of films by collective members. This show of 4th June has films by, Donal Ruane, Duncan Reekie, Colette Rouhier, Andre Stitt and Lepke B, who are all collective members, as well as work by Ken McDonald and Vivienne Dick. The text on the front cover and inside front cover celebrates film as 'a magic process', 'a chemical conjunction of light and matter'. It goes on to explain 'the persistence of vision'. Further inside the programme are images of zoetropes and a very simple and effective 'Make a Film' graphic sequence which explains establishing shots and cut-ins. These references to moving image production techniques refer back to early cinema as well as relating to the Do-It-Yourself ideology of the counter culture.

Apart from this didactic theme there is an odd letter to the Daily Mirror (dated 1937) which purports to tell of the effectiveness of 'capital punishment' on three seventeen year old schoolgirls by a schoolmistress. The programme also contains an odd anecdote about a home movie that is said to have been made by John F. Kennedy two months before he was killed. The subject of this fictional amateur movie is purported to be an assassination. Headed *Ripley's Believe it or Not* it is probably 'disinformation' which reflects the counter-cultural interest in urban myth. This reference to home-movies glamorises the amateur genre and asserts its historical

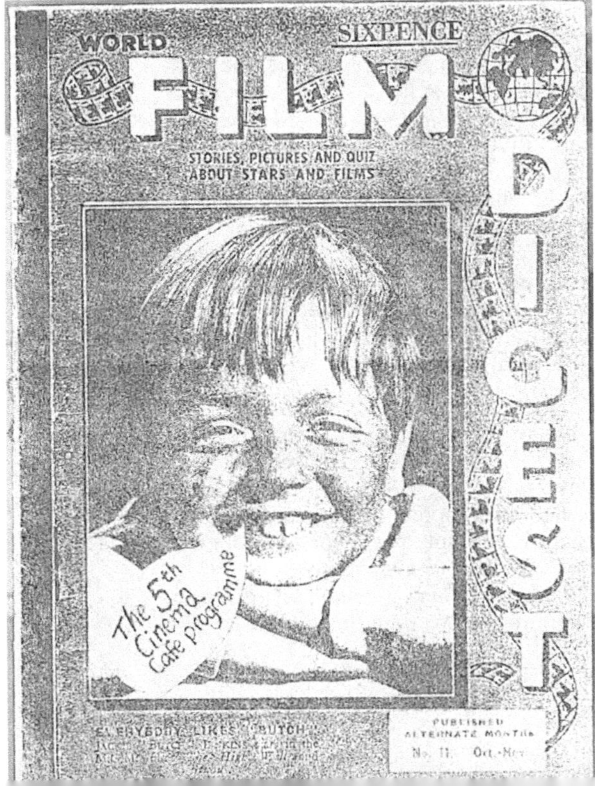

Programme February 1992

significance.

By now the Exploding Cinema formula is well established and there are regular shows every two weeks, with a paying audience of 50 - 100 or more. The next show was on 18th June. In the programme, 'Captain Porteus' reviews the show on the 4th June declaring it a 'great success' and talks of an 'encouraging and energetic' audience. Mention is made of impromptu music by *The Murphys*, showing films at the wrong speed and unexpected power failures.

This programme continues the didactic theme. Inside the front cover is a found text defining the underground, first with an unreferenced quote from Marcel Duchamp; *"The only solution for the artist of tomorrow is to go underground"*. It then quotes a text on film in the US beat scene of 1959. Although I have not been able to find the source of this quote it shows how the history of the underground was associated with Post-War USA scene. The centre spread contains a short text about the gruesome Manson Family rituals with Super 8 and dog's blood. Further on is a Union Jack with picture of the Queen, corsets, and the text 'ENGLAND R.I.P.' Clearly, ten years after *Anarchy in the UK* the punk spirit was alive and well in the Exploding Cinema collective. These references to punk and hippie antiheroes are all somewhat retro in the context of 1992 when the contemporary underground was involved with music raves and techno music, but they serve to give the angry, even threatening, tone of Exploding's oppositional posture at the time.

The cover graphic of the programme of the 2nd July show is a pastiche of the famous Black Panther photograph of an armed and beret wearing black man peeping through a curtained window. In this stylised drawn copy, signed by Donal, the Black Panther is holding a home-movie camera instead of a gun

with the slogan: *'Liberate our minds, by any means necessary'*. A found text in the inside cover talks about how the exclusiveness of the mainstream cinema is tied up with the large amount of money required to achieve the slick illusionistic narrative. He ends by calling for a compelling alternative. The programme includes a documentary about William Burroughs by Ellie Jeffreys to complete the parade of retro Sixties underground signifiers.

Returning again to the punk era the centre-spread text is a reproduction of Nick Zedd's *The Cinema of Transgression Manifesto*, which had first appeared seven years before. Captain Porteus' reviews start off by exhorting the audience to get out there and make new films; *'Don't be shy, even if you haven't made a film before, all you have to do is point the camera and shoot, Go for it!!!'*. Several eye dissection graphics throughout exhort the audience to see things anew.

Donal, Jennet, Lepke, Andre and Duncan seem to be prolific moviemakers. They all have something in the show on 20th July. The centre-spread of the programme of that date contains a much-reduced DIY graphic guide to drawing directly onto film.

Captain Porteus describes the last show as 'a heady mix of High Art, camp trash and documentary expose'. Marc Conway's Super 8 film *Mantis Part1* featured footage from the last year's Anti-Poll Tax riots in Trafalgar Square. The contacts given are Duncan or Jennet who share a short-life terrace house in Rodwell Road in East Dulwich. They continue living there until 1998 and during that period it became the main Exploding Cinema headquarters.

In an undated but minuted meeting that followed this show, the collective decided to limit the number of longer films to a maximum of one half-hour film per show. The use of an MC, live performers and games were agreed to work well to break up any possibility of monotony. A healthy bank balance of £420 is reported.

Duncan Reekie's rant 'FUCK OFF AVANT-GARDIST' takes the centre fold in the next programme. There is also reference to the world's most famous home movie: Abraham Zapruder's amateur footage of the assassination of President John F. Kennedy. Captain Porteus comments on how the audience 'was engaged in top gear, cheering, hurling insults and arguing amongst themselves over the merits or demerits of the work on view'.

Cathy Gibb's Super 8 film and loop *Scratch in the Park* was a double projection. A simple but highly effective piece achieved by scratching onto the surface of some footage shot in a London Park on a summer's day. The film loop, of a bird's head, was constantly moved around the space, sometimes even projected onto the audience itself.

In spite of the apparent high energy of this show the minutes of a meeting on the 2nd August reflect some boredom; '*It went on too long... too many projected works*'.

The inside cover of the next programme on the 13th August shows us 'How to Make a Zoetrope' again. The centre-spread is copied from *A Directory of Alternative Society Projects* (1973). It gives detailed advice on '8mm and 16mm FILMS FOR SHOWING IN PUBS'. 'Paddy Payne' (aka Donal Ruane) has taken over writing the review section. There is another rant entitled 'DEMOCRATIZE ART!' which is a tirade against the passive audience.

Democratize Art! Audience, what a shame it is that you are constantly travelling from venue to venue and once arrived you are forced to sit in the darkness or wander around sterile

Programme 30 - 7 - 92 Rant by Duncan Reekie

galleries. Audience, how lamentable it is that you are all the time confronted with closed sacred objects produced by ambitious professionals. You are excluded from the art process and the trouble is that, if you seek to end this exclusion by becoming an artist, you will no longer be a member of the audience. Rather, this blissful union of art and audience must take place at the venue.

A democratic spirit was certainly part of the collective ethos. Minutes of a meeting at the beginning of October mention a 'New constitution and positive discrimination to get all members to voice their opinions.' The programme of the 27th August has a 'Fuck Off Avantgardist' graphic signed by Donal (no other Exploding Cinema graphics are signed). Inside the front of this programme is an unreferenced text about Punk filmmakers, including Vivienne Dick, who rejected the academic formalism of the earlier Seventies avant-garde and made 'a partial return to the underground of the 1960's'.

The show on 10th September has another surrealist style programme cover graphic signed by Donal with the text: 'WE WILL RENDER YOUR SYMBOLS MEANINGLESS'. Inside there is a witty and subversive glossary, as an *Independent Film A - Z* examples from which are:

> *Experimental:* A type of avant-garde film made by artists who think they're scientists.

> *Underground:* A seething rabble of no-budget film/video makers who don't give a fuck for the 'independent' film industry.

Ripley's Believe it or Not! is a story alleging the Queen Mother had an affair during the war. 'Paddy Payne' starts off the review section by addressing the audience; *If you need any assistance or equipment just ask. Don't be afraid, anyone can do it.* The back-cover

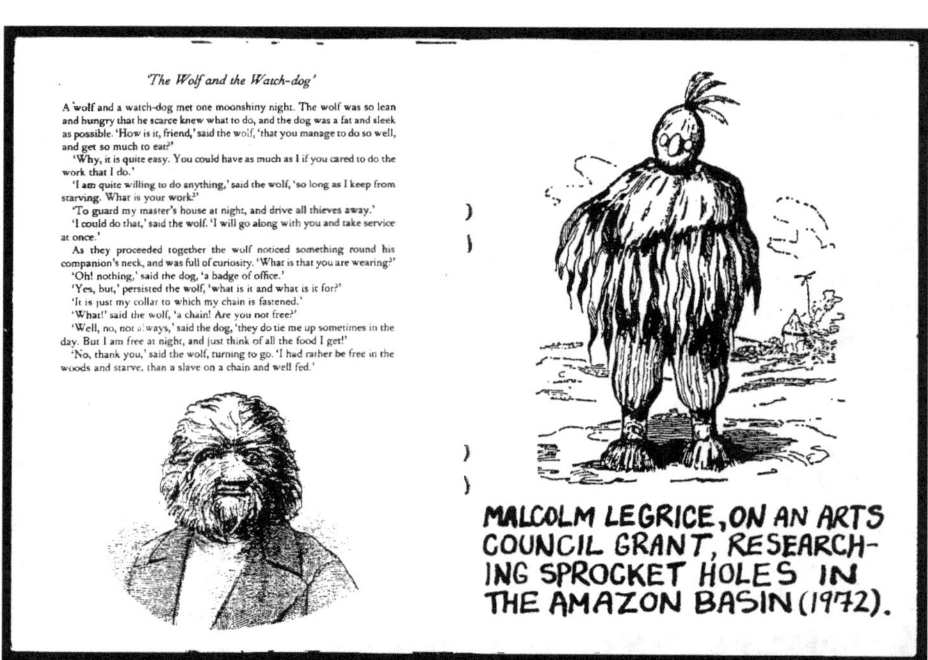

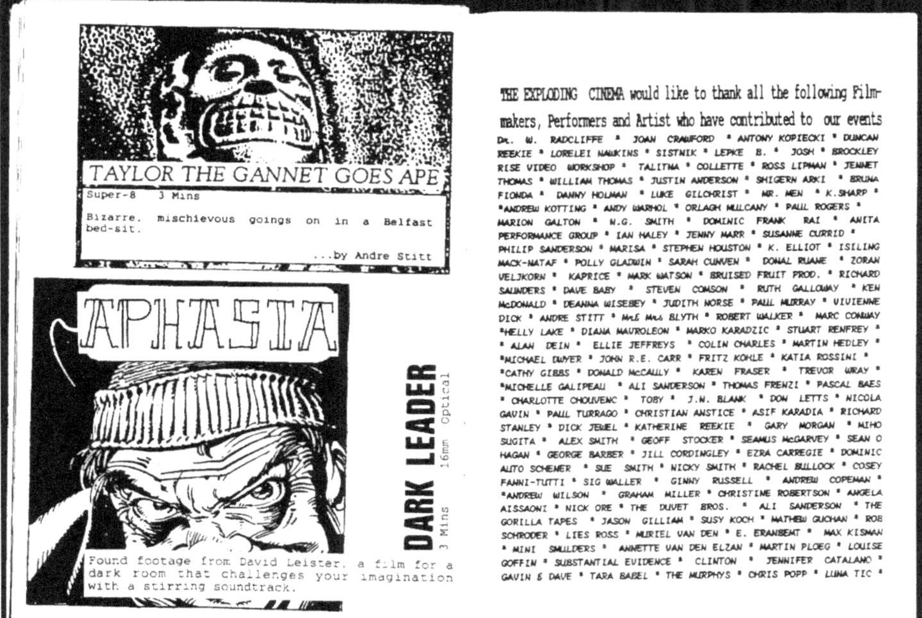

Programme 17 - 12 - 92

graphic has the word 'ANGRY' under an eerie drawing of a child's doll.

An unusually well-minuted meeting on 13th September was critical about the last show which was considered 'a bad show', in which a member of the collective got drunk and insulted the audience. 'Sloppy… Some films were too long… It started too late… The team is becoming complacent.' A mail-out to filmmakers was mentioned. Publicity for shows is being circulated to student unions, independent cinemas and record shops. There was a prescient mention of the need for a policy regarding the lending of vital pieces of equipment.

In a meeting on 20th September a door price of £3, with £2 concessionary rate, was voted in. It was also decided that musicians and other live performers should get their travel expenses reimbursed. This was a practice that continued throughout the Nineties and is the only instance of anyone getting any personal expenses paid.

The programme of a show on 24th September shows the image of a young girl's face on the front cover with the text; *A fairy inside, Mummy?* The style of this goes back to the more handmade scribbly style of the earliest surviving programme. This seems to indicate the end of the period in which Donal made the programmes on his own. Indeed, there is a minute of 4th October which suggests that the programmes are now being made at collective meetings, something which became a regular ritual.

Jennet was MC for the first time at this show. The show is described in the following programme with the usual hyperbole: *The night was a sublime mixture of poets, films, impromptu performance, edible opera, high noon shenanigans and curious goings on involving much rubber and human flesh.*

'After weeks of talk Anthony is going to buy a (video) projector' with help from £50 loans from collective members

Andy, Suzanne, Donal and William.

A show programme in November is undated but has a cover graphic which declares that 'Guy Fawkes is a Hero', so it will be early November if not on the 5th. The programme has a satirical cartoon of Malcolm LeGrice, on an Arts Council grant, 'researching sprocket holes in the Amazon Basin' (1972). There is a short report on Exploding Cinema's multi-screen contribution to *Fanny Adam's Big Ball* in the West End. These smaller excursions to contribute to other events tend to go unrecorded but would have been an important part of getting Exploding Cinema known to a wider non-experimental film audience.

The minute book shows there was some excitement at the possibility of a continental show coming up in Amsterdam, which indicates that international contacts had started to bear fruit and that the influence of Exploding Cinema had already spread beyond London.

On the 17th December 1992 there was a one-year anniversary show. The programme contained an acknowledgement of all the contributors so far. In this first year there were around thirteen people taking regular active roles. The series of events at Las Casas had established an identity for the group, which became quite separate from the mother collective of Cooltan.

The regular events twice a month at Las Casas seem to have tested and developed the basic format of Exploding that had evolved in the Cooltan Cafe; the core network of filmmakers and the cultural presence of Exploding Cinema in London had expanded enormously. It had developed a kudos, which was to induce a continued expansion and subsequent fracturing in the coming year or two. In many ways it was to become a victim of its own success.

A founder member, Stephen Houston, left the group to return to Australia having shown only one of his own works. Lorelei Lisowsky had also left to

Programme 20 - 3 - 93

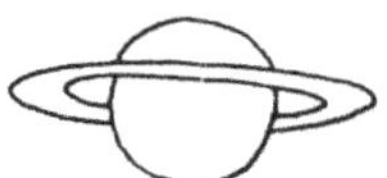

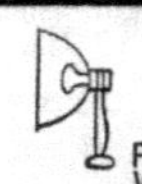

FUCK THE FUTURE...WE WANT THE PRESENT

Nineteen Ninety Three and how predictable that the British cultural establishment should offer us a (non-) choice between the failed modernist project and the same old Oxbridge romanticism...to make myself plain I mean that these shallow bureaucrats were the last to realise that the shiney future of cat-suits, monorails and anti-grav scooters wasn't going to happen. This was already plain to the non-class of loungers and scroungers, we knew that the vid-phones and matter transporters were destined for the ruling class anyway, while the rest of us were trapped in the community theme park No-Go areas. And when the vision of white cities, blonde citizens, pure sound and abstract form fell away the establishment discovered popular culture which they thought was dreadfully sweet and they christened it 'Postmodernism'. They said to themselves ..'We want a cinema which shows how we live, what we feel, who we are !" So they began to adapt Edwardian novels by E.M.Forster and Virginia Woolf. Turn on your T.V. and catch some so-called New Age guru telling you that only a few 'artists' have the sacred shamanic power...oh no..different words same tune..looks like we can't all be Sylvia Plath, the rest of us are going to have to hang around in AWE while the real stars express our lives for us...when is this anyway ? The psychedelic sixties ? The Elizabethan renaissance ? That's right creatures if you don't understand history you're doomed to repeat it. We're living in past tense. Fuck that because one out of focus bedroom camcorder video has more integrity than the last ten years of British feature films.
Close the fucker down.

THE EXPLODING CINEMA

FLOOD
WITH C

Yes you are right...this is not Clapham!..this is not Las Casas!..and this is no-longer Thursday!
Due to unforeseen circumstances Las Casas, our previous venue closed for good, making our "Anniversary show ", on 17th of December, our last. Since then we have been searching high and low, far and wide to find the venue that would be capable of providing THE EXPLODING CINEMA with exactly what's needed for its events.
So now we welcome you, not only, back to THE EXPLODING CINEMA, but also to our new venue " The Jugglers Arms " where we will be staging our Happenings every second saturday from now till the end of time! So I have only one question to ask you: Are you having fun yet?

OUR NEXT SHOW:

The EXPLODING CINEMA returns in two weeks time on Saturday the 3rd April with another exciting show. Starts 8.00pm sharpish!

SUPER 8 SUPER 8 SUPER 8 SUPER 8 SUPER 8 SUPER 8 SUPER 8 SUPER 8 SUPER 8 SU

THE FLYING TEA POT.

For THE EXPLODING CINEMA on the 13th February " Love " was in air. We had breath taking Standard 8's by Paul Torrago and Ant Kopiecki and the world famous " I LOVE YOU " performance Duncan Reekie. For THE EXPLODING CINEMA had arrived in Southamp for a one night only show, in a squatted cafe called The Flying Tea Pot.
One of the many highlights of the night was Donal Ruane's "I your musical lass" a searing indictment of the side-effects alcohol on North of England and another memorable film w Duncan Reekie's self proclaimed favourite: "SLAVE RIDE" certai a film for any discerning Masochist.
But without a doubt the film that really stole the show wa nameless Super 8 shot on Brighton Beach, starring William with a live sound track improvised by Mungo, a truly unexpec and unscheduled delight.

start her own 'New Cinema' in the South West of England.

The Jugglers Arms.
March to August 1993

By the end of 1992 the wave of illegal Raves or warehouse parties had already passed the height of their popularity. The Exploding Cinema was a refreshing change from the usual warehouse party, with a larger more visible crew and even a reaction to that scene's lack of content or overt political direction. The Alternative Comedy scene had also lost much of its initial excitement as many of the early performers began to be offered their own TV shows. Donal Ruane thought that rave and Super 8 screening events were incompatible.

After a foray outside of London to do a show in a café in Southampton on the 13th of February, a new larger venue had been found in London to accommodate the rapid expansion of Exploding. This was a cavernous ground floor room in an old pub called The Jugglers Arms. It was situated in an old industrial area of London SE1, quite close to Borough tube and London Bridge station. The events in the new venue were high-energy events with audiences of 200 to 300 people run by a collective of 10 to 20 people. T-shirts were produced and there were side stalls.

The first show was planned for the 20th March 1993. There were performances by Jane Bombane and Hermine. The programme is notable for a lively rant entitled, *Fuck the Future... We want the present.*

An undated meeting after 20th March reports on this first show at the Jugglers: Jennet was the MC again, she complained of needing more back-up and wanting to be kept better informed. It seems that there were gaps in the programme. The need to start on time was stressed and Danny made the point that there is a fine line between fun and sloppiness. The food was good and generally people had a good time.

The second Jugglers show on 3rd April had a programme cover, which declared; *It's exploding time again, Jumping over barriers of taste.* There was a meeting the next day that discussed the show: It was noted that 'We rely on Ron too much' for leads and sound. Ron Briefl worked at Morley College as a sound technician.

In a meeting on 25th April a proposal for a guest list for performers and filmmakers was discussed. There was a vote of 14:1 against filmmakers that were showing films, or collective members, paying. In any ambiguous situation the host was delegated to decide.

The fourth show on the 1st of May had AVI, Active Visual Intervention, the billboard montagists, showing slides and talking about their work and a performance by Ian Hinchliffe, the notorious performance artist.

In the minutes of a meeting on 5th May Suzanne pointed out the need for more women's work. There is talk of plans to travel to Dublin, Holland and Berlin, which indicates the extent of the Exploding network at this time.

Putting on regular shows of this size was certainly tiring. However, the Jugglers audience produced a healthy financial situation allowing the purchase of a range of equipment. A report on the show on 26th June: 'Pissed off with Jugglers, can't use phone, trouble with power.' Suzanne C. Generally the feedback was good but the show did not run smoothly. Planning begins for a monster event at the Brockwell Park Lido in August.

In spite of the problems voiced above the run of shows at the Jugglers came to

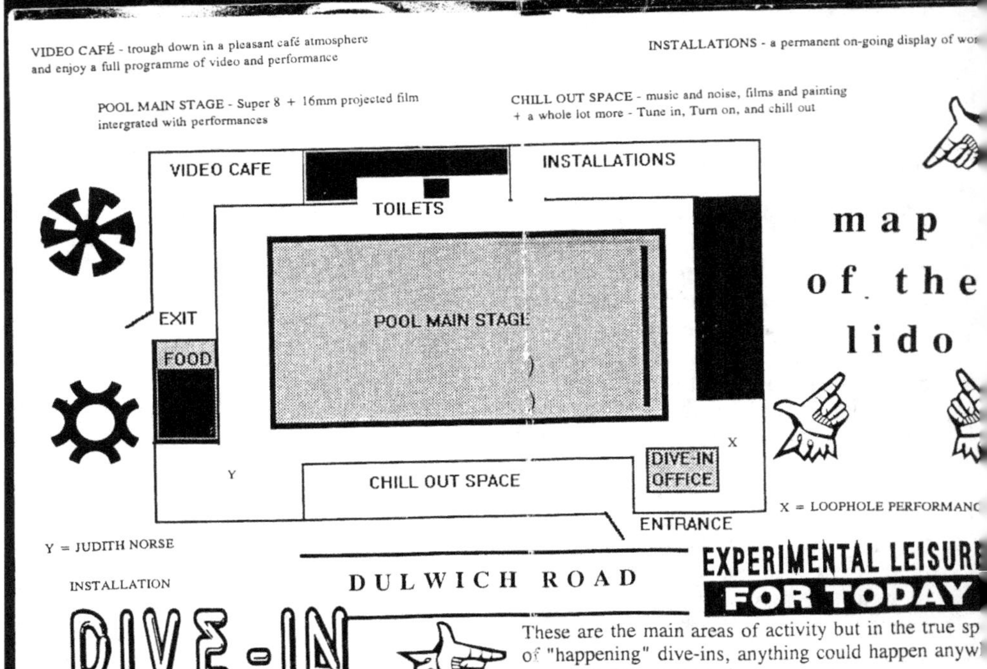

Programme 7 - 8 - 93

an end because of the pubs licensing problems, and a show after the Brockwell Lido show in August is the last show there.

Although the series at the Jugglers showed the mass appeal of the Exploding Cinema format, this success also brought problems for an unpaid non-profit collective. What was fun to do for a network of friends can get to be tedious and stressful for a larger crowd of strangers.

On a more positive note Duncan observed:

> *The Exploding Cinema are showing films in a way that hasn't happened since the 1960's - large, regular audience - diverse, populist.*

The audiences at the Jugglers were regular and large. The Exploding Cinema had already become a unique and well-known event in London's underground culture.

The 'Dive-In' Show Lido Show (7th August 1993)

The *'Dive-In Show'* at Brockwell Park Lido was announced in a centre-page advert in an Exploding programme of 24th July 1993. This was a major event showing at least seventy five works with a budget of £1200 and a paying audience of over 2000. Along with the media attention it generated this was the event that established Exploding Cinema as an underground institution and myth.

Brockwell Lido at that time was unused and the pool was dry. It was a medium sized open-air municipal swimming pool with a simple modernist architectural charm. Changing rooms and other spaces make up about half of the perimeter. These derelict spaces were used to house installations and screenings. The pool had previously been squatted and used for various parties and raves.

This was the Exploding Cinema show

that many people remember for the simple reason of its scale. At the time the collective numbered more than 20 people. It is not remembered fondly by some of the 1997 - 1999 members who were in the collective at that time. Although for Caroline Kennedy it was the event at which she joined the collective. It provided technical headaches of mammoth proportions. Several screenings ran in parallel using the outbuildings and the poolside cafe as well as decor projections in the empty pool itself.

I attended this event and as an audience member my memory is of experimental no-budget film culture on an incredible scale. Impressive because of the amount it concentrated into one space, on one evening. Never had I seen so much projection equipment brought into action in one venue. The later Volcanos were bigger but spread out on various sites over a week. On top of that the empty pool did provide a uniquely memorable setting.

The Lido has a place in the hearts of most people brought up locally. Perhaps the event played some part in the revival of the pool which has since be taken over by private enterprise and regained its former summer glory and has itself been the subject of several documentary films. Here is an account from the interview with Caroline Kennedy:

> What I did in the Lido was quite a good installation. It was in the shower room and changing room. I got loads of tiles, and I put that… magic stuff which you paint on white tiles and you can print on to it. And I had taken loads of photographs of lidos, people just swimming and lounging. I printed them all on these tiles. And a lot of the tiles were falling off the wall, it was like a really wrecked shower, and I just put them on the ground. And I had a loop of, I think it was me swimming under water, filling the entire space. And there was

sound, and smells like bleach. And the sound of water, and people showering, and distant voices.

A video document was made by Mark Saunders of Despite TV.

The Union Tavern. October 1993 - May 1994

The sixteen shows that Exploding Cinema put on at the Union Tavern were the longest series of shows put on in one venue in the Nineties. The Union Tavern is on the corner of Camberwell New Road and Vassal road in South London. The Union Place community print workshop was next door at the time.

The Union Tavern was a slightly down-at-heel old music pub about quarter of a mile down the Camberwell New Road from the Oval Tube. A narrow bar space gave way to an increasingly wide back space with a large raised stage. At a push there was room for an audience of about 200. This venue was a bit smaller than the Jugglers Arms. The shows were fortnightly and it used to get 'jam packed'. You often couldn't get in if you arrived after 9pm.

This was close to where I was squatting in St Agnes Place, Kennington and so I went fairly regularly. The social networking was lively and the audience were often vociferous, especially in their exchanges with the MC. These regular shows seemed to generate their own ongoing energy. People got used to them being on every month. There was a regular audience, which reduced work on publicity but also induced a steady stream of films to show. During this series alone over 300 works were projected on the main screen.

The first show was on 2nd of October 1993. It included a packed programme of 22 works. These comprised: One 16mm film, twelve Super 8mm films, five VHS tapes, two live music events and two performances. They included work by Steven Eastwood and Andrew Kotting both destined for future prominence. At this time a high proportion of the work being made is still on Super 8 film. By April 1994 a change in the balance of film to video seems to have taken place. At the show of 16th April in that year there were sixteen works of which only four were 8mm film and ten were on VHS.

The high audience numbers provided a good income and soon the collective were considering buying a van and getting an office. The office was obtained by the end of November and lasted until November 1994. No vehicle was bought until Colette bought a Cortina Estate in October 1996. Equipment was moved using cars owned by Anthony Kopieki and John Carr.

In 1993, Katya Rossini left the group and moved to Belgium where she was active in independent cinema with a group called Kino Trotter. Paul Tarrago had joined the group in late 1992; Colette Rouhier joined in the spring of 1993 and Caroline Kennedy joined after the Lido Show in August 1993. So, by the beginning of 1994 the members who were to provide the stable core of the collective in the next six years were in place.

Little feedback on shows exists in the minutes for this period and it seemed people were putting all their energy into the ongoing shows and had got used to the highs and lows of putting on shows on a regular basis.

At a General Meeting on 21st of April 1994, Jennet, Duncan, Danny, Caroline, Robyn, Anthony, Michael, Dennis, Fiona, Hassan and Paul are present. Although the last show was profitable Jennet reckoned it was the most uninspiring Exploding Cinema ever, with an annoying 'beery' audience and a 'sparse' programme. Repeated shows at the same venue were starting to feel *like going to do a job*. People voted to do just two more shows at the Union Tavern and then have a break.

The show on the 14th May 1994 was to be the last at Union Tavern in this series. Work included a performance by Ian Hinchliffe and a 16mm film by tENTITATIVELY a. cONVENIENCE a performance artist from Baltimore in the USA who had become famous through the International Postal Art Network.

The Collective split. 1994 - 1996

This is not a show report but needs to be inserted into the chronology of show reports to make sense of the changes that happened after the split.

I decided not to focus my research on the contentious details of the collective split which occurred formally in October 1994 nor to make any attempt at a formal judgement which would serve no purpose at this time except to open old wounds. It was a very acrimonious disagreement but, referring to the published accounts, it is not easy to see what the argument was about. It seems to have built up for at least a year previous to October 1994, but even before that there were inevitable stresses in doing regular shows on a voluntary basis.

The programme for the sixth show at the Jugglers on the 29th May 1993 shows dissatisfaction and tiredness creeping in: Inside the front cover John Carr or Andy Lowe wrote:

> WHO ARE YOU? Do you care about the films you watch or are they just pretty colours and something arty to accompany a social evenings drink? Certainly the Exploding Cinema has

worked hard developing an exciting atmosphere for filmmakers and performers to show their work but have we lost our way?

Once the Exploding Cinema audience was just a large group of friends but now it is edging towards a faceless crowd and it is becoming hard for the people organising the event to feel quite so at home. WHAT CAN BE DONE ABOUT THIS NEW DISTANCE? MAYBE IT'S JUST A QUESTION OF FEEDBACK?

After all the Exploding Cinema belongs to everyone and that includes the audience. It would be nice to see some new blood emerging from that faceless crowd to help to run the event.

This may be simply the stress of putting on regular shows or it may indeed be a premonition of the disquiet to come. Later at a meeting on 1st June 1993, John, Duncan and Jenny complain of being overworked and that there has been a 'loss of control and fun'. They ask the question; 'Is the Jugglers Arms too big?' In a subsequent meeting on 6th June it was noted that Las Casas had been more intimate. Bigger audiences are inevitably audiences of strangers. But worse was to come - after the Lido show the collective had grown to an unwieldy size.

There seem to have been personality clashes, disillusionment and general angst which created conflicts, which then snowballed in reaction to the animosity generated, as much as any substantive issues.

An account, published in Donal Ruane's *KinoKaze* magazine gives the following as reasons: 'The group, it was felt, had become stale and oppressive, the shows formulaic and boring.' The 'anything could happen' feel of the early shows in which 'every show was different' had evaporated leaving a predictable formula. The collective had grown, it is reported in *KinoKaze*, to nearly fifty following the Lido Event. Open meetings became impractical leaving people feeling unheard.

In September 1994 after a series of 'crisis' meetings very little was resolved and many felt it was time to call it a day. Soon after this, the treasurer Anthony Kopiecki froze the Exploding Cinema bank account. Nearly £1000 has remained there to this day (it was never his intention to steal this money as some have alleged). On the 2nd October 1994 the last Exploding Cinema meeting was held at the 121 Bookshop in Brixton. At this meeting it was agreed to formally dissolve Exploding Cinema whilst keeping all the equipment together in a common pool for all the Exploding people to use.

Paddy Payne in *KinoKaze 3*, 1995.

This meeting was not recorded in the minute books that I examined and the Kinokaze account does not record who attended. The remaining group had a meeting, a short time later, on the 20th October which is recorded in the minute books I examined in dramatic but cryptic fashion:

As of this date the Exploding Cinema (group) is SPLIT (not really) into various creatures [rubber stamp of cow] and /OR the Exploding Cinema hard core become the EXPLODING CINEMA COLLECTIVE.

This is witnessed by sixteen signatures, four of which are illegible. They include Duncan Reekie and Jennet Thomas, who were in the initial Cooltan group, along with Caroline Kennedy, Paul Tarrago, Colette Rouhier, Kerry Sharp, James Stevens, and Anne Brus. A further four are represented by initials, one of which is likely to be Katia Rossini and another Danny Holman. Rosalind Grainger, Silvy da Silva, Ghisli Bergman and

Fiona Lord were also part of this group.

The group's collectively owned equipment was kept in the house in Rodwell Road, East Dulwich, that was occupied by Jennet Thomas and Duncan Reekie. A year later the ownership of the equipment was still a serious bone of contention.

> On September 2 1995, after a film show in a North London pub, The Exploding Cinema video projector was repossessed by myself and some colleagues. Paddy Payne in KinoKase 3

A possible explanation of the acrimonious nature of this split could lie in the question of ownership. As a voluntary worker, producing income which is then spent on equipment, one feels some ownership of that equipment after a certain amount of unpaid time is put in. If a collective member is forced to leave, this 'investment' is not easily recouped and can become a source of resentment. This resentment can then become entangled with more inter-subjective disputes, leading to outright conflict.

In July 1995 it had been unanimously agreed that the Exploding Cinema, 'no longer rents or loans the video projector to anyone'. This would prove to be a resolution that was hard to adhere to strictly. e.g. In a meeting on 11th February 1996, attended by Sheik, Duncan, Colette and Steve, Sheik put pressure on the group to allow him to borrow equipment, with no hire fee, for 'no profit' events. Later there is a report of Fiona wanting to borrow equipment after she has left the collective. A change to the constitution was made in July 1997: *Membership of the Exploding Cinema confers no absolute right of access to equipment outside of the Exploding Cinema's activities but does give members priority and discount on equipment hire.* This was voted in unanimously. People borrowing equipment are now asked to pay a deposit of £50 per £100 of value, plus a hire charge for 'profit making' use. Damages to be deducted from deposit. Membership definitions were set to be debated later. Sheik borrowed the equipment he needed on the new conditions. Things worked out OK with the loan to Sheik. He was even charged £4 for a missing take-up spool, but the effect of this new policy seems to have put people off borrowing equipment altogether.

Even in collectives where this difficulty is faced and hours worked are recorded and reflected in their rights of ownership, there still exists the problem of people's different levels of productivity. This still results in ill feeling, and 'survival of the fittest' types of resolution are prevalent.

The people who left have not as far as I am aware formed any other film groups in the same public arena as Exploding Cinema.

Such conflicts leave a terrible legacy of negative feelings that poison wide areas of the underground. Personal attacks on Duncan and Colette through abusive stickers were still evident at our shows at George IV in May 1997.

The extent to which such unresolved conflicts and their resulting emotional pollution have stunted the growth of radical networks can only be guessed at. These aspects of collective working are seriously in need of solutions. At present they are in the head lock of a machismo which will not allow caring for each other and the use of interpersonal methods of conflict resolution, which have been seen as 'female' realms, to become a part collective practice.

The questions which probably need to be answered before this can be approached are; How can voluntary collective work be properly validated? How is critical feedback handled? And what methods of conflict resolution can be offered at an early stage?

Two Decades of Exploding

That's :
OVER 300 SHOWS
5400 FILMS SHOWN
500 PERFORMANCES
632 TECHNICAL HITCHES
230 ANGRY FILM MAKERS
214 BURNED 35mm SLIDES
709 SPILT PINTS OF LAGER
72000 CIGARETTES
1400 HOURS OF LOVE

HAPPY BIRTHDAY TO US !!!

WWW.EXPLODINGCINEMA.ORG

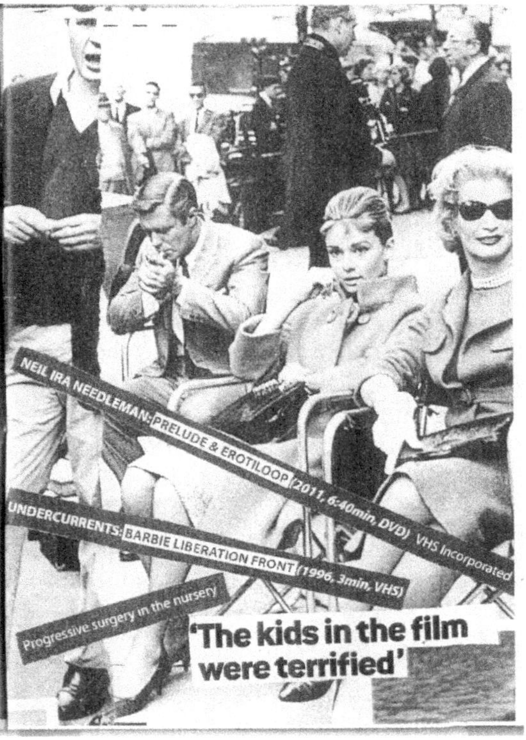

NEIL IRA NEEDLEMAN:PRELUDE & EROTILOOP (2011, 6:40min, DVD) VHS Incorporated

UNDERCURRENTS: BARBIE LIBERATION FRONT (1996, 3min, VHS)

Progressive surgery in the nursery

'The kids in the film were terrified'

Twenty Years of Vitriol...

Back in the early nineties short film in London was controlled by an incestuous clique of academics and bureaucrats who had developed an undemocratic, and frankly creepy, network of agencies funded by the British State. They called this nepotistic circle jerk the "Independent" sector and the best work it produced was about as interesting as the fluff you'd find in the pocket of a coat. In 1991 the Exploding Cinema entered this cosy milieu like a zombie at Glyndebourne. We proved that it was possible to make films without state finance and that there was a popular audience for short film.

20 years later and anyone with a laptop can make a broadcast quality film for a vast international audience. So can the EC get off the barricade? Take a trip to the Tate Modern and you'll find out why not. Tacita Dean's new vast installation 'FILM' has been hailed as a moving elegy to a dying Art form. But anyone with an eye in their head can see that this pompous spectacle is uniquely uncinematic. Moreover Dean's narrative of loss masks the actual triumph of 'Artists Film and Video' the rebranded son of circle jerk.

Oh... and Dean's FILM is sponsored by Unilever, who by the way have a despicable history of forced labour in the Congo and who are now a leading producer of skin whitening products in India ....

Stay Vigilant !

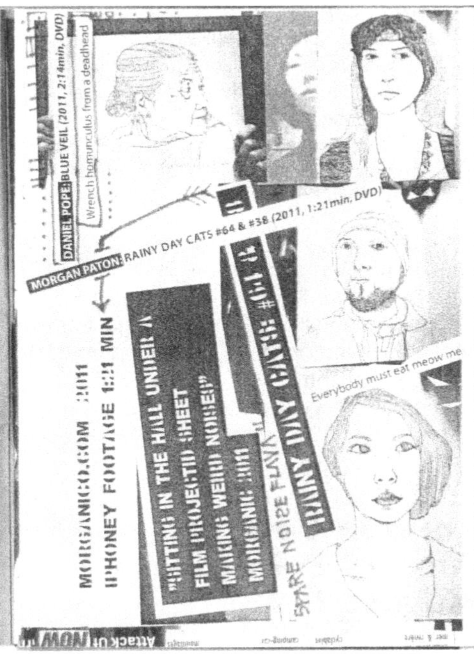

To pump the mood back up we can see these four pages from 15 years later. They show that the Exploding continued to enjoy rude health. Programme 29 - 10 - 2011

It is remarkable that after such a traumatic split Exploding Cinema Collective remained 'open' to any interested newcomer. This means that anyone in the audience can join the collective and 'get involved' in putting on shows and have an equal say in meetings. This policy may be declared more enthusiastically when there is a shortage of members (remembering that the core group can maintain the collective but to put on shows at least eight people are required).

However, it was hard for me to feel a sense of equal ownership even after two years and quite a lot of work, which is probably due to the depth of identification that early bonding and surviving a crisis gives you. This is the perennial problem that such collectives face - how to renew themselves and take on fresh blood.

> "The kibbutz, the commune, the co-operative, are all striving after the person culture in organisational form. On the whole, only their original creators achieve any success. Too soon the organisation achieves its own identity and begins to impose on its individuals. It becomes, at best, a task culture, but often a power or a role culture".
> Charles Handy, *Understanding Organisations* (Penguin, 1993 page 189)

During the period of study, 1997 - 1999 the collective seemed very stable. Colette dropped out for a year but Paul Motel and Damon Herd joined and made strong contributions. There were no collective rows of any substance.

London Venues: August 1994 to August 1996

After the first four venues, which hosted regular series of shows up to the middle of 1994, there is, for the next two years, a much quicker turnover of venues. Is this because of a boredom factor which means regular venues get dull quicker? Or it could have been that venues were being sought out for their spatial interest rather than longevity. Or was it attributable to the disruption of the collective by the arguments and subsequent split? Whatever the reason, in the following period venues do not last for more than three events.

Farringdon Studios. Station Chambers, EC1, 27th August 1994

Station Chambers was an odd assortment of literally underground spaces against the Farringdon Underground station cutting. Stairs led down into a long open courtyard off of which there are a set of small subterranean rooms. The main space is at the end of this courtyard and has further spaces that lead off it. This space lent itself to a range of installations and sideshows.

Unusually the event started at 2pm in the afternoon with a 'Sub Media Pow Wow'. This was a successful break from the usual format although a contemporaneous description of the event does not exist. This following is from the press release:

> "Beneath the streets of the City of London, below the finance houses and the banks, in the stifling darkness, amongst the ruins of Empire... Something terrible is happening. In a maze of dusty corridors that once housed a strobe light factory the infamous EXPLODING CINEMA a gang of reckless no-budget film/video makers will be holding a day to night media carnival featuring Super 8 romance, experimental food, video trash, porno animation, direct action loops and radical shadow play... Beginning at noon the audience will be given the chance to scratch and colour their own films, to mix their

own videos, to perform live film soundtracks, to become their own idols! Then as night slowly falls the Cinema will become a labyrinth of narrative, installation and subversion."

The venue was used again as part of the first Volcano Festival in 1996.

St Johns Church, Brixton, 29th October & 12th November 1994

A deconsecrated medium-sized Victorian church just to the north of Brixton. Plain white walls - somewhat cold in atmosphere.

This was the first show by the new collective after the collective split. Security was clearly a priority with the perceived threat of disruption by the other parties in the conflict. After these two shows there were no more shows at the church as Lambeth Council cut-off the electricity. The need for an independent bar operation was noted. Feedback from the collective on the first church event ranged from: 'A bit sedate', to 'A Good show'. The expenses were high due to running a café and bar as well as the usual show costs.

The Rivoli Ballroom, Brockley, 22nd December 1994

An old barrel vault cinema that was converted into a ballroom in the 1930's. It is a long rectangle with separate long bars to the side. The fittings were very ornate with a lot of more modern cheaper additions which are all somewhat tatty. It was run by a family and has a quirky Country and Western sort of atmosphere, which can also be quite surreal. The hall is capable of taking an audience of 300 or more. The trio of filmmakers known as Lovely Movies compered this third birthday show.

The Sanctuary Cafe, Brighton, 23rd February 1995

No description of this venue was found, but a report appeared in the programme of a subsequent show.

Oh I do like to be beside the seaside… watching low budget movies. So it is true; the virus is spreading. On Thursday evening 23rd February Brighton had a tasty little cine snack with their very own Exploding Cinema at the Sanctuary Café. Some London critters had the rare pleasure of watching nineteen lil' ol' movies fruitfully slung together with the Lovely Movies gang. The joint was a jumping - in fact it was packed with people sitting on all manner of things craning to see them treasures. Oh the joy of being a punter - now I know why you all keep coming back. Yes - some films were so fab we've included them in tonight's programme for your delectation. Films like *Love Me Tender* are only the first to be pulled from their merry seaside recluses to be thrust onto the feisty London screen. When the show rolled to a tardy close the audience groaned with the prospect of no more pictures and forced the Lovely Movies to make promises of another show. Yes - there it is. The unstoppable forces of cheap and fast films in full effect, twisting fresh minds and leading them down the promenade of low budget frenzimania. Take a bite and talk to Jamie, Lovely Movies about showing your film at their next show."

Programme 19-3-9

Loughborough Hotel, Brixton, 19th March, 14th May & 11th June 1995

The upper floor of a large pub. From the main staircase you turn right into a main room which has an interesting dome ceiling, but can only accommodate less than a hundred people. This is the main projection room. Turning left from the staircase you go down a short corridor and enter a back room with a food bar and a few seats around small tables. The decor is fairly funky.

My own memory of this venue is that the showing room was quite small, which forced a lot of people to stand. I arrived late and couldn't see the films comfortably. However, along a corridor I found a chillout room, which provided refreshments and other sideshows, and which had a good clubby atmosphere.

The programme of the first show at the Loughborough had a home movie photo captioned with 'LOST IN SHAME, HOLISTIC SUBVERSION'. The Back cover of the programme of the third show at the Loughborough shows a picture of a drive-in movie with 'GO HOME' on the screen (+ 'to show work ring this number...')

Benhill Hall, (as part of Camberwell Arts Week) 17th June 1995

A church hall painted in the 'you *will* have fun' cheap and cheerful colours used in community arts buildings. It is a simple rectangular box with a high roof and a proscenium stage. This show included films by Andrew Kotting and Nick Gordon Smith. In spite of the quality fo the works shown it was one of the few shows that only just broke even due to a small audience.

One of the problems of changing venues is that the audience has to make the effort to find it, whereas going back to a regular venue is easier.

A Circus Tent, Mountsfield Park, Catford, 8th July 1995

A small circus tent. Films shown included: *Top Gear* by George Barber and *Bitchorama* by Colette Rouhier. The Exploding Collective were not able to provide the swift set-up and get-out required by the circus management which caused frayed nerves. There was also a problem with the door takings.

At a Annual General Meeting on 22nd of July 1995 there was a vote to discontinue the 'Mambo space' (The Loughborough Hotel) and look for a more less cramped space as a priority.

The Old School, Catherine Grove, Greenwich, 30th September, 28th October & 25th November 1995

A small Victorian redbrick school in which the old classrooms were now used as a collectively run artists studios. The shows were in the old school hall, which had a parquet floor and still had exercise ropes hanging from the wall.

The second show here was 'tough' with electrical problems with the P.A. and trouble from the Council, due to the lack of an entertainments licence. Described in subsequent minutes as a 'sad debacle but fun!'

Hackney Anarchy Festival, 25th May 1996

Exploding Cinema took part in this festival on an industrial estate in Shelford place, Clissold Park in North London. The venue was described by Paul Tarrago as 'a concrete bunker squatted by Spanish youths'.

There were only two other shows in 1996 apart from the experiments at the Ritzy Cinema. These were in:

Subterrania, W10, 4th August 1996

A substantial music venue in Notting Hill (no description was found of this event).

The Duke of Edinburgh Pub garden, Brixton, 16th August 1996

A 'secluded, sleepy, very brown, lovely garden'. The garden of the pub is approximately 20x45M running alongside a railway track. Copiously planted with bushes which screened the railway. At night trains passing at speed create a dramatic backdrop to the cinema screen. There are quite a number of wooden tables and chairs. A barbecue food stall in one corner did a brisk trade.

A meeting towards the end of 1996 noted the continued success of Exploding Cinema. It was also noted that a few people were doing the bulk of the work. An equipment inventory at the end of 1996 was noted in these minutes.

In the summer of 1996 several major subsidiary projects came to fruition...

'Vacuum'. A compilation tape was finished, with funding from James Stevens. It is, however, 'a copyright nightmare', so can only be sold informally and cannot enter commercial distribution. It was launched on the 2nd of August 1996.

'Exponet'. The Exploding Cinema worldwide web-site was launched in January 1996. This was hosted by *Backspace,* the alternative cyber cafe run by James Stevens in Clink Street near London Bridge. By July there was reports of it 'really taking off, it was registered with all the search engines' and achieved eighth place in Internet Magazine's 'choice of the month'.

'Volcano!' is the name of a new London film groups film festival. It was launched in parallel with the London Film Festival in the Autumn of 1996. The programme was announced in July. A full report on Volcano is given later.

Transport. There is a proposal to get a £300 grey Ford Cortina estate. Colette agreed to pay maintenance costs until these equal or exceed the purchase cost - The car will then be hers. Colette also agreed to pay the cost of insurance. Exploding Cinema will pay one third of the road tax. Colette will be keeper and driver. Came to be known affectionately as The Slab.

London Venues: March 1997 to June 1998

I have grouped these together, as I was part of the collective in this period. My own participant observer logbook, which I started at the beginning of 1998, will be the source of data for the shows from this period.

George IV, Brixton Hill. 28th March, 1st May & 29th May 1997

George IV was ten minutes walk from Brixton underground station up Brixton Hill. George IV was a well-known music pub with a black painted back room with a large stage and projection/ sound booth and two or three DJ booths. There was space for about 120 people in the main room (we needed to bring in extra chairs). The main show was relayed to a smaller bar in the pub using the pubs own video circuit. We had arranged for a van to serve 'Soul food' out in the front yard and a bouncer was provided by the pub.

The collective's feedback on this first show at George IV was upbeat.

I was MC for the first time at the second show at George IV and had my head painted a deep blue. I found being MC rather stressful as several of the collective were shouting at me and there were a few technical breakdowns to talk the audience through. The landlord became overbearing and sexist. We tried having a disco to follow the films, but the audience had drifted away. Feedback on this second show was considerably more downbeat than the first.

In the third and last show at George IV I did the decor with Thomas. We prepared special slides and had the idea of changing the atmosphere in each of the three programme sections. DJ Nat played his retro collection in the intervals - to great acclaim, and at the end of the show.

These shows were all on a Thursday night, which, along with the pub atmosphere, was not popular with some of the collective. Understandably a lot of people want to leave before last buses on a weekday night. We then began a long search for a new venue.

Kennington Park Community Centre, Kennington Oval, 14th March, 10th April & 9th May 1998

Kennington Park Estate is a very large estate on the South West of Kennington Park. It is a five storey 1930's tenement estate with external walkways. The more recent Community Centre is situated on the southern edge of the estate over the road from the Oval House Theatre. A plain brick building with no external architectural facade it faces inwards onto a battered courtyard. You enter a small corridor, which leads to toilets, two committee rooms, an office and a kitchen. The main space at the end of this corridor is square with an impressive pyramid roof held up with four laminated timber beams and lined with pine board. The space can seat 150 or more with the chairs supplied by the venue. We projected diagonally across the square.

I found and set this venue up. I had asked Roz, a director of the Oval house Theatre, to lend us their aluminium rigging tower so we could put décor screens up high into the pyramidal roof. Thomas helped me do this at 10am on the morning of the show. I also made some cheap projection shelves that clipped onto the timber trunking that ran around the walls. The idea was to have 360-degree projection. The problem with projections close to the main screen is that of their light bleeding onto the main screen and washing out the main film. But it worked and the whole room looked spectacular. By 9pm it was packed out and people were being turned away.

Duncan was MC dressed as an 18th century French Sans Culotte. He did a rousing performance poem called *England My Frankenstein* which was accompanied by specially made slides. The show ended at midnight and everyone was high after a good show. We should have helped Bill the caretaker to mop the floor, which was covered in spilt beer, but people's need to talk and socialise was too great. He wasn't happy as he had to work clearing up until

PROGRAMME 10TH APRIL 1998

BATTLE OF TRAFALGAR EXCERPT	Mark Saunders	VHS 15mins
HEADCLEANER	David Leister	VHS 4 mins
CRIME AS A MEANS OF GENTRIFICATION	Ipek Threlli	VHS 5 mins
COMMONS SPIRIT	Stefan Szchelkun	VHS 10mins
ANNABEL	Chris Saunders	VHS 6mins
KX	Boot Motel	S8 10 mins
interval	Capt 3D	35mm slides
SPARKASSE !!	The Vectre Spectres	VHS 10mins
HOMETOWN REEL	Paul Tarrago	Super 8 5mins
PARADIGM LOST	Shaheen Merali	VHS 10mins
SORTS	Christian Dyer	VHS 8mins
Tommy Fate	Comedian	15mins
interval	Capt 3D	35mm slides
LMX SPIRAL	Richard Wright	VHS 8mins
IF	Rozann Nobilet	VHS 10mins
AN ARACHNA IDEAL	Jay Gibson	VHS 8mins

HISTORY IS WRITTEN BY THOSE WITH PENS

" A man whose limbs had been bound from birth, but who had nevertheless found out how to hobble about,might attribute to the very bands that bound him his ability to move" Errico Malatesta 1907.

That's right citizens, it's in the interest of those who control the media to present media technology as an immaculate organic product of social evolution. As if one evening Marconi invented the radio, housed his mechanism in an attractive bakelite cabinet and tuned into the latest jazz combo on the BBC Home service. But hold on!!If Marconi invented the radio then there couldn't have been any radio stations to tune into!!!

Exactly....all the early radio sets were transmitters as well as receivers - it was only after the British State outlawed transmission and monopolised broadcasting with the BBC that the airwaves were silenced. Same thing with cinema- it wasn't always 90 minute feature films in dark auditoriums, cinema started out at fairgrounds and as an act on the music hall. That's right, every time a liberatating technology comes along it gets industrialised, professionalised and legislated out of reach. This time we've got the camcorder, the internet and desktop publishing, it's going to be hard to close down but they will try.

So be vigilant!

Make your own culture
Kick out the JAMS

2.30am to get the hall ready for an Alcoholic Anonymous meeting the next morning. We collected our equipment the next day. The next show was set to be on the 10th April in the same venue.

I had pushed for this show to coincide with a celebration the 150th anniversary of the Great Chartist meeting in the nearby Kennington Park that same afternoon. The timing was not ideal as the rest of the collective had just returned from Germany three days before - so I was left doing the publicity and programming on my own. I was also the MC. As if this wasn't enough I tried to make a film of the anniversary celebrations in the park that afternoon, featuring myself with a green head. The idea was that my cameraperson, Ana Kolpy, would make a crash edit from the camera straight onto VHS and we would screen it that same evening. I drove off with my green head to get the video projector from James Stevens in Tooting. The weather was stormy.

This turned out to be a somewhat flat show with a programme that was somewhat serious in tone. The audience numbers were small, probably on account of most of the collective being away and the poor weather.

The final show at this venue was on 9th May: I was the floor manager and there was a lot of stress and bad feeling around that was difficult to find the source of. We had problems finding people to do door duty. This job meant being out in the corridor and being hassled by the housing estate's youth, who were curious to know what was going on. A few people wanted their money back and started to argue with Duncan because the admission charge of £4 didn't have 'a concessionary rate'. Then there were latecomers who wanted to come in free and Paul wasn't having it. The bouncer, we had hired, was good but couldn't alleviate the ongoing stress.

The Oval was a good one actually, yes. Even though it was a Youth Centre it looked alright, and the people running it were sympathetic enough… It looked like a tent of some description, like a tent-full of projections. It was a really nice screening space in the end.

Thomas Zagrosek, interview

Wilsons Annexe, Camberwell Arts Week, 26th June 1998

A baronial styled hall on the first floor of a Victorian school building with a lot of dark timber and a large balcony that was not accessible to the audience. Access was from the large car park then up a wide stone staircase. Pretensions to grandeur were undercut by its institutional usage, as it is now an annex of Camberwell Art College.

Report from my log: 'Colette took on organising this and had a constant battle with the Camberwell Arts Week organising group. This was a miniature bureaucracy which wanted to have a say on every aspect of our operation and the show. They had a whole battery of petty regulations to pester us with. There were many letters, minutes and special meetings. This is the sort of gig you can do without as a voluntary collective.

Still, with perseverance from Colette the event itself turned out surprisingly well. The interior architecture of the hall had suggested a secret society with an adherence to animal spirits. We all decided to make full-head animal masks and Duncan wrote a script in which a person from the audience was apparently sacrificed with a lot of fake blood. Many of the Exploding Cinema were good at making stage props and there were some excellent masks which set a strange atmosphere at the start. As people came in Duncan was standing up on the balcony dressed in his ram's head. The Camberwell Arts Week people took care of the door and bar and the Wilson's Annex caretakers saved us any worries about security. This freed us up to enjoy our own show more. This was a memorable themed show'.

The 'Roof Shows' Peckham, August 1997 & 1998

These were two spectacular large-scale shows that were the nearest the collective got to repeating The Lido Show of 1993. The venue was a large rooftop on an old factory in the centre of Peckham, overlooking the railway. The roof was five floors high, with panoramic views of London in all directions. It was a long roof with a four-foot high parapet wall. The whole roof was about 90M x 20M divided into two halves by a lift tower and staircase housing. The western half had a white roof surface. The Eastern end was covered with grey pitch and has a set of derelict buildings at the eastern end. The main screen was attached to these buildings. The roof of the central lift tower and stairwell was also used as a projection point and place for a set of TV monitors. The stairs up to the venue were steep and enervating and the old service lift was unreliable. One floor of the building is used as artist's studios and it was this organisation, SANA, which had invited us to use their roof.

These were large-scale shows with audiences of 400 or more. For the 1998 Roof Show I can quote from my own log notes. Feedback on the 1997 show was recorded in the minutes book.

These large scale open-air shows were much more work than the usual pub show and were financially and in other ways much more of a risk. The cinema space had to be built from scratch. Rain protection needed to be thought about for the equipment, and an alternative venue found so the show could go on even if the rain was persistent. In the event we were lucky both years as the weather was perfect.

The seating had to be constructed. The first year we devised a method of using 4" x 2" timber planks that were found on site. These were made into benches by gaffer taping them onto short stumps of heavy cardboard tubes that served as legs. The edges of the boards needed taping to protect the audience from splinters. We hauled these long timber planks up the outside walls of the factory using ropes. This seating was used later at our Volcano show in Fashion street and after that by the group *My Eyes My Eyes* in Greenwich. It was cheap but labour intensive.

The next year we bought fifty polypropylene storage boxes in the Pound Shop nearby (for fifty pence each) and hired short scaffolding planks that fitted into the factory lift. The rough scaffolding planks were covered with material off-cuts from the sweatshops below and a large old carpet we found was put down at the front underneath the screen. This seating was used again at The Blue club in Loughborough Junction in June 1999.

The free availability of timber at the first show inspired me to make a pyramidal projection platform and another structure to give rain protection to the equipment on the bridge. This heavy structural work met quite a bit of opposition from the older collective - it seemed I was going beyond an undeclared cultural boundary of Exploding Cinema activity. This seems to have been about reworking existing space with light projection rather than making transformations with actual construction work.

A timber frame had to be made to stretch the large screen we had borrowed. All in all, with having to fill two vast spaces with projections and activity, the work was the equivalent of doing two shows at the same time. We worked flat out for two long days before the show. A lot of this time was under a baking hot sun. There was constant driving work for Colette who felt isolated and got very pissed off.

The result, though, was spectacular! The structures, projections, environments and activities created a kind of club/ village in the sky - which lit up as the sun went down. A weather balloon on the bridge was used as a 3D screen and the row of monitors beneath it made it look like some eastern cyber city. Some of the other film group people pretty much gasped when they arrived and saw the overall effect we had achieved.

This was a great show for everyone with the possible exception of Colette. She didn't have a good time because driving was followed by an isolated door job. The door person needed to share with the person video projecting so as not to get isolated from the main show. Transport was arduous and did not end until all equipment is put away back at home. A future big show like this might need to employ roadies!

The next summer some of the structures had survived and the seating design cost a bit more but was less effort to construct. My pyramid projection tower had not survived and the overall effect was less architectural and more ramshackle but still effective. And it was still a lot of work.

James got paid £500 cash on the night for what we owed on our new video projector, which gave a bright, and blistering performance and proved its worth. Over 200 people had paid to get in and we took over £1000 on the door.

The week before I had worked on the show almost every day. The work had started with a meeting on Sunday evening at Colette's. Monday night I'd fly-postered Brixton and Kennington with Thomas. On Tuesday evening I went for a swim with a friend, who then helped me to machine up three or four red felt fez hats until late. On Wednesday evening the collective made the programme at Paul's. Thursday night I baby-sat for another friend and was on the phone as I was the programmer. On Friday I worked all day on the roof, went home early (and went straight to bed!). I worked from noon on Saturday right through the show. We were humping on the prospect of another night of pupil punching pop. movies from the toppest notch film screening gang in the world. It is with the ocean deep gratitude that we toast **South And North Arts** for flinging open stu stu studio world and exposing us all to this honey of a view. And now, as the sun sets and you have a cold drink in your hand, you're probably deep in thought as you gaze across London.

"Why do I live in this part of the world?"

"I wounder where he / she is"

"Tomorrow It is all mine mine mine."

Enjoy them! For tomorrow your mind will be a vortex of random shock and dark matter... The night is upon us, and our projectors are beginning to purr.

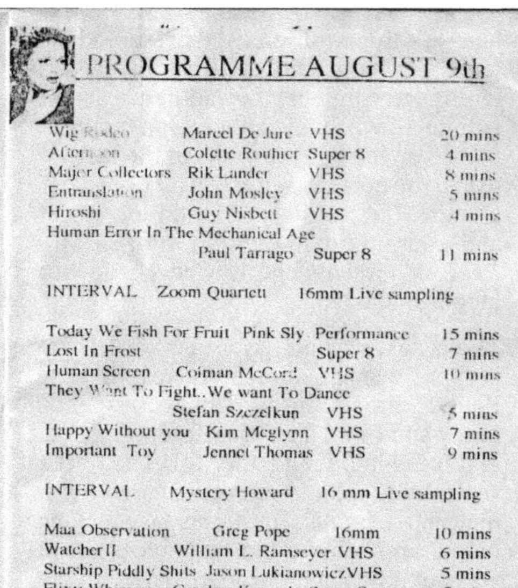

PROGRAMME AUGUST 9th

Wig Rodeo	Marcel De Jure	VHS	20 mins
Afternoon	Colette Routhier	Super 8	4 mins
Major Collectors	Rik Lander	VHS	8 mins
Entranslation	John Mosley	VHS	5 mins
Hiroshi	Guy Nisbett	VHS	4 mins
Human Error In The Mechanical Age			
	Paul Tarrago	Super 8	11 mins

INTERVAL   Zoom Quartett   16mm Live sampling

Today We Fish For Fruit	Pink Sly	Performance	15 mins
Lost In Frost		Super 8	7 mins
Human Screen	Coiman McCord	VHS	10 mins
They Want To Fight.. We want To Dance			
	Stefan Szczelkun	VHS	5 mins
Happy Without you	Kim Mcglynn	VHS	7 mins
Important Toy	Jennet Thomas	VHS	9 mins

INTERVAL   Mystery Howard   16 mm Live sampling

Maa Observation	Greg Pope	16mm	10 mins
Watcher II	William L. Ramseyer	VHS	6 mins
Starship Piddly Shits	Jason Lukianowicz	VHS	5 mins
Flixy Whimsy	Caroline Kennedy	Super 8	5 mins
Snowball	Stephen Ashurst	VHS	7 mins
Downloads	Dan Schott and Justin Chin	VHS	8 mins
My Dinner with Eddie Bahar	Arthur Lager	VHS	4 mins

heavy equipment downstairs to a storeroom at 3am, so it could be picked up another day.' I was completely exhausted! I give this account in some detail not because I was a special case but to show the amount of intensive voluntary labour that can go into a major show.

Following our Camberwell Arts Week show we also had a theme for this show. The roof was to be a foreign country called 'Exploitania'. The Exploders were its officials and we made red or black Fezzes and wore cheap suits. The programme was styled as a passport that was stamped as people came in.

Caroline was MC and was very enthusiastic about the theme. During the afternoon she'd made a sort of spoof promotion video from the 'tourist board' of Exploitania. Part of the interview with Caroline Kennedy focused on her experience of being MC at this event:

I was really, really nervous for like days beforehand, and then I thought I won't be able to get my trousers on... This was in the loo downstairs. It was like five minutes before the show was on. And then I couldn't get them on, and now I thought now I can't get them off either, and then I managed to get them on. And that sort of like expended all my nervousness, and then I was MC and it was like a breeze.

The person doing the compering does miss out on other more social activities. For this reason, Caroline only did the MC role this one time and preferred doing décor projections.

The roof was a different country - Exploitania. I made little videos saying that it was actually a different land and, 'Welcome to our land'. I had a national flag and stuff and, 'This is what we eat, this is what we drink'. This is something that I really enjoyed doing. I think the audience liked that as well, because people can go to any film show, they can go to the pictures. It is something to make it something more interesting. There is something quite juvenile and amateur about Exploding Cinema, and quite heart-warming.

As she drank more beer she believed in the Expoitania land more. Talking to the audience in role to which some in the audience responded encouraging her to go on.

I made posters of 'our leader', a grinning Fifties woman with a fez and stuff. And loads of mottos in the toilets, stuff about our customs or whatever… At one point there was lots of music playing and people had taken the flag down and were dancing with the flag,

On the other roof people were dancing in the beam of projectors and really enjoying the summer party atmosphere. Caroline pointed out the advantages of having two spaces so the audience aren't trapped into only watching the film (or disrupting this activity by being rowdy). People like to move around. To Caroline, having only one screen is a bit

like being in an illustrated lecture.

It does expend a lot of energy, and tempers can fray, at the end of it you sort of go: 'I never want to do one of those again!'. A week later, you go; 'Wouldn't it be great if we did another one like that!

Continental Touring - 1993-1998

Tours have came about in two ways. By making contact with similar groups abroad such as the *Chaos Filmgruppe* from Germany or by collective members moving abroad and starting up groups or running venues. This happened in Prague, Belgium and New York.

The touring shows have been a different format to the regular shows in that they were <u>not entirely open access programming</u>. Although they may have included films made by people from the place visited it is more likely that such films are brought back and shown in

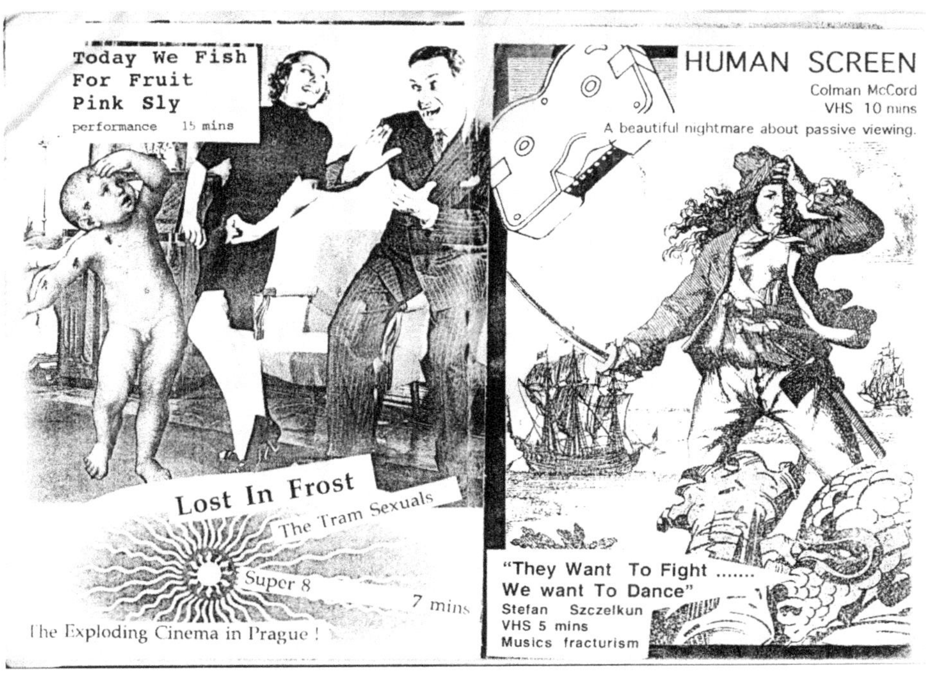

London. The films are often a selection of current favourites that the collective has copies of, or can get hold of easily, along with works by the collective. However, the selection would have included any film submitted for showing in the period preceding the tour.

There may also be less decor due to the limitations of the amount of equipment that can be comfortably be transported.

The usual multi-page A6 programme was not usually produced although some sort of simpler programme was usually put together. Only a part of the collective went on such trips and they would probably have had to pay most, if not all, of their own expenses.

Berlin, May 1993

The first recorded show abroad was in Berlin sometime between 16th and 23rd May 1993. According to Paul Tarrago 'Suzanne Currid went on her own and brought back some films which she showed at The Grace Theatre, Battersea'. This Berlin show lost money due to bad publicity by the venue and it was agreed to only do such shows in the future if there is a guaranteed £150 to cover costs.

Dublin, 11th September 1993

Organised by Donal Ruane. The venue was a disused building on a Quayside of the docks. This was the first group visit abroad but no detailed report was found.

Germany tour, December 1994

A tour of Northern Germany with the *Filmgruppe Chaos* from Kiel. "This was the first contact with Karsten, he was living in Deptford and came to an Exploding show. A whole mob went in two shifts. As I remember it was me, Colette, Caroline, Jenet, Danny Holman, Lepke B, Mick Farrelly, Mark Pawson, Rob Stanley, Andy Lowe, Anthony Kopieki and Les (a friend of Ron Briefl's)." Duncan Reekie email 16-8-2001

A show in San Francisco - 8th April 1995

An early collective member Danny Holman had gone over to visit his brother and had been to a film show in one of the many Micro Cinemas on the West Coast. These are little independent cinemas in spaces that take maybe thirty to one hundred people. He'd been impressed by the two people who ran it, Rebecca Barton and David Sherman, who went by the name of *Total Mobile Home*. They had a cinema in the basement of their home and were interested in doing exchanges of work. Naturally Danny thought of his old friends in Exploding. Jenet and Paul from Exploding already wanted to make a trip to San Francisco on the way to a holiday in Mexico. So they put together a package of films and made up some flyers:

> It was really pretty scary because we had to go through customs... wearing our Exploding Cinema badges and they are going; 'What's that?' and we were saying; 'Oh it's the film group that we are part of'. And they are going; 'I hope you're not going to be doing any shows whilst you are in America'. And we were going; 'Oh no', and our bags were just kind of crammed full of films and flyers advertising the date and what the entrance charge was, and all the rest. Anyway, they didn't look through our bags, thankfully, even though they kept X-raying them. (PT)

The *Total Mobile Home* show wasn't in the cellar of their house after all. It was in an artists' studio called *The Victoria Rooms* and there were about fifty people in the audience. It seems that it is easy to get such audiences in San Francisco.

> The show was packed quite tightly and it went really well. There was an incredibly good positive feedback. The great thing about San Francisco is that it's easy to do

publicity very quickly because you can actually put fly-posters on lamposts and just hand out stuff to people. Lots of people use an Internet connection to see what's happening that week so you put the information there. We were there about five days ahead of time and loads of people came along.

There's a filmmaker called Scott Stark who's also based in San Francisco who runs a website called *Flicker,* which has a listing of all the different screening initiatives and festivals, and distribution networks, and experimental friendly festivals and other festivals. He brings all the information together and has links with these websites all around the world. Exploding Cinema's actually got a link on there as well. Total Mobile Home told us about *Flicker* and since then we've used it quite a lot to check out other festivals and shows. (PT)

(Jennet and Paul returned at a later date.)

Tour of Benelux with Kino Trotter from Brussels - 1st to 16th December 1995

The tour encompassed a hectic schedule, which took in ten or eleven shows in two weeks, travelling to Belgium, France, Luxembourg and Holland. It was considered a great success but made no money. The collective members who went included Sylvie, Duncan, Colette, Caroline, James, Duncan and Arthur Lager. Old Exploding Cinema collective member Katia Rossini, her partner Gwen and Karsten, of *Chaos Filmgruppen,* had put their contacts together to organise it. Colette took her first car a rusty Cavalier, Sylvie had another car and the rest went in Katia's green VW Transporter. I asked Colette what was the most memorable gig out of the eleven.

Brussels was great, I don't even remember where we were in Brussels, we just arrived at a certain place. You know, it was just mad finding the venue … It was quite a cavernous venue, it was great, and it was filled with people who went absolutely berserk for it, they loved it. It was just a big party, party-time kind of thing, and it really made us realise how much of an impact Exploding Cinema had made on the continent, you know. (CR)

The show may have been helped by the German tour of the previous year, which had got the film network in NorthWest Europe talking. These shows used the full Exploding Cinema environment with loops and slides onto sheets. I asked Colette what the venues were like:

The best one we loved was in Ghent. That was fantastic, that was called *Demo Crazy*… Demo Crazy was like a classic venue… It was like an old movie theatre that once upon a time had been a playhouse or a theatre. So they all had balconies that you could look down from and so it was great for us to do projection, because you could put your projectors up there and bend the images across these huge expanses, so you'd get really large projections. (CR)

Another memorable venue was the *Freeze House America* in Amsterdam, which is down by the harbour. It was a series of bunkers in a cold storage building. There was a skateboarding rink on the bottom and then a Go-Karting loop on the first floor. The Exploding show was on the second floor in a fog of dry ice. The smallest gig was in Niemegen, in an empty shop which had been stripped out and covered with white parachute fabric, which was perfect for projecting onto.

Prague - 26th January 1997

A report on the Prague show was published in the programme of the next Exploding show after their return. I quote in full to give the full flavour of Exploding's prose style.

> In January Colette 'Cat Woman' Rouhier, Jenet 'Five Bottle' Thomas and Duncan 'Branch Davidian' Reekie took the Exploding cinema show to Prague, Gothic capital of the Czech republic. We arrived at twilight as the last rays of the sun sparkled on the black slush. The show was set up by Exploding émigré veteran Danny Holman and was staged at The Roxy, Prague's top underground hot spot, an old cinema with a weathered plaster interior which makes it look like a nightclub in a vast cave. The programme included the Czech premiere of *Faster Pussycat Kill! Kill!* about twenty British films and a few local works. The audience was around 300 and the beer was delicious. The reaction to our incoherent spectacle was most pleasing and hopefully we planted a tiny sapling of DIY Cinema that will grow a twisted yew of no-budget media.

New York and Athens, Georgia USA - 20th and 26th July 1997

Jenet and Paul took a selection of work to show in New York. The New York show was set up by Jane Gang of *The Pink Pony Club,* which operates on a sort of exchange basis with Exploding Cinema. The club is in a theatre screening space on the Lower East Side of New York. Jane Gang (aka Higgins) had showed her work regularly in Exploding shows and had then moved to New York to set up her own Micro Cinema. Jane took part in the subsequent Volcano festivals in London. Paul Tarrago tells of a further show in Athens, Georgia.

When we went to New York last time we also did a small show in Georgia, in Athens, that was a very small show and a couple of filmmakers gave us their films to bring back which we've shown a couple of times since and they are very good. I've got copies of my films now on NTSC because it's easier for me to show in North America than it is to show in this country or Europe… I've got a film at the moment which is in a London Electronic Arts package which is showing around Europe… Every six months they tell you where it's shown (and give you money for the times they've shown it). I am really interested to see where in Europe my film gets shown, because I've got no sense of who I can approach to try and show my work (in Europe). It's just a really discreet hermeticised world. (PT)

Germany 2 Frankfurt and Cologne - 4th & 5th April 1998

This was a two-day trip to *G. Werk-Ost* in Frankfurt and *Gebaud-9* in Cologne set up by Thomas Zagrosek and Karsten Weber from Chaos Filmgruppen. Transport was provided by Colette's Cortina estate. The personnel were Duncan, Colette, Thomas, Jenet and Paul. A report on the German Tour was published in a subsequent programme.

> **Thursday April 2nd.** Up at six, packed the car, then drove to Dover where we boarded the Sea Cat bound for Ostend. Narrowly escaping planting my Brothel Creeper in a pool of vomit in the Sea Cat bogs. Disembarked and drove down the autobahn through rain and night to Frankfurt. Checked out the venue *G Werk-Oust,* a factory space on a godforsaken factory estate by the river Main. Met the venue girls Biggy and Misha and their frisky hounds. We were much impressed

by the illuminated atlas globes that hung above the bar. Went to Didi's flat and slept in a row of sleeping bags like kippers.

Friday April 3rd. Walked around Frankfurt, which is like Croydon with more money. Dined on felafel and beer and then went down to the *G Werk-Ost* for a screening of German film and video which was most pleasing, especially an animated symphony starring garage doors. Drank lots of beer, back to Natalie's flat to kip.

Saturday April 4th. Woke up, halfway through breakfast Natalie turned up with Lemmy a Motorhead look-a-like and assorted coke fiends. Went to *G Werk-Ost* and set up our show. Ate pizza with capers. Show went down a storm and was packed out. Drank more beer.

Sunday April 5th. Woke up jaded. Drove to Cologne and met notorious Karsten Weber underground film impressario and infamous didgereedoo player Phil Cunningham, at the venue *Gebaud* 9. Set up the show amidst much hungover tempers flaring. Audience arrived late but keen, until our Super 8 projector broke down. But in spite of it all it was a great show. Afterwards we danced to Screaming Jay Hawkins in the bar and drank beer. Went back to Jan's flat and passed out.

Monday April 6th. Bid farewell to *Gebaud 9* crew and set off for home, but we got as far as Aachen and discovered we had the keys to Jan's flat. Bollocks. Arrived in Ostend and drank Hoegaarden in a bar playing loud FM rock. Caught the Sea Cat back to Blighty, Hell we could have gone on to Bremen.

(from programme 10-4-98)

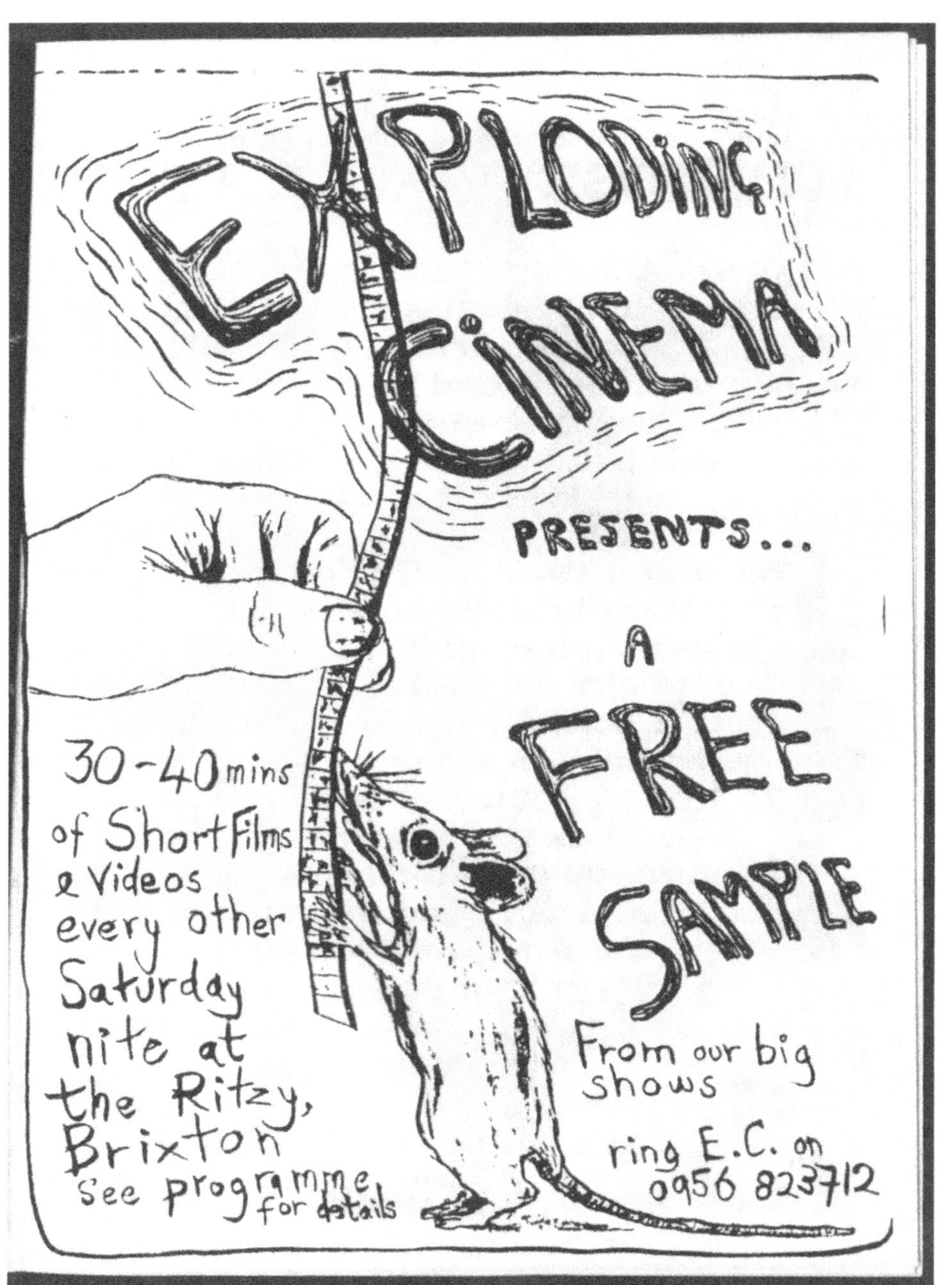

Programme 28 - 10 - 95

The Ritzy Shows - October 1995 to September 1996

This series of eleven or twelve shows was a deviation from the usual open access format. Differentiated from the main shows by the designation 'Exploding Cinema Presents'. This was motivated by the idea of integrating short film within the programmes of commercial cinemas, giving mainstream audiences a side-helping of short film.

The Ritzy Cinema is housed in what was an Edwardian barrel-vaulted cinema in the centre of Brixton, that closed in 1976. It reopened two years later as an independently run arthouse cinema called 'Little Bit Ritzy'. In the Nineties it underwent a conversion to a multiplex, reopening in 1995 as The Ritzy but retaining much of its independence and commitment to supporting non-mainstream film.

Two approaches were tried: the first, called *'A Free Sample'*, was a selection of four to six shorts shown between the regular midnight double feature spot programmed by the Ritzy in October and November of 1996. An advert for the Ritzy showings was included in a show on the 28ᵗʰ October. Paul commented on this in his interview:

> This didn't really work that well for various reasons. The feature films chosen weren't very interesting so they didn't get much of an audience. We had very brief turn-around time to actually set things up and the audiences weren't aware that this was going to be going on and thought it was a break - so it was a reason for them to leave. Some of them even came in and thought they were in the wrong auditorium so they walked out again... So, it was a bit frustrating. We felt like we were a little side bar that wasn't really publicised. Another thing that really complicated it was, some of the time, when we were doing those shows, we couldn't actually project from the booth. The Ritzy cinema spaces were pretty badly designed and they didn't make enough projection port holes in the projection booth. (PT)

Communicating between the stage/ screen and the projection booth was also a problem. You could only ring it by telephone and this was before the time of mobile phones. To communicate you had to go down a corridor, up a staircase and then down another corridor to the projection booth. This architectural form clashed with the Exploding ethos in which the separation between consumption and production is challenged, partly by having the projector in the midst of the audience.

The second format was slightly more successful. Entitled *'Exploding Cinema presents six to nine 'lo/no' budget films bubbled up from the underground'*, which were followed by a 'mystery feature'. After about forty-five minutes of short films there would be a break. People would sneak in cans of drink. So the formal aspect of mainstream cinema, in which the audience does not talk amongst itself and is constrained by fixed seating, was broken down to some extent. There were seven or eight of these shows between 7th March 1996 and the 26th September 1996.

> What actually happened with this though, because it was the Ritzy, they still had to charge their normal door price, which was annoying, they are charging six pounds or three pounds concession which obviously is a far inflated version of what we usually charged for our shows. Also, they took half the door takings after VAT so we actually ended up getting very little money for putting shows on there.

The new format was well received at first but the next show was considered by Paul Tarrago to be a 'pointless and fruitless fiasco'. A meeting on the 14th January 1996

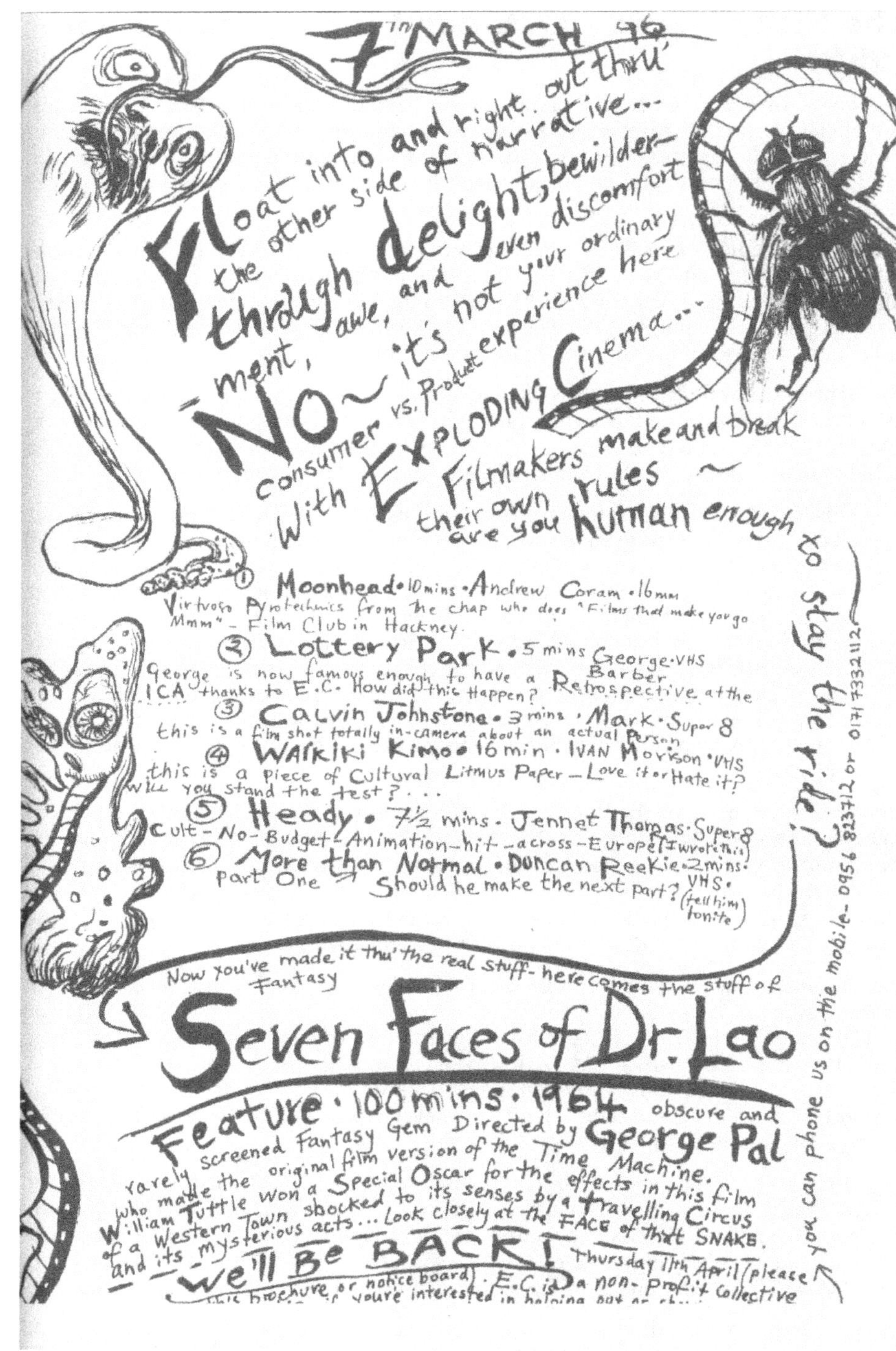

Programme 7 - 3 - 96

discussed the Ritzy Shows. They discussed the different nature of the Ritzy as a commercial cinema and the problems of programming short film for this context. At a subsequent smaller meeting on the 29th January there is a minuted report which is critical of the show that *The Halloween Society* had put on at the Ritzy:

> Halloween Society at Ritzy was packed, but thought to be depressing - lots of naff gimmicks - really mainstream. High production values and white upper-middleclass culture - smug, bad scripts with 'farting in the lift' gags. Confirms your worst suspicions. Andy Johnson fell asleep. The Exploding Cinema shows are completely different; the audience is very different. Halloween doesn't have a sense of being cutting edge.

Later on in the year, the Ritzy shows are still coming under fire at meetings: Someone called Mandy Barefoot makes the point that 'The Ritzy show did not have the buzz of a Loughborough show… The problem with the Ritzy is that we can't show open access films there.' Duncan Reekie countered this: 'No cinemas are showing short film as a matter of principle… We are making a gesture towards this.' The meeting voted to continue with a bimonthly showing at the Ritzy. The next shows were programmed for 26th September & the 28th November.

Exploding's 'mystery feature' format included the following feature films:

The Seven Faces of Dr Lao, Dir. George Pal, 1964

Pretty Baby, Dir. Louis Males, 1977

Quatermas and the Pit, Dir. Roy Ward Baker, 1968

Beyond the Valley of the Dolls, Dir. Russ Meyer, 1970

Morgan a Suitable Case for Treatment, Dir. Karel Reisz, 1966

The Man Who Got His Hair Cut Short, Dir. Andre Delvaux, 1966

Bronco Bullfrog, Dir. Barney Platts-Mills, 1970

The Ritzy shows were initiated by an invitation from Claire Binns; one of the original collective owners of what was then called 'A Little Bit Ritzy'. The Ritzy was being re-launched as a new multi-screen venue with a policy of relating to the local community and was interested in getting local arts groups in. She had been to Exploding Cinema shows and asked Danny Holman if Exploding were interested in being involved. There were a lot of good reasons that Exploding had rejected conventional cinema spaces so rather than trying to bring an Exploding show into the cinema space it was thought that a new approach was needed.

> Exploding Cinema is about redefining space and the whole aspect of watching films. But there were several of us that actually felt that the reasons why we got involved in film was because of going to see films in cinema auditoriums and to actually dismiss that was a trifle nonsensical. We should try and look at the positive aspects of what we could get from feature film screening facilities. (PT)

The features were chosen by Paul, Duncan, Colette and Caroline. They were chosen as idiosyncratic films that had had a personal influence on them as filmmakers.

> We had to do a 'mystery' cult feature because we were hiring the films from a film society screening sort of list and you can't actually advertise publicly otherwise you get charged about twice the amount of money, so we had to go under the name of. . . this is all slightly illegal anyway - we had to go under the name 'Swollen Hearts Film Society'. (PT)

As we have seen the Ritzy shows were controversial within the collective. Often it was left to Paul and Jennet to make these shows happen. Others in the collective were not so committed to the experiment and found the Ritzy too formal and constrained.

> We had to operate around their scheduling. We had very little time to set up. We'd be kind of rushing in there trying to set things up, once their previous feature had finished, before our slot came on. Then they'd want us out by a certain time so it was working against quite a few voices, including the ushers and projectionists. It wasn't ideal. But when it worked well it was pretty engaging because you were in this kind of little cosy auditorium, showing films and having a bit of banter. (PT)

But, as well as its brief, to be responsive to the community, the Ritzy also had a desire to be a respectable tidy space and in various little ways this went against the Exploding culture. At one point someone in the collective designed a noticeboard decorated with little creatures and so on. This was a contact point for people to buy and sell equipment or show films or whatever - a little filmmaker's forum. But it was soon taken down by the Ritzy management on the grounds that it was a fire risk.

Some people were attracted to the format because a showing at an arthouse cinema was better for your CV than a showing at Exploding Cinema. It could have been a bridge between the 'independent' film world and that of the underground. In the end there was too much of a culture clash, which as we have seen, ranged from the architectural design of the Ritzy, to the institutional aesthetic as well as the basic economic conditions. For collective members like Paul who had been so influenced by arthouse cinema it was an important experiment. In terms of this book the Ritzy intervention is useful for what it uncovers about conventional cinema space. Some of its limitations, which are usually invisible, are here made explicit.

Volcano! Annual Film Festivals, 1996 and 1997

Volcano was the autumn festival of the London film groups that had arisen from the networking in the early Nineties in which Exploding Cinema was a central forum. This short study of the Volcano! Festival is intended to give some idea of the wider underground scene in London that came out of and was a context for Exploding Cinema activity. I was involved with the preparations and running of the 1998 Volcano and attended as many shows as was possible. Short interviews with selected leaders of the participating film groups were videoed at the event called '*Aftershock*' which happened at the Oval House.

Volcano seems to have arisen from an idea of Steven Eastwood's:

> Steven Eastwood wants to set up a pan London Film gathering - defining an independent league…   We'd involve ourselves in a London-wide Indie Film Festival.

By the middle of May 1996 the planning of an event involving all the film groups active in the underground was underway: OMSK, One Pink Tuesday, Halloween, Films that make you go Hmmm, Cinergy, Critical Sync, and Vito Rocco are the groups mentioned at that time.

> EXPLODING CINEMA is not an isolated faction, over the last five years a NO WAVE of new cinema groups has emerged including Loophole Cinema, the Kino

Club, The Halloween Society, Films That Make You Go Hmmm, Speckled Eye, Red Dog Films, M2C2, Cynergy, One Pink Tuesday, Critical Sync and Peeping Toms in London, Vision Collision in Manchester, Head Cleaner in Birmingham and Conscious Cinema in Brighton. Two other EXPLODING CINEMA groups are also active, one in Brighton and most recently one in Amsterdam.

By July the name 'VOLCANO!' had been agreed as the name of the groups film festival. It was to run in parallel with the London Film Festival. The first Volcano ran from the 8th to the 23rd November 1996 and included the following London film groups: The Halloween Society, KingKey Movies (Vito Roco), Films that make You Go Hmmm, OMSK, My Eyes! My Eyes!, [SIC], Cinergy, Backspace, Kinodisobey, Renegade, Peeping Tom, Uncut, Shaolin and Exploding Cinema; with an additional international night at the Ritzy.

By January 1997 the network contact list of the Exploding Cinema stretched way beyond London, whilst some of the 1996 London groups had already disappeared. This was the impressive underground film scene in 1997:

OMSK, a club orientated event run by the charismatic Steven Eastwood,

THE HALLOWEEN SOCIETY with regular screenings at Notre Dame Hall in central London; run by Philip Illson and Tim Harding.

FILMS THAT MAKE YOU GO HMMMMM... were holding screenings at the Samuel Pepys pub in Hackney, North London. This group was run by Mmoloki.

KINODISOBEY, a short film cinema that specialised in underground music video and held regular screenings at The Chamber of Popular Culture; the organiser was Ian White.

UNDERCURRENTS, an Oxford based documentary video group who bring out regular compilation videozines of radical protest and agitation; our contact was Ted Oakes.

BACKSPACE, an underground media centre and 'internet web boutique' run by the new media entrepreneur James Stevens.

CONSCIOUS CINEMA, a Brighton based radical protest video group.

RENEGADE ARTS, an international underground film Exchange organised by Robert Robinson.

MY EYES! MY EYES! a short film and performance cinema based in Woolwich South East London, run by Grace Connor and Clive Shaw.

[SIC], an eccentric performance cinema based in Islington north London.

HEAD CLEANER, a Coventry based screening group. A contact was Anne Forgan.

THE TERMINAL BAR, an underground cinema and cyber cafe based in Prague, in the Czech Republic; run by ex-Exploder Danny Holman.

KINO TROTTER, a Brussels based Belgium film group run by ex-Exploder Katia Rossini;

FAKE, an Amsterdam based no-budget film/video group who organise the ROUGH AND RUINED FESTIVAL. The contact given was Liz Wendelbo.

ALL NIZO RESTRICTED REVOLUTION PICTURES, a Hamburg based no-budget Super 8 group who specialise in outdoor screenings. The contact person was Lutz Kayser.

THE PINK PONY CLUB, a low budget film screening event in New York, run by Jane Higgins.

TOTAL MOBILE HOME, a San Francisco based 'micro' cinema. The contact was Rebecca Barton.

The changing nature of these lists suggests that the scene was fairly volatile with groups forming and disappearing on a regular basis or at least network links changing. *Filmwaves* magazine regularly listed the current groups on its 'Film Societies' page.

The 1997 **Volcano!** took place from 1st to the 15th November. By now it is just called a 'film festival' not an 'independent' film festival due to the problematic nature of the term independent which by now had come to be used to describe practically all non-Hollywood filmmaking. The following London groups ran separate shows as part in the 1997 Volcano Film Festival: Exploding Cinema, Undercurrents, The Halloween Society, OMSK, Scooter, Shaolin, Pink Pony Club, My Eyes! My Eyes!, kinoKULTURE, Films That Make You Go Hmmm..., Renegade Arts and Backspace.

I was now part of the Exploding collective and took part in Exploding Cinema's Volcano! show at the venue *Strike* on the 1st November. This was an arts space in an old sweatshop in Fashion street, East London. I also attended *The Pink Pony* show in a riverside gallery near London Bridge; a Ritzy special showing of films from the British Independent Film Movement of the 1930s arranged by Duncan Reekie; a show by Scooter at the Spitz in Spitalfields, which was enlivened by tea and cake served by women in C18th costume; My Eyes! My Eyes! showed in a disused concrete mill in Greenwich with a live performance by John Bentley; the final show in a small warehouse behind Kings Cross station included a 'best of the festival' selection, was put on by all the groups involved but mainly using Exploding Cinema's equipment.

London's *Volcano Film Festival* was the nearest that Britain had to a low budget film festival that was truly independent from both public and commercial sectors. In 1998 it was organised, without any public funding, by six London based 'underground' film groups.

Volcano! in 1998, had a raw excitement that other festivals, from the lifeless BBC British Short Film Festival to the ponderous London Film Festival, could never hope to attain. In 1998 it had box office attendance of over 2500 people who went to nineteen events over eight days. At least 280 films and videos were projected, plus dozens of performances and many installations. International in scope, there were groups attending from Germany and New York. Perhaps the most distinctive thing about this festival and the London underground film scene generally was the way that film wasn't isolated as a media. In *Volcano!* in 1998 film coexisted with music, performance, club-culture, publications, market stalls, cabaret, installations, debates, food and what have you. This made it open to life rather than being a closed media form. The films themselves are also as diverse as the contributing groups, which ranged from the Halloween Society's short film promotion, which merges with the calling card production values of mainstream short film culture, to the Kung Fu cultism and street-wise posture of Shaolin which was run by Ben Slotover.

Volcano! was successful because it was an immense concentration of skills and experience. The nineteen or more people who put unpaid time into making *Volcano!* happen included skilled organisers, technicians, curators, copywriters, and graphic artists. This diverse agglomeration of talent seemed to work well in concert.

1998 was the festival's third year and the first time there has been a base for guest shows in a single venue. The Oval House Theatre in South London provided serviced space, box office and cafe facilities in exchange for a 20% cut of ticket sales plus the income from beer and food sales. *Volcano!* didn't make much profit but it was good to have the luxury of a base for the guest shows. The organising groups each put on their own shows around London in venues of their own choice - some days this meant that four shows were going on simultaneously.

In addition to all the film and performance there was also a debate set up by Duncan of Exploding Cinema at the Lux in Hoxton on the Thursday evening. This was intended to confront the radical establishment and the funding agencies of independent film and video. Of course, filmmakers turned up in force but the establishment didn't. Nonetheless even with just a few of them there, it was like trying to have a debate about political change whilst under surveillance. Unsurprisingly, the debate was generally mild if not stilted. For a while it revolved around the question of labels and especially the fluffy notion of 'independence'. However, in spite of the atmosphere of timidity a few good points were finally made by both sides. The academic John Thompson pointed out the need for writers who could articulate a critical and historicising discourse. Jenet Thomas, of Exploding Cinema argued that the rise of the professional curator had meant that art was mediated by a professional elite and that artists rarely had control of resources. This led to what Colette had called an 'exhibition lock-down'. The historically pernicious nature of third-party management of culture, especially if it is professional or elite, was pointed out but not explored in much detail.

This third *Volcano!* Was undoubtedly very successful. It raised the profile of autonomous film in London, but may have been its high point. Voluntary effort on this scale may have worn out the participants.

The next year the 1999 Volcano! was smaller in scale. It had a small base in *The Annexe* in Dean Street, Soho, for early evening free shows by people such as Chip Karney and Ian Robertson, but little sense of occasion was generated. There was no big poster, fewer shows and none of the visitors from abroad. OMSK put on a show in the Hoxton Hall, an old and unspoilt music-hall, which had its moments. There was a show of George Kuchar's classic underground film *The Devils Cleavage* at the Horse Hospital. The Exploding Collective put on a show at the Union Tavern. The set-up included an interesting argument as to whether we should be getting the maximum number of people seeing the films by putting the chairs in rows, or whether we should stick with the more social arrangement of chairs around tables.

I didn't attempt to attend all the Volcano shows in 1999, so this report is based on seeing less than half of the shows. There was another Pow Wow organised by Duncan, this time at Backspace near London Bridge. Jenet made a point about the lack of critical discourse on almost any of the work. Duncan put forward an imaginative proposal for shifting national filmmaking resourcing from production to enabling the whole population to make short films through local access facilities. Steven Eastwood suggested that *Volcano!* should become an all-year-round institution with a building, but he found few backers. There is a lack of any strong agreement about future collective directions. The underground consensus seems to be wary of hard-edged proposals that do not have a groundswell of opinion behind them.

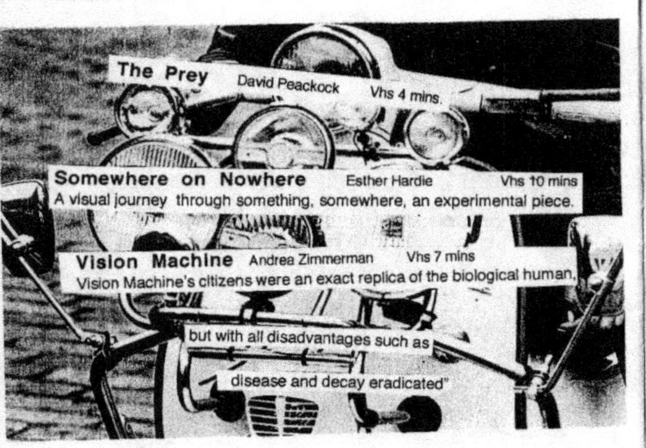

WHY WE ARE VOLCAN

The VOLCANO !! Underground Film Festival is not a new, dig
Postmodern phenomena, it's not art, it's not research for the advertising indust
it's not a talent contest for the state funded media agencies.
It is the latest resurgence of an alternative cinema tradition that began in the
fairground booths and music halls of the 1890's, reappeared in the Independe
amateur film movement of the 1930's and flourished in the Underground c
culture of the 1960's.
It is the **cinema of carnival,** where the codes and conventions of the n
picture house are swept away, where the audience can become the event.
And the carnival cinema exposes a dangerous truth...anyone can make film, a
can make television, anyone can make a cinema and find an audience. This t
dangerous to the media establishment because it threatens their monop
expression, because it turns consumers into producers and because it open
space for subversion. So, like every other form of carnival it has been suppr
and appropriated.

Programme 1 - 11 - 97

VOLCANO ! 1998 (in more detail)

Sunday the 27th September saw the 'Death of OMSK' in Hoxton. **OMSK** was a club with inbuilt cinema(s). A place were it was promised that 'anything can happen'. The organiser Steven Eastwood had decided to put this project aside for the next year and make a movie, so this was the last in a series. Run simultaneously in three venues, the roomy *333 Club* and two nearby pubs, it had over 800 people on a Sunday night. Just about every type of artist under the sun had a slot in this extravaganza from poets to V-Jays, with cinema rooms in each venue running alongside a dance floor, bars and chill-out spaces.

Meanwhile in South London, **Real Fiction's** 'kinetic candlelit cabaret', organised by Paul Johnson, showed fifteen 'Gothik' films and four ethereal performances above a pub in Balham. That same evening, at the base camp at Kennington Oval, lanky Ian White, who had made a name running the Horse Hospital's *Kinoculture* programme, put on his own 'transgressive' evening of hyper-camp, starring the performance artist The Divine David and the author Dennis Cooper.

Monday night saw the **Hallowe'en Society** do their show at the glitzy Notre Dame Dance Hall off Leicester Square. Philip and Tim ran a tight ship and do things properly right down to projecting from a Beta VCR rather than the VHS machines most of the groups make do with. Each film was introduced by an MC who also ran an occasional quiz with daft prizes. The audience sat around tables with drinks entertained by occasional cabaret style acts.

Back at the Oval, hot off a plane from Havana, Robert Robinson was running his **Renegade Arts** show in the upstairs theatre. Renegade is an international exchange of work with an emphasis on what slips off the agenda of the mass media.

Tuesday was the turn of the **Exploding Cinema.** They were the only group with a firm open access/ no selection policy - showing whatever they are given. Duncan, Colette, Paul, Jennet, Caroline, Stefan and Thomas, had taken over the George IV pub, near the infamous prison on Brixton Hill. The interior was swathed in the lights from a myriad of slide projectors and Super 8 loops. More uncomfortable, raunchy, radical and unpredictable than Halloween, they showed 16 works including four by collective members. The Exploding had a wide collection of old projectors and leads and, along with the Kiel based Filmgruppe Chaos, supplied much of the decor at the Oval house.

Meanwhile, back at the Oval James Stevens, proprietor of the open access cyberarts workshop *Backspace*, was running his chaotic **Blink** show - apparently programmed and organised on the spur of the moment. *Backspace*, situated on the riverside near London Bridge, is home to the Volcano web site amongst others.

The Wednesday saw Ben and Jap of **Shaolin** do their show at The Foundry near Fleet Street. One of the things that makes Shaolin different from any other group is the live computer fighting games which are projected on a big screen. Possibly a kind of nascent ritual resolution of male aggression. Anyway along with its obscure Kung Fu feature films, the Shaolin attracts a more youthful audience.

On the same evening further out in South East London, **My Eyes! My Eyes!** run by Clive, Grace and Damian Abbott, were running a show of home-grown underground classics to a mostly local audience they built-up in the previous two or three years. Clive was the layout artist who had designed the slick poster/programme which was reminiscent of the old *Scala Cinema's* programmes.

These groups total about 19 to 25 active personnel, although it is perhaps only ten of these people who did most of the work this year. Most of them are hardened underground impresarios with a pioneer like level of urban survival skills. The point of listing the groups, is to convey some idea of the diversity within the host groups and their audiences. Audiences varied from the local to the 'cult'. One way the underground might be defined is by its diversity and inclusiveness, especially to outsiders. This diversity expands when we take into account the guest groups:

The guests groups in order of appearance:

The first Saturday night of the festival was dedicated to a **Jeff Keen** retrospective. This Brighton based film-maker is a master of the multiple exposure, along with animation and studio based performance. Veering wildly from raunchy home movies to exquisitely composed drum rolls of coloured light and form; oscillating between the lyrical and the banal; the movies provided a retinal roller coaster ride. Jeff, who has been making movies since the early Sixties, appeared looking somewhat awed by the adulation of the younger audience. His film works had been avoided by the film establishment in the 1980s and 1990s, perhaps because of his underground style. This was his first show in London for over 10 years. In fact only shortly before he did have a show at the Tate Britain Gallery. His most recent work was a live multiple projection of stuff that he'd had digitally recoloured. It appeared to be attempting to escape the screen, jittering, flashing and jumping the frame like a cinematic demon. It was this latest stuff that the younger audience seemed to like most.

On Sunday evening there was a selection of German films from the **Frankfurt** group that Exploding had met on its recent short tour of Germany. Organised by Thomas Zagroszek. By this time there was a problem of overload.

The next night was a double bill by **Jack Sargeant** who shared the Oval with Renegade. Jack had a couple of books out by Creation Books and is an expert in the area of underground which is obsessed with death, schlock horror and the so-called dark side.

The main international guests and old friends of Exploding Cinema were the notorious **Filmgruppen Chaos** who have been going since 1975. They had come over in force with five or six of their member present. They were joined by members of the Munich based **ABGEDREHT**. They decorated the passage to the main theatre space with a variety of environmental projections. Rotating mirrors threw images over the walls and ceiling. A chattering face was projected onto a polystyrene head on a high shelf creating a surreal illusion. Inside the theatre large Gothic picture frames contained lurid loop projections. The show, with three presenters, was a quirky mix of animation, cryptic drama, collage and found footage made all the more interesting by the lively presence of the film-makers. Memorable for me was a film about an androgenous Elvis whose life and suffering becomes increasingly Christ-like. His guitar was the cross. Finally, with this burden slung across hir shoulder, s/he climbs Calvary and is finally buried in the guitar (which magically grows to accomodate hir body). Particularly funny if you grew up Catholic in the late Fifties.

The same night at the Oval, Philip from Halloween had programmed a selection of short film and video from the USA in the smaller upstairs theatre.

From here on in the Oval became wilder and wilder. The next evening was taken over by the **Frank Chickens** who were a broad London based collective of about twenty Japanese women, cultural refugees, who not only show films but also VJ, sing and dance, and do uncategoriseable performances.

In parallel with the 'Jap-chick' madness downstairs Halloween Society presented **Rocketfish** the quirky films of Mark Locke and Guy Powell from Tamworth, Birmingham in the theatre upstairs. Lower class suburban culture at its most idiosyncratic and fascinating.

The next night was a double bill of **Arthur Lager** and **VaVaVoom** downstairs and Jane Gang's personally presented selection from the New York Underground upstairs. The VaVaVoom evening had been set up by Colette of Exploding. VaVaVoom was Brighton based and are a kind of total sleaze cabaret with a swamp/ Gothic undertones. Lots of skulls and writhing around half-naked. I'm not sure they were at their best in the Oval theatre, as there was not enough room for a table-based audience, which is what they seem to be all about. Nonetheless they did provide the perfect environment for Arthur Lager's first retrospective. Arthur is a kind of suburban greaseball Nineties version of Jeff Keen the beatnik and in fact the two had connections. His films also use goofy pop imagery along with multi-layering and animation. There is a lot of coarse and comical sex between unlikely (toy) creatures and seaside pier style humour. All of which comes at you like a luminous freight train and is sometimes accompanied by Arthur's live drumming. Arthur has been an Exploding favourite for years and Colette's inspired programming with VaVaVoom made it an unforgettable occasion. Nevertheless Mr Lager was, contrary to his presence on screen, still his usual surly, nervous self.

Upstairs, the tattooed lady, **Jane Gang** had her New York 'Zipper' show. Two of the film-makers had come over and were somewhat shocked at our lack of basic hospitality for international visitors. US underground festivals are much better resourced although they don't sound as much fun. Nor do they include the transmedia live dimension that made Volcano so exciting. *The Zipper show*, which was a 'best of' selection, veered from the darkly comical to the horrificly vulgar. Annie Stanley and Patty Chang produced 'Hub Cap' in which two women have sex in a motor car. Cut! Their limp and naked bodies are drapped across the seats. The cops arrive. Horror enough? No way! A cop then appears to proceed with a variety of necrophilic acts. Too shockingly unpleasant for any aesthetic appreciation to seem appropriate. But it was well made!

On the other hand Mr Mean's, 'Glamour Puss: How to Keep Your Man Happy' was a delightful and funny celebration of sexual seduction for the over-seventies. Mrs Means enjoys trying a variety of approaches to seduce her newspaper hugging spouse. Finally she does succeed in getting his amorous attention and we could all join in with her sense of achievement. Lisa Barnstone was one of the film-makers who had come over from theUSA. Her *Sleepwalk* was a lyrical Super 8 animation in which an ethereal woman appears to hover through woodland glades. Old fashioned effects which achieved a sort of retro poesy.

Upstairs and down, this was indeed a wild night. The large Oval cafe was packed and had four market stalls selling wares which ranged from dominatrix bone china mugs to second-hand super eight cameras. Sandwiched in this cacophony of commerce was Mark Pawson with his lurid selection of publications, pop trash ephemera and toys-as-art. This self-dubbed 'Mail Art Superstar' and ex member of Exploding Collective now makes a regular living with his stall at Camden Market. *VaVaVoom* contributed their own Tequila cocktail bar and a record amount of heaving cleavage. The final nights **Aftershock** was mainly curated by Grace Connor of *My Eyes! My Eyes!*

The whole of the Oval House Building was used for installations and a continuous series of performances. The range of work on show that night was mind boggling. In a dark room a weird group, including a eight year old girl with a false beard, played cards around a table bathed in red light. Behind them was an audience of rigid (dead) rabbits seated on raked chairs. Very strange and unsettling. This was *'Toolroom Salon'.*

Just around the corner, Tim Flitcroft had a sound laboratory, in which sounds of the previous evening were transferred to film mag stock and then looped and passed through a series of table mounted professional film editing pick-up heads. The resulting sounds were then modulated by a small team. A evocative electronic music experience which seemed like it had come straight out of the Seventies. And so it went on, in every corner of the building, using the full firepower of the combined projection resources. An incredible selection of artists working without pay. The ambience was a cross between a lurid street market spectacle and an ancient autumnal festival of light.

Issues and Themes

A. Division of Labour (1991 - 1999)

B. The audience (1991 - 1999)

C. Filmmakers & performers (1992 - 1997)

D. Programme texts (1991 - 1999)

E. Politics and Policies (1991 - 1999)

Division of Labour - 1991 to 1999

From the early events various roles or jobs evolved. These would generally be rotated amongst the collective. Although compliance with this format is not required in the constitution, it is a standard practice which defines the Exploding quite precisely when doing the main collective shows. Some of the roles have even been defined at length with the idea of compiling a manual of 'how to roll your own film group' on the Exploding model. Here is a short job description of each role.

The Programmer: This is the person who must start work first, locate the films to be shown, make arrangements with the filmmakers and compose the programme entry for each work.

> It's a good idea to alternate GENRES, so that the audience gets a diversity of forms. This grabs their attention. For example :- HOME MOVIE - ANIMATION - DRAMA - DOCUMENTARY... As the night wears on the audience will be getting pissed, their attention span drops, they get rowdy, so bear this in mind when programming longer work that requires audience sensitivity. Finally make sure to programme intervals roughly every hour. (efile: PROGRAMMER)

Publicity designer: The job is to design a poster and flyer, which will be photocopied and circulated in different ways. This job is rotated amongst the more graphically adept and is usually considered a desirable task; In my time it was usually done by Duncan or Colette, but Jennet and Thomas have also done flyers.

The Floor Manager: This role requires a person to think about the logistics of materials and equipment before the event and to co-ordinate and take final decisions during the event. He or she would also liaise with the management of the venue. (efile: FLOOR MANAGER)

'Decor': One or two people prepare slides and loops sometimes making work especially for a venue. Their job is also to maintain, and ideally vary, this 'decor' during the show. People like Duncan, Caroline and Paul Tarrago have worked up sets of slides and Super 8 film loops. These recur regularly giving Exploding Cinema a particular kitsch /trash aesthetic. The intense decor give shows a distinctive edge over other film clubs, which can look drab in comparison.

Usually now, if you are doing floor managing and you are doing an installation at the same time, and doing decor, you tend to (end up) just chucking things together. And you are too busy to really get it like how you want it. But it is something that I am thinking about doing; more installation stuff. I enjoy the combination of things; filmmaking is a bit flat. (Caroline Kennedy, interview 16-10-99)

Host: In the first year the host would greet filmmakers and guests and do active PR. This role was dropped sometime in 1993.

Projectionist: The job used to need one person on film projection and another operating the video projector, due to their very different focal lengths. The new video projector (bought in 1998) allows slide, 8mm film and video to be projected from one stand. It is still necessary to have a second projectionist when showing the odd 16mm film.

Sound Technician: This person, often not a member of the collective, used to bring the P.A., set it up, run it and get paid expenses or a nominal fee. In 1999 Exploding Cinema bought its own sound system. As well as keeping an eye on sound levels, this person also puts on music tapes during the intervals.

Transport: From 1996 to 1998 this was done by Colette after the Exploding bought her a Ford Cortina estate, nicknamed 'The Slab'. She in return paid the running expenses and repair costs, as I have said elsewhere. In a large show in which many resources need to be brought from all over London (e.g. the Peckham Roof Shows) this could be a thankless task as the driver also has to load and unload, as well as deal with London traffic. When Colette took a year out from the group in 1999 the role was taken by Paul Motel with his ancient Land Rover.

Door person: This is often a trusted person on the edge of the collective helped by friends, or done on a rota system. Sometimes he or she is backed up by a professional paid bouncer if the place or time seem to require such precautions. At a meeting on the 5th July 1992 it was decided that the only people who should get in free apart from the collective were the filmmakers. This was later extended to a reciprocal arrangement with other London film groups who could get two members each in free.

Drinks: Usually supplied by the venue or subcontracted. If done by the Exploding Cinema collective this job can easily over-stretch resources and muddy the financial situation. Drink sales income is often instead of paying a hall hire fee.

Stalls (including food stalls): These were always run independently by people from outside the collective who show interest in doing them. This is an occasional feature of Exploding Cinema shows, which is hardly ever recorded in the programmes. Mark Pawson has run stalls of his artist's books and ephemera on many occasions. Another type of stall is one selling second-hand filmmaking and projection equipment. Such stalls can have a considerable impact on the space and atmosphere.

The food aspect of the early shows at Cooltan, Las Casas and the Jugglers seemed to be an important part of the formula. In later years, with a leaner collective, food was not such a regular part of the shows.

Programmes: For most of the 1991 - 1999 period making the programmes was a collective act and invariably done in a single evening. At the centre of this process is the programmer who is responsible for typesetting the film entries and making up descriptive captions. Another person has to deliver artwork to the copy-shop, pick it up later and bring it to the venue for collation, stapling and folding.

The programme-making meeting is an important ritual; it generates energy before the show. The programme of films is now fixed and becomes known. The collective are all 'creative' and together produce this object which will act as an aide memoire of the show. Its format is both well-known and complex at the same time. Even if you don't have a film to show you can at least make a page in the programme. Once the programme is made the show shifts a gear into production mode.

Publicity distribution: Generally each member of the collective takes a bunch of photocopied flyers and posters and agrees to distribute them in an area of London that is convenient for them. Occasionally a mail-out is done to filmmakers or to film colleges. A single person informs the Time Out and other listings. Since 1999 an email list has accumulated and seems to be the most efficient and low-cost method of publicity. Along with other pressures email has made flyposting less important. Occasionally flyposting brought the wrath of the Local Authority down on Exploding Cinema. This could also highlight other extra-legal aspects of the operation such as a lack of an entertainment licence. During the period of my study (1997 - 1999) publicity came to rely more and more on email although a flyer was always produced.

Webmaster: This is, of course, a recent role. Duncan made the first website at James Steven's Backspace in 1997. It was phenomenally successful and was reputed to have made the top ten website list in some web magazines. Colette also trained in web design and made a site for Volcano! Damon Herd took on the job as webmaster at the end of 1999 and since then Ben Slotover also contributed.

Finding Venues: In the time I was with the collective locating suitable venues, going to survey them and arranging a collective visit was often the prime activity between shows. Responsibility of finding new venues is shared by the whole collective.

Decision making: There were usually one or two meetings between each show. All decisions that effected the group are made in open meetings. This included the details of the shows, but also equipment purchases and other key business. Sub roles within meetings include a minute's writer and chair.

Equipment Maintenance: Whilst I was with the group this mainly fell to Paul Tarrago who ordered new bulbs and other esoteric matters concerning the maintenance of projectors. There was one meeting I attended which sorted, marked and repaired equipment.

Treasurer: This role was mainly done by Paul Tarrago, although Colette did the job for a year in 1997/98. The account did not have a chequebook. Transactions had to be made in person at a local branch of the Halifax Building Society.

Secretary: This was not a formal position. The contact phone number from the earliest days was often the house in which Duncan and Jennet lived, or Colette. These people answered general enquiries but it also led to them making contacts and occasionally being spokespeople. When Duncan and Jennet's short-life house in Rodwell Road, East Dulwich came to an end in 1998 the phone contact number circulated around the collective more. The role is now more concerned with answering the emails enquiries that the website attracts.

Movie Making: Most of the regular collective are active filmmakers who could show their work regularly. There was an old rule which stated that a film made by a member of the collective can be shown only once every six months. Paul Tarrago comments: "This has rarely if ever been a problem, but it was informally devised lest such a situation arose".

Opinion varies as to what extent getting work shown motivated collective membership and effected filmmaking practice. Jennet saw the opportunity to show as important and has even suggested that it was what first encouraged her to make short works, whilst Duncan says it is less important. Both still clearly enjoyed the opportunity to present their work regularly. Another frequently asked question - 'Does the Exploding Cinema help people to make films? Do we have was production equipment?' Well, the answer was no, but people did help each other out and lend each other equipment on an informal basis, based on interpersonal trust. And there is a lot of knowledge within the group that members could draw on. And then of course, members always had somewhere to screen what they produced (even internationally).

The Exploding Cinema did not provide any formal psychological support for members who made movies. A person who joined Exploding Cinema for support in making work might well be disappointed. Quoting from my logbook: 'On the way back from a meeting at Paul Motel's house in Streatham on 7 February 1999. We had a pint at the Oval. Paul was grateful for feedback on his (new) film and seemed to agree that Exploding Cinema wasn't a particularly encouraging environment for people making films.' Later that year Jennet said she was 'completely starved of feedback' after a showing of her work at the Lux on 2nd September 1999. Other collective members like Thomas rarely showed work.

M.C. (Master of Ceremonies): This is the person who introduces, announces, attempts to make links between films, and runs a raffle, games or other entertainments. The MC was often called on to hold the audience's interest whilst technical changes or even repairs were carried out and to invite any filmmakers present to come up to answer questions. The MC can be a crucial element that helps to transform the show from a normal short film screening to the vaudevillian show that is Exploding Cinema. Here is a detailed account from the early Las Casas shows from the interview with Jennet Thomas:

> I was MC for the first time in the middle of the Las Casas period and I was very nervous about it because, really… I had never done anything like that before. (I had) never considered that could possibly be my role. But it was a good place to start because it was very friendly there, and the audience wasn't too big, and it wasn't too scary. Duncan and Jenny tended to be MC before, both of whom had a much more theatrical (background). Jenny was a professional singer and Duncan used to be in a band and has done a bit of acting, so he was more confident about it… Things often went wrong. So you had to be able to fill in, so as not to let the whole situation get too demoralising. (Jenet Thomas)

She then remembers being MC at the first show at The Jugglers Arms in which the audience was much larger and more rowdy, and keen to participate and harangue anybody on stage. It would have been easy to be humiliated by the audience without some confidence and experience of returning heckles.

> We sold bagels, and as a promotional thing, I actually dressed up, not as a bagel, but… I was 'bagelled'. I became Bagel Woman. I made this costume and I was covered in bagels, and I had a giant bagel on my head. I came on to the stage announcing myself as Bagel Woman and it was time to eat. That went down so well, then whenever I appeared on stage again, even to (talk about) a film, people shouted 'Bagel Woman!' So, for that period of time, I was Bagel Woman. Which was quite sweet. To become recognisable in that way was nice, and I started realising that there was quite an element of Vaudeville in what we were doing

potentially. (JT)

Following this Lepke B decided to MC as the Emperor Nero. He was utterly transformed complete with toga, huge gold belt and laurel. The programme was announced from velum proclamations. Nobody could believe how well he filled the role. Another notable costume was provided by Duncan, who would dress as a Sans-Culotte.

At a typical show each person would take several of these roles, but below about six people the collective was seriously under-staffed. Each show costed between £150 to £250 depending on the venue so we needed to get a minimum paying audience of 40 to 65 to cover costs. Rarely did a show not cover its expenses.

This format takes about 150 to 200 hours of labour per show plus the time it took to make the work shown. If this labour were paid, the audience would have had to pay a ticket price of around £20 per show. It also means that Exploding Cinema shows are the result of a great concentration of resources. This is sensed as a quality of experience that is outside of the ordinary.

The Audience

The audience for Exploding Cinema ranges from commercial film professionals to eco-warrior type radicals. The connections with Reclaim the Streets, Undercurrents and the Anarchist Bookfair will define some of the audience but others will be less political, with an interest in film from any number of angles.

No audience surveys have been completed. It is difficult to be an active member of the collective and spend the show talking to as many of the audience as possible. The tendency is to talk to people you know, the filmmakers and other underground film contacts, so one does not get to know whole sections of the audience who are on the edges of these scenes. I once set out to do an audience survey at the post Volcano event in 1998. The clipboard formality of the questionnaire clashed so much with the dark, loud, informal atmosphere I abandoned it.

The questionnaire is associated with marketing and this style of investigation is antithetical to the underground and to the informal atmosphere of an evening event. It is a methodology associated with the commercial world with associations of an invasion of privacy and a manufacture of 'need'. Perhaps the indeterminate nature of the audience is the whole point. It means that Exploding Cinema functions as a forum in which subcultures crossover or clash. It is a place where the commercial and professional mix and merge with the amateur. In short there were thought to be unacceptable costs involved with using a questionnaire methodology.

The Exploding Cinema events seem to cross-pollinate other areas of culture, or involve people lives that are not part of the 'no/lo budget' film scene. These oblique effects could easily be missed by even the most sophisticated survey. Firstly, because effects are often subconscious and would not be easily articulated. Secondly, because important effects might not be statistically widespread and so not register. The diffusion of democratic discourses is about the quality and innovativity of singular messages a well as the quantitative density that can be sensed in the general buzz of an audience.

Obtaining an audience profile for those who attend Exploding Cinema shows may be difficult to achieve on the basis of empirical evidence without destroying what you are studying. The problem of reducing the diversity of the audience profile in the attempt to label it is also a serious problem. The profile may also change over time, which implies a prolonged and costly study that again would tend to intrude into the 'atmosphere' and radically change it.

At the same time a central slogan of Exploding Cinema is 'The Audience Decides' and the aporia of research data on the audience is a place where further research may be needed.

At the centre of my thesis are ideas about how the public realm and culture, effect each other. I am interested finally in what comes up from the underground into the public realm and its effects on society as a whole. This is inevitably a set of communicative effects that is carried into society by the audience.

So, the audience and how they take in what they experience, how they make use of it is something of an unknown at least in terms of empirical evidence. This is partly because of methodological difficulties and the resource limitations of a self-funded solo research programme.

One thing we do know about the Exploding Cinema audiences is that they are more or less active. They often will be drinking, eating and talking through films. Sometimes they will even lose any balance of attention and the films can be sidelined. In the minutes of the 5th May 1993 the club atmosphere, in which people talk through all the films, was noted. Sometimes the audience would become drunk and 'too active'.

It may also be fair to say that the Exploding Cinema and the Volcano network are to some extent their own audience. The Exploding Cinema Collective, the filmmakers who show their films and the audience are not separate. I would certainly expect the Exploding Cinema audience to include a higher percentage of practitioners and counter cultural types than you might find in a typical cinema audience. I could also expect a large part of any Exploding Cinema audience to be organically interrelated by complex network connections. Although it would also be a valid criticism that Exploding Cinema does too little to encourage further networking beyond what happens organically. In contrast to the commercial culture at 'Peeping Toms', a Soho based film society for those working in the film industry, only very few of the Exploding audience would declare needs for contacts in the shows. Although people do announce shows and events, and it may not be easy to meet the people you want to at an Exploding event, although they might be there.

I did however take an artistic approach to 'capturing' the audience. On two or three occasions I videoed portraits of members of the audience as they entered the venue. I then copied this onto VHS and showed it back to the audience in one of the intervals. This reflected the genre of 'local topicals' which were common in cinemas up to the 1930's. The audience for local community activities, like carnivals or processions, were filmed and shown, uncut, to the cinema audience when they had been processed. The cinema would often announce 'come and see yourselves on the screen'. In the North West Film Archive these now constitute some of the most important early film records of working-class life.

One version of this video work is available on my YouTube collection of Exploding Cinema materials.

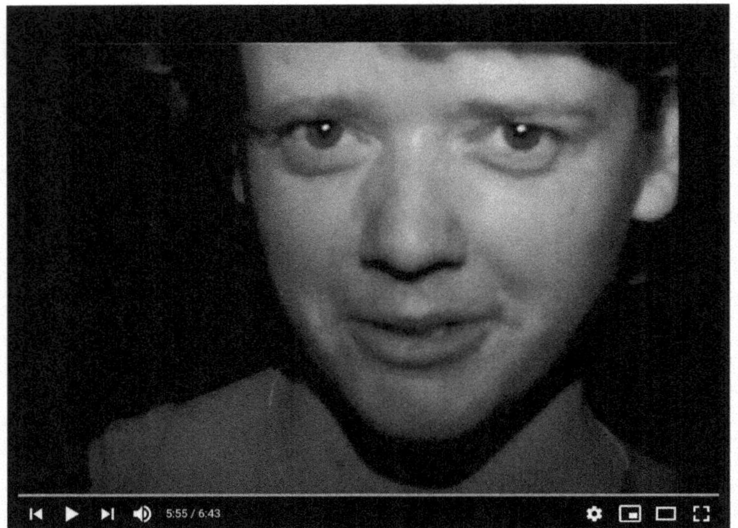

The Audience Sees Itself

Programme Texts: 1992 - 1997

The programmes are the most important trace left by the Exploding Cinema events, and their visual content will be discussed in a separate chapter. Apart from the first six months, for which I found only two programmes, very few programmes have been lost. The surviving set of over 70 programmes up to June 1998 were scanned and transferred to a set of 8 CDRs and deposited with the BFI Special Collections.

The films and filmmakers are covered in another section, so this section will catalogue and comment on the remaining contents of the programmes. I have classified the texts found in the programmes up to May 1997. I used the following headings:

> Reviews;
>
> Pop diversions (1992 only);
>
> Self descriptions and reports;
>
> Lists & glossaries;
>
> Critiques;
>
> Intervention reports;
>
> Rants and polemics;
>
> Quotes and reprints;
>
> Satirical and propaganda graphic texts;
>
> Adverts for political events or other film groups.

I will only discuss the first four categories here. The following six types of text are covered by the discussion that follows on 'Politics and Policies'.

Reviews: From June 1992 to June 1993 very short reviews of work from the previous shows were included in every programme. There are fifteen of these short review sections in all, which review about 50 movies. After this the review sections become sporadic.

It should be emphasised that after June 1993 the individual works shown at Exploding Cinema are rarely reviewed anywhere. The media coverage of Exploding Cinema that does appear is of a general nature, so although the reviews in the programmes are slight they are important due to the absence of any other critical literature.

Extracts from some of the Early Reviews:

In the light of the lack of critical study of the films shown at Exploding Cinema these reviews by three members of the collective are useful in giving us a flavour of the kinds of movie material that was shown.

Published in the programmes from June 1992 - June 1993. The dates refer to the date of the programme the review was published in. The first batch of reviews were attributed to 'Captain Pat Porteus' aka Duncan Reekie (until cJuly 1992).

4-6-92 (The last Exploding Cinema event at Las Casas): "One of the highlights of our last show was 'The Diary' by Yugoslavian filmmaker *Zoran Velijkovic*. Unfortunately because of his hurried departure from his war torn homeland, he only managed to take this one VHS copy of the film with him... Sheer visual delight."

18-6-92: "*Vivienne Dick's* Super 8 'home movie' 'Let Me Tell You a Story' shot with sync sound was a pleasure to watch. Featuring a haphazard cast of family and friends it had the depth, directness and magic of Super 8 that video unfortunately lacks."

2-7-92: "'That Stage', by *Steven Houston*, an Australian filmmaker, was a complex multi-layered examination of communication and information dissemination in our ever more complex modern world. Using a cinema verite style we were invited into the private world of a series of individuals, while the multi-layered soundtrack conveyed a variety of information: telephone conversations, answering machines and internal monologues vied with each other to communicate some sort of 'essence' of the individuals view. Fascinating!" Houston was the founding member of Exploding Cinema but showed only this one film.

16-7-92: "'Seven Deadly Sins' a video documentary by *Ellie Jefferies* about the godfather of the underground himself William S. Burroughs was fascinating. Shot mainly at a private view of Burrough's work at the October Gallery, here in London." "*Marc Conway's* Super 8 film called 'Mantis Part 1' in our last programme should in fact have been called 'Blood and Money'. Featuring footage shot at the anti-poll tax riots in Trafalgar Square in 1990."

"*Suzanne Currid's* 'Up Your Arse' a brash hand-held camera probe into the torrid shenanigans of the Gay Pride festival at Brockwell Park was both hilarious and revealing."

30-7-92: "'Peregrine' by *Karen Frazer* shot on 16mm while at Farnham School of Art was a highly accomplished slick piece of film making."

'Paddy Payne', aka *Donal Ruane*, seems to have taken over the reviewing at around this time and continued until cJune 1993.

13-8-92: "The evening kicked off with *Bruised Fruits* '234 Dog' a searing slice of life docu-drama set amongst the Bohemian cafe society of London's Soho. *Stuart Renfrew's* 'Jack the Rubber' took an affectionate look at rubber clothing and those seduced by its skin tight charms."

27-8-92: "*Andre Stitt's* 'Kincora' took the history of child abuse at the Kincora Boys Home and cut it down to a moment of degradation: a child is woken and bribed with sweets. This image repeated endlessly became a waking nightmare in the auditorium. Oh no, its happening again... A powerful work. *Paul Tarrago's* 'Requiem for an Ice Baby' shot on Super-8 was a highly individual piece featuring a wind-up baby doll. The baby dolls head is encased in a block of melting ice and the baby's eye view of the world through melting ice in truly inspired."

10-9-92: "'Mash' by *Asif Karadia* explored cultural identity and alienation in the life of a young Asian student. Loose acting and tight dialogue held the drama in focus, and the writing was sharp, driving the whole thing to an ambiguous, open ending."

24-9-92: "'Let's Go To the Beach', the latest performance work by *Jenny Marr* and *Cris Popp* took the audience on an all too familiar odyssey to the desolate shores of the family holiday where children whine, dogs bite, and parents devolve into twitching neurotics."

8-10-92: "*George Barber's* scratch video, made in the piratical Eighties, deconstructed and reconstructed pulp Hollywood features into a subversive montage of repetition and spectacle. Turning incidental dialogue and car door slamming into a visual song of terror and hesitation."

13-2-93: A collectively run cafe in Southampton called 'The Flying Teapot' invited the Exploding to do a show in February 1993. The following report on this gig was included in the next show's programme: "For THE EXPLODING CINEMA on the 13th February 'Love' was in the air. We had breath-taking Standard 8's by *Paul Tarrago and Anthony Kopieki* and the world famous 'I Love You' performance by *Duncan Reekie*. One of the many highlights of the night was *Donal Ruane's* 'I am your Musical Lass', a searing indictment of the side-effects of alcohol on the North of England and another memorable film was Duncan Reekie's self-proclaimed favourite: 'SLAVE RIDE', certainly a film for any discerning Masochist. But without doubt the film that really stole the show was a nameless Super 8 shot on Brighton Beach, starring William and with alive sound track improvised by *Mungo*, a truly unexpected and unscheduled delight." programme 20-3-93 p14

20-3-93: This was the show at which *Victoria Kirkwood's* 'Dead Dog' film was first shown. This was considered a classic of the no budget genre (Minute book 1 p105). Five of the movies listed for this first show at the Jugglers are on Super 8 film with just one video.

17-4-93: "Even technical hitches can sometimes be outdone by the resourceful talents of our more lively filmmakers. Such was the case at the last Exploding Cinema when *Andrew Copeman* stepped into the breach and gave a powerful impromptu performance of the voice-over of his film 'Just Harry'."

1-5-93: "With 'Dead Dog Film', *Victoria Kirkwood* plumbed to the depths, 'Sue 86' went one stage further and dropped out the other side. From a fuzzy superimposition of a stroll down the aisle, we gasped as marriage led to prostitution! Drug-taking! S & M! This b&w odyssey on S8mm dealt a laudable kick in the teeth to narrative sequentiality."

26-6-93: "'Berlin Rickstrasse' was filmed in Berlin by *Alan Dein* on his first visit
there in 1986. Dein's cheap Super 8 eye roams the city, beyond embarassment , often
confrontational, observing the mundane, the pathetic and the strange. To the beat of
an obscure sub Kraftwerk '80's techno-pop, a nun rumbles along in an electric
wheelchair, a drunk is arrested, two small boys take turns at shoving each other, a riot
cop adjusts his helmet strap. Dein transforms a documentary into a personal
consciousness, an eye that smiles."

The reviewing is now taken over for a short period by Jennet Thomas:

19-3-94: "*Ashleys King's* 'Life of Brian' b/w Super 8... He shot time lapse Super 8 of a
snail placed (with obvious artificiality) on a large daisy. It thrashed round and round
about 5 times (our time 1 min) (it's time half an hour?) teetering near the edge and
then it fell." .

2-4-94: "With I'm so Sorry' *Jennet* demonstrates that what takes Industrial Light and
Magic Inc millions of dollars of shooting and re-shooting to achieve, can be done
simply by means of a lens cap sellotaped to a piece of string."

Pop diversions: These die out after 1992. There is a series of four mini articles called

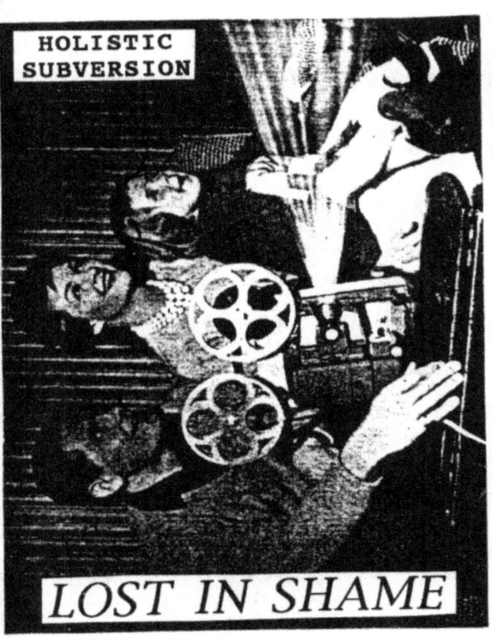

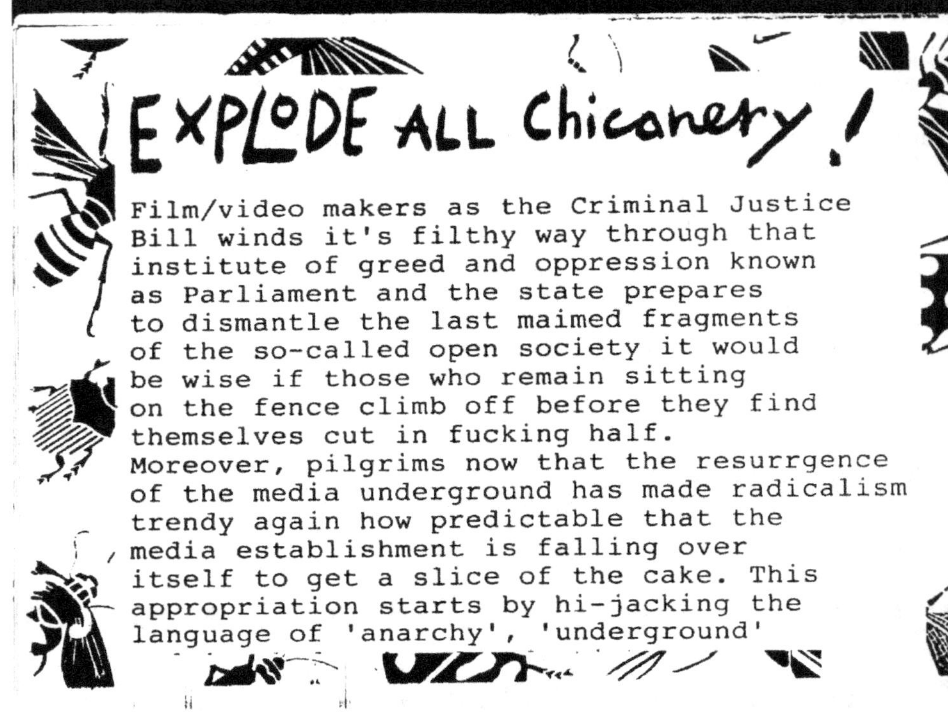

'Ripley's Believe it or Not' that include snippets about Bette Davis and John Cage. These show how people were keen to use popular magazine rather than more literary idioms to produce written material. Which we can assume was an effort to avoid the studious tone of establishment film discourse and to align written texts with oral culture.

Self-descriptions and reports: Nearly every programme has an, often jokey or poetic, introduction, which will often include elements of self-description.

Lists and glossaries: This is another format from popular publishing. These range from a 'definition of underground', to satires of independent film and the avant-garde. They include a satire of Aesthetics with a 'We Love / We Hate' list by *Donal Ruane*, and a seven point guide on 'How to Be a Successful Spectator'. There is an Exploding Manifesto and a satirical glossary.

There are programmes that mark the seasons, such as the 'Up Your Maypole with the EXPLODING SINEMA' in the programme of 2nd April 1994. That text is on the front cover. The back cover has a blasphemous anti-Christ graphic. Part of the counter cultural stance is to be pagan and generally anti-Christian. The tendency to mark seasonal holidays is quite strong.

The text content of the programme does give a very good idea of the concerns of the Exploding Cinema and the range of their counter cultural ideas. The literary forms used also give us clues as to the broader cultural forms that they wish to relate to. Basically, they are 'inferior' literary forms such as the list, the satire, the report, the rant, the quotation, the graphic proclamation, the cheap advert, the comic. There are

and no 'no-budget' and ends with RTZ
funding and a cheese and wine party
at the I.C.A. A documentary 'about'
radical organisation is not a radical
documentary, what begins as evidence
of police violence can end up as rave
visuals in a chill out room.
Underground film/video is not about
being trendy, if you want to be trendy
get your eyebrow pierced.
We replace industrial hierarchy with
free collective association.
We replace wage slavery with voluntary
co-operation.
We replace private ownership with collective
distribution.
Accept no substitutes - KICK OUT THE JAMS

no poems and the very format itself makes any extended prose style difficult. The rant polemics are the most common forms that approach what would be defined as prose in the literary world. I will discuss the polemics in the next section on politics. These stylistic forms do have precedents in the early chapbooks and penny books. They are signifiers of forms that emerge from and address oral culture and create links with a wider counter-culture.

Programme texts about Politics and Policies - 1991 - 1999

The Exploding Cinema seems never to have held or promoted any particular political ideology - except that which is broadly implied by the collectivism of the practice and the traditions of the underground, which are left-libertarian or anarchist. Different members of the collective will support such ideologies to different extents.

The Exploding Cinema does have an implied political stance through alliance and contextual preferences. Instead of seeking the ICA as a context for its activity it would in preference choose much rougher and more low-culture surroundings like those of the Cultures of Resistance in a squatted factory on Tower Bridge Road or the Hatcham Social Club which was an workingmen's club in New Cross.

It is also a model of open collectivist action promoting 'no' budget films within a general underground ethos of oppositional creativity. The political implication of open access is that it would allow the occasional viewpoints to be shown that would never get through the mainstream filters. A point I will argue in some detail.

Apart from the sort of politics implied in its practice Exploding Cinema has made more explicitly political actions:

1. The programmes contain texts that are written in a colloquial style of polemic, the rant, and are often unsigned. It should be pointed out that the programme is open house for contributions from collective members. Whilst they do not represent collective policy, taken as a whole they do represent a coherent political ethos within which the collective operates. These rants also take other forms such as the graphic poster or the populist list of likes and dislikes. There are also straight adverts for key events in the counter cultural calendar.

Examples of Graphic poster texts:

> **Annoying Performance Artist** (13-2-93) A spoof magazine cover as advert, satirising performance art.
>
> **Leisure, virtual reality** (26-7-93) An anti-work rant.
>
> **BoysBoysBoys** (1-5-94) A satire on male violence.
>
> **Explode the UK'**(2-4-94) A plea for the spread of alternative media.
>
> **Things that Art Students Say. Part 1.** (2-4-94) A satire of performance art.
>
> **Representation Is Not Democracy** (28-3-97) Comment on election choice.
>
> **You'll Enjoy These Other Exploding Features** (29-5-97) Pulp novel titles imagined as B movies.

2. The promotion of *Undercurrents*. an alternative newsreel which was founded in 1993 and was based in Oxford. The first annual news compilation came out in 1994. In the following five or six years they released ten compilations each containing 12 - 15 short radical films directed by video activists involved in direct action campaigns. Selections were sometimes shown within the shows. Duncan and Thomas have been keen to contribute to the launch of the *Undercurrents Newsreel* each year, whereas others, whilst not opposing it, did not see it as important business for Exploding.

3. Videos from the Exploding collections have been shown twice at the *Anarchist Bookfair* at Conway Hall (1997 & 1999) eliciting widespread support from the collective. One show was put on at *Hackney Anarchy Week* (1996) and another at the *Cultures of Resistance* a large show of counter culture artists in a squatted warehouse on Tower Bridge Road in December 1999.

4. The organising of networking and discussion meetings amongst the independent film groups. The *'Pow Wows'*, organised by Duncan, have been a part of each Volcano! Festival from 1996. The first of these meetings was held in Farringdon in August 1994. Here is a description of the Pow Wow as used in the publicity:

> Calling all film/video makers, all media subversives, all chill out visualists, all electronic image makers, all collectives, all anti-artists, all careerists, all funders, all academics, all media students, all bedroom animators, all workshops, all T.V. professionals, all avant-gardists, all home camcorder users, all cinema ushers, all no-budget feature fans, all art patrons, all perverts...
>
> CALLING ANYONE AND EVERYONE WITH SOMETHING TO SAY OR WHO WANTS TO LEARN ABOUT UNDERGROUND INDEPENDENT EXPERIMENTAL ALTERNATIVE NO BUDGET FILM AND VIDEO
>
> COME AND SHOOT YOUR MOUTH OFF AT THE SUBMEDIA POWWOW. (efile: POWWow June 1994)

5. Interventions into the world of elite art and film have been on the agenda since 1992. The first record of this is in the minutes of a meeting on the 18th of October

1992 in which there was mention of the need for 'interventions at the film festival'.

From 1995 - 1997 there was a public critique of the term 'independence' and the exclusive practices of the establishment through engagement with events at the ICA. A definition of 'independent' film and video was expressed in an ICA showcase of Independent Film, the third ICA Biennale, in 1995. At a debate at this event, members of the Exploding Cinema questioned just how 'independent' the selection was. The work shown consisted almost exclusively of films funded by the establishment.

In an account of this first intervention at the ICA in 1995, John Wyver was quoted saying there is no independent film culture outside of TV. This was contradicted by Duncan. Wyver then referred to Exploding Cinema type activity as 'bedroom cinema'.

WHAT YOU SEE IS WHAT THEY SHOW

In the catalogue essay for the third ICA Biennial of 'Independent' Film and Video the guest 'curator' John Wyver states that 'In the mid-1990s in Britain there is no independent film and video culture'.

This comes as a shock to the EXPLODING CINEMA (London), THE HALLOWEEN SOCIETY (London), LOOPHOLE CINEMA (London), THE KINO CLUB (London), PEEPING TOMS (London), VISION COLLISION (Manchester), EXPLODING CINEMA (Brighton), THE FREAK SHOW (Brighton), SMALL WORLD (Oxford) and all the other UNDERGROUND media groups and NO BUDGET film/video makers who have created the thriving DIY cinema circuit.

Nevertheless, undaunted by the non-existence of INDEPENDENT FILM AND VIDEO Wyver goes on to re-define it not as an economic or political practise but as a 'TRADITION', a tradition which is alive and kicking thanks to the benevolence of the state funding agencies and the enlightened television companies...

Seems like the term INDEPENDENT as used by John Wyver and the ICA is open to interpretation.

Like ... 'INDEPENDENT' of no/low-budget film/video makers, 'INDEPENDENT' of all democratic access and consultation or 'INDEPENDENT' of box office or critical success. (efile: ICA 1995)

Exploding had handed out flyers pointing out that only two of the twenty six works selected had not received official funding and that no-one from the Biennale had attended any of the film club events that were thriving at the time.

Hats off to the L.F.F. and the ICA for screening the 'in-your-face, raw, sexy and sometimes sleazy'. DIRTY AND DANGEROUS package of AMERICAN Underground film and video. Those of us in the London Underground are most encouraged by this historic breakthrough and also by so many anti-art and revolutionary tracts for sale in the ICA Bookshop. No doubt this first 'transgressive' step against establishment values will be followed by a wave of RADICAL REFORMS: Open access screenings of British Underground film and video... The abolition of hierarchical work practises... Democratic collective management meetings attended by all staff including catering and cleaning staff... Common ownership of the Institutes resources... Scandalous, sleazy, sexy, happenings in the ICA toilets.

DONT HOLD YOUR FUCKING BREATH !!

The truth is that all the radical action at the ICA stays firmly on the screen and the bookshelf, if you really want transgression join the LONDON NO BUDGET NO WAVE where hundreds of makers produce toxic gems despite the apathy and hostility of the LAUDANUM FILM FESTIVAL and the INSTITUTE of CO-OPTION AND APPROPRIATION. (efile: CLEAN AND SAFE. 1996)

In 1995 John Wyver said they would try to view work from the underground, but two years later none of the groups had been contacted, despite the fact that the Volcano festival had a high profile. The 1997 Biennale had the same high proportion of funded films.

> What is not acceptable is that is that they represent the Biennale as being a showcase for the best British 'INDEPENDENT' film and video and tour this pap all over the country spreading the lie that the only way to make 'INDEPENDENT' film/ video is to apply to the state funding agencies or join the mainstream. (Reekie, 1998)

Many other texts in a similar vein were published in the show programmes at the time.

6. Alliances: Occasionally there are political issues, which threaten underground cultures in general. *The Criminal Justice Bill* of 1994 was one such. The Bill threatened to control raves, new age travellers, squatters and road protesters and was seen as a direct attack on the anarchic DIY culture.

The programme cover text of 23rd February 1994 proclaims:

> XPLODING SINEMA, KILL THE BILL, 'We Shall party on the beaches' speech bubble from image of Winston Churchill. The twenty-four-page programme has several pieces on the Criminal Justice Bill.

The back cover has an exploding policeman graphic with the punning caption: 'Kill the Bill'.

This is followed up in the following months by further texts published in the programmes including a 'Rant against Criminal Justice Act in olde Ranter style... signed Kerrence, ye bold flag-bearer and bard'. A campaign of this sort does serve to give what is a diverse group of outsider cultures a common identity. The Criminal Justice Act was not an immediate threat to Exploding Cinema, but by taking part in the campaign Exploding showed it was part of a broader underground cultural resistance of the time.

An advert for the *London DIY Gathering* within a programme and an advert for the *Stop the Arms Fair* blockade (28-10-95). An advert for a public meeting opposing welfare cuts and an advert for the *Reclaim the Streets* march on 12th April, starting at Kennington Park (28-3-97). A front cover text (1-5-97) declares: 'I will escape from your bogus scam democracy into a realm of total and reckless abandon'. Inside there is an advert for a 'post election gathering of resistance' and an advert for the *PinkLove Cabaret.*

It is clear from the above examples that there were explicitly political actions and discourses that the Exploding Cinema engaged in. The focus of this book is not to engage with these themes in detail but to note them as part of the broad non-verbal, written and oral discourses that flow from and through the Exploding Cinema. It is the value of Exploding Cinema as a forum of democratic culture that is at stake here, rather than the effectiveness or rightness of any particular argument or campaign.

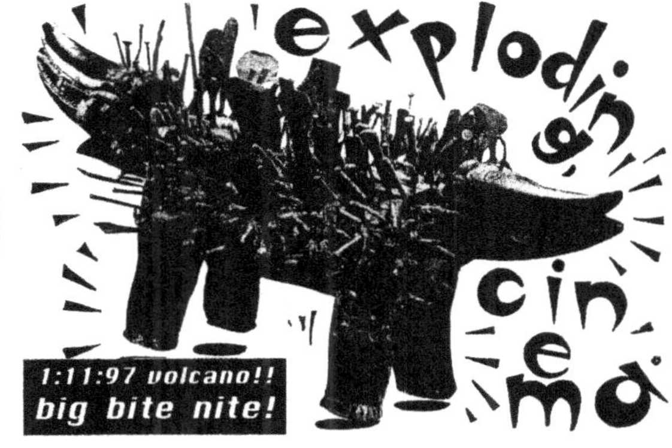

Performers at Exploding Cinema

An important aspect of Exploding Cinema shows is the inclusion of live performance and this is one of the elements that give it a connection to the music-hall tradition and early cinema history.

The range of performers has been as diverse as the movie material and has included: Performance art in the European tradition by *Ronald Fraser-Munro* who did at least five performances, *Andre Stitt, Hermine* and *Ian Hinchliffe*; singing by *Jenny Marr* and Mongolian singing by *Cat Von Trapp*; music by *The Murphys, Bing Selfish, DogRack, Dave Powell* and many others; live painting by *Wendy Chandler*; percussive sculpture by *Wendy Welder*; sound Sculptures from *Lepke B.* and the *Bohman Brothers*; dance by *Yasunari Maeda*; poetry by *Vanessa Richards and Poets of the Machine;* prose readings by *Stewart Home.*

The Exploding Cinema collective has provided *Duncan Reekie's* 'Theatre of Sad' group performances and a short-lived collective member *Vanessa Woolf* once put on her ambitious 25min musical 'Supermover', an extravagant 'rock music time machine'.

Performance has been a category problem as many include projected work of all types and some projected works include a live element. It is not possible to make these sorts of distinctions from the extant records. Both Duncan Reekie and Jennet Thomas regularly do projected works with a live voice-over. But it seemed confusing to include straight performance (without projection) within a list of film - the main focus of the Exploding Cinema effort. Nonetheless, performance *is* much more than a diversion for the audience. The merging of live performance with movies underlines the close relation between the live performer and the historical resonance of the music-hall, circus, magic lantern phantasmagorias and early silent film with piano accompaniment.

If the filmmaker is present the films are backed up by her live presence. One's perceptual framework is changed when a poorly made movie is followed with an interview with the maker who turns out to be a teenager making hir first film. After s/he has talked about his work process the film can be seen within a different frame. This constitutes another kind of live presence.

The role of MC can become that of a performer and this has been discussed in some depth in a previous section. The MC is an intermediary or a medium. The audience are themselves celebrated as rowdy, as 'active', as being a part of the process and can often be performers in their own right. This is contrary to the historical pacification of the theatre audience by the forces of good taste.

From another point of view, it is the diversity of media that strikes one again and again in the process of classification of Exploding Cinema material, whether we look at the genres of projected works or performance. In terms of any ideas about the discourse function of Exploding Cinema as forum, this diversity may be crucial, undercutting any simplistic notions of language and communication as a cut-and-dried system. For written cultures, as dominated by their alphabets as the Europeans have been, the notion that language is essentially oral is simply beyond comprehension to the literary establishment.

A detailed description of performances by *Andre Stitt* and *Steven Houston*, along with 'games with the audience' was related in the interview I recorded with Jennet Thomas:

> I don't think Andre Stitt had been that long in the group. But he said that he was going to do a performance. He was fairly well known for getting up to some strange things. And of course… what was nice about Las Casas was that people did come and they watched the shows, and they would eat, they would have a nice big vegetarian meal and they would sit down.

> André came along on stage, and took all his clothes off and got out all these jars of mustard and ketchup and I think these frankfurters as well and then proceeded to shove the frankfurters up his arse. And then squirt the mustard up his arse and put the mustard on the frankfurters and did the same thing with the tomato sauce and mayonnaise as well, and shoving this anywhere he could. And it was sort of flying all over the place. It was very alarming, and he was shouting as well at the same time, and there was some kind of sound track, and possibly a projection going as well. It was quite a shock for people that had come to have a nice vegetarian meal and see some super eight films!

> What was so shocking was that the mustard looked like puss and the tomato ketchup looked like blood. And he was naked and covering himself in this, and it looked pretty unpleasant. You know, it did look fairly. . . and it stank as well. (JT)

I then asked her about a performance she had mentioned by Steven Houston.

> Yes. At Las Casas. He wrote quite interestingly, and he took slides from lifestyle magazines - very, very smart interiors. It was this narrative about a woman who felt that she was the centre of the world, but in fact it was kind of about an incredibly depressive state of mind, and sort of falseness. I played a part in this - I was speaking what he had written, with these slides being projected. And then he played his trumpet, and he was pretty good actually. He had written a little trumpet piece to go with this slide text performance thing. It would have been good it he did more actually. (JT)

We discussed the aspects of vaudeville in Exploding shows especially in terms of audience participation. The raffle is the most mundane way of doing this and Exploding show almost always has a raffle with silly prizes. There have also been competitive games as well, such as *Utopian Bingo*. In this version of the classic game of Bingo, the point at which all the numbers are completed is reached by the whole audience at the same moment. In an ideal version many people in the audience simultaneously leap up to shout 'Bingo!' Jennet went on to describe a 'Seats Lotto' she organised at some of the Ritzy shows.

> I did a floor plan of the cinema at the Ritzy and, I made an animation… of this

little ball rolling around, and it would stop at one seat. You had to be aware of what seat you were in and what number and then stand up and wave your hand if the ball landed on your seat. So, it was like an animation, but you kind of knew that it was a predetermined thing for people that came previously to the shows. So I did two versions of it, but if you came for more than a few shows, the same seat would win. So, if you could remember where it was, you know, but we pretended that it was a random thing. The audience would do an odd double take. (JT)

A couple of weeks ago a friend of mine asked me to take a look at his Pathe Baby 9.5 cine camera. We walked back to his house, and all the way I was thinking about what was going to happen. As soon as we got to the bedroom he took the camera out of it's case. As the lens cap slipped off he pressed his body up against mine, I put my arms around him and ran my hands down his back. His pistol grip was firm but more shapely than a Bolex and the difference really turned me on. I pulled his shirt up and stroked his bare buttocks. He wasn't wearing any knickers, and as I squeezed his arse-cheeks he started to kiss my neck. The Pathe Baby was introduced in 1922, later came the Pathe-Rural 17.5 (now abandoned for amateur use) and finally, thanks to the production of very fine grained emulsions, the Kodak 8 mm. That really gets me going. When his lips fastened on my nipple I let out a groan. I could feel the Dallmeyer 15mm F.1.5 lens nudging against my leg and I reached down and gently gripped the focus ring sending

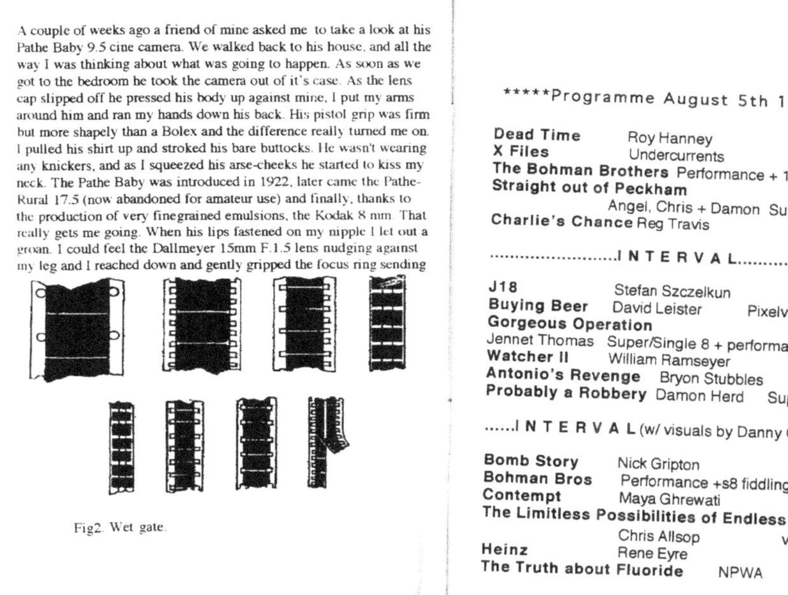

Fig2. Wet gate.

*****Programme August 5th 1999*****

Dead Time	Roy Hanney	vhs 3½ mins
X Files	Undercurrents	vhs 5 mins
The Bohman Brothers	Performance + 16mm	10mins
Straight out of Peckham		
	Angel, Chris + Damon	Super 8 4 mins
Charlie's Chance	Reg Travis	vhs 26 mins

........................I N T E R V A L........................

J18	Stefan Szczelkun	DV 10 mins
Buying Beer	David Leister	Pixelvision 3 mins
Gorgeous Operation		
Jennet Thomas	Super/Single 8 + performance	8 mins
Watcher II	William Ramseyer	vhs 8 mins
Antonio's Revenge	Bryon Stubbles	vhs 4 mins
Probably a Robbery	Damon Herd	Super 8 4 mins

......I N T E R V A L (w/ visuals by Danny Cooke).......

Bomb Story	Nick Gripton	vhs 1.5 mins
Bohman Bros	Performance +s8 fiddlings	10 mins
Contempt	Maya Ghrewati	vhs 2 mins
The Limitless Possibilities of Endless Repetition		
	Chris Allsop	vhs 11½ mins
Heinz	Rene Eyre	vhs 5 mins
The Truth about Fluoride	NPWA	vhs 13 mins

Programme 5 - 8 - 99

Filmmakers and Films - 1992 - 1997

In quantitative terms the statistics of Exploding Cinema productivity are without doubt impressive: Twenty-five filmmakers in the collective showed about 207 films in the period 1992 - 1997. A further twenty five filmmakers, who were not in the collective and had shown four or more films at Exploding Cinema, had in total shown 212 films in the same period. A further twenty three filmmakers had shown three films each. Altogether over a thousand films have been shown by around seven hundred filmmakers in the period for which records were available. A full content analysis showing the filmmakers who showed most work follows.

I did not study the filmmakers in person in this research programme. However a thumbnail sketch may be of interest here in the form of an extract from an email sent to me when I was doing the programming:

"I would like to come down and see the screening, but I am on limited budget. I live in rented accommodation and the rent is phenomenal, and my latest project has come entirely out of my pocket, so money is tight at the moment to say the least. I will try though; having 'The Reckoning' screened is a first for me.

Later: I won't be able to make it to the screening I'm afraid. I cannot arrange transport and I cannot get Friday evening off work. I only work two frigging hours, I've offered to lick my bosses boots clean, even the soles but 'no'. If you can give me some feedback I'd be very grateful." *Nathan Hughes*.

A self-description by *Rosalind Grainger*, a collective member between 1993 to 1995 is a unique text in the programmes and is worth quoting here:

"I started making videos last year in Sydney after attending adult education class in filmmaking for beginners. I chose video rather than film because it seemed less technical, cheaper and more immediate.

I managed to meet other people who had skills and equipment to share and were happy to let me be the director and writer. In a year we made four very low-budget productions (under £50). Obviously as we were beginners the quality of this early work is not good, but more importantly we were learning fast and not too dependent on others for favours.

'The Bastard in the Basement' was my most ambitious project. It had a budget of about £150, £90 of which was spent on the editing process. The rest of the money went on expenses (food/ petrol/ lighting hire). I still feel there are things I could have done better, but of course everyone says that. We were very lucky to be lent a camera and microphone for the day, saving about £100.

Although I would like to study film/video in a more formal setting, to do so can be extremely expensive and often it is difficult to get a place if you have the 'wrong' background (no previous art involvement, too old etc). I am therefore committed to learning through skill sharing and continuing to make as many very low budget productions as possible now I am back in London." (from Programme 11-9-93)

In this next section I will show the range of subject matter covered by the films projected at Exploding Cinema by extracting genre self-descriptors from the captions given in the programmes.

A listing of the filmmakers and their films that have been recorded in the programmes has been compiled and bound separately. In the content analysis chapter that follows I have made an analysis of the filmmakers from this list that have shown most frequently.

Analysis of film types:

I made a list of the self-descriptors of works extracted from the short texts found in the programmes. These are the nearest we get to a consistent description of each film shown. Often cryptic and sometimes ironic, the captions are written by the programmer of the show. She or he will often view the work before the show, or question the filmmaker as to the movies content. In an estimated 10 - 20% of cases, the captions are based on a written description supplied by the filmmaker.

These descriptors tend to extend and play with the terms of existing cinematic taxonomies. Particularly using labels that are in circulation in the underground dialect. New categories could arise out of a discursive relationship with an audience over time. Presently these self-descriptors rely on the terminology of existing genres but may also be ironic or playful usages.

They indicate a wide range of filmmaking styles and approaches. At the same time, we should note that work that falls outside the existing terminology might not find an adequate label. Duncan Reekie's rant poems, with slides or video as counterpoint, do not have an obvious existing cinematic category. Jennet Thomas's digitally animated or collaged narratives with their strange anti-aesthetic hover between kitsch, and a sort of protected naivety. Other works mix genre in innovative ways.

One of the values of Exploding Cinema is exactly this boundary hopping which may seem to negate the utility of this sort of analysis which tends to draw representation back to existing verbal categories. A value of underground films is that they evade normative taxonomic definition. But I would argue that the conventional descriptors need to be at least listed to allow the uncategorisable to be critically appreciated by default, or for the linguistic aporia which hover vertiginously around the unnamed are allowed to announce the problematic of their immanent tension. A tension that is generated by the lack of symmetry between the world of words and the world of things and their relations.

Along with the paucity of critical response to the work shown, there has been little attempt to develop a new critical language to describe and appreciate this body of work beyond what occurs in these seemingly flippant captions and the short early reviews. Without this critical mediation the work has its cultural effect only directly through the experience that the viewers have whilst watching the film together. The value of any discourse in response to such experiences may lay claim to an unmediated authenticity - there are no preconceptions set up by critical previews or advertising. But this may also be seen as a romantic and naive position which basically leaves this whole area of work undefended and vulnerable to easy marginalisation and for the most part, as there is as yet no archive, plain extinction.

Exploding Cinema movie genres 1992 - 1997

Animation (11); abstract; audio visual; buried history; campaign film (2); celebration; chiller; classic pastiche; collage (see montage); comedy (2); cult classics (2); cyber glam; deviant; dance video; documentary (10); dream sequence; epic story; fantasy; film noir (2); found footage (3); Gothik terror; hallucinatory (2); hard-core experimental; home movie (3); holiday movie (3); horror, kitchen sink; independent short film (2); interview; legendary; lesbian vampires; light patterns; L.A. trippy; melodrama, fifties; montage, collage (2); musical (2); musical medley; mystery shocker; narrative (2); nostalgia; opera for film; parody, gross; performance poetry; philosophical tirade; pop promo/music video (2); porno pastiche (2); propaganda; public info film spoof; psychological thriller; road movie(2); sadomasochistic; sci-fi shocker; scratch video; scratched film; short film; student film; Super 8 epic; surreal; techno pagan meditation; terror; trash biker classic; video sampling; wedding video (3); western (2); work in progress.

Clearly the films shown cover a lot of ground both in reflecting mainstream genres, and amateur genres such as wedding videos, holiday movies or home movies. There are also underground categories like trash or Scratch-video and cult sub-genre crossovers like 'lesbian vampires'. Animation and documentary are the most popular broad genre descriptors. They are general umbrella terms that occupy neutral territory in underground critical polarities.

Only one film is described as 'horror'. Perhaps this is surprising, as this is a leading pop trash genre of the commercial feature film. Only two are labelled as 'porno' and both of those are pastiche. Notable because the underground still has its Sixties US image for exploring sex taboos and we might expect more sexual 'transgression'. However Exploding Cinema shows are welcoming to all ages and so there is a intuitive tendency to avoid material that might be overly offensive in sexual terms.

The descriptors do indicate how the films shown at Exploding Cinema seem to embrace popular references and show a great diversity of approaches to filmmaking that find their place within the show. It is remarkable how little repetition of descriptors occurs.

MEDIA TUTOR.....

First you told us that our popular culture w
rubbish and that the only way to freedom was A
Then you told us that everything we thought and
was determined by economics and that o
language was really a code which only y
understood.
Next you told us that our personalities were writt
in code when we were children in parts of o
minds that only you knew about and then you to
us that our popular culture was really a means
control us but that you had discovered a way to fr
us. So you studied our popular culture and taug
your discoveries to the Artists who took it a
displayed it in galleries and you called th
Postmodernism. Finally you told us that everythi
had become either a code or an image and that w
really dont exist anymore. And now you tell us th
it's all been a big mistake and that the future is
the world wide web making Art with machine
which we dont have access to in a code which on
you understand.
You told us Art would make us free, it hasn't'. Yo
told us understanding culture would make us fre
it hasn't and now you tell us digital technology wi
free us.....but it seems like the only one that's fre
is you.

Love from your Other

**********Programme November 4th 1999**********

Chemical Warfare in the Supermarket
Corrin Little VHS 5min
The Hole Oliver Griffin VHS 10min30sec
Broken Glass Paul Synott VHS 1min
The Bohman Bros Performance + VHS 10min
Life Model Claudia Lee VHS 23min

..................…......INTERVAL…......................

4 Ways He Tried To Tell Her
Jennet Thomas VHS 7min
3 by 3 Jason Cunningham VHS 4min
Virgin Birth Vesna Cudic VHS 13min
Coup de Vent Megan Bedell S8 4min20sec
Words Teething Trouble
Roy Hanney VHS 5min
Impossibility Of Mortality In The Mind Of The Cyclist Andrew Vallance VHS 4min

..................…......INTERVAL......................

The Bohman Bros Performance+16mm 10min
Bad Korma Annie Bailey VHS 7min27sec
N Oliver Griffin VHS 10min
Animal Paul Synott VHS 1min
Get Out Of My Way Superfly TNT's VHS 3min
Eddy Meatbeater Gennie Rose VHS 10min

Chapter 5

Content Analysis:
The collective and the filmmakers

Thinking critically about this methodology

An analysis of attendance at meetings gives an indication of who was in the Exploding at any time and how active they were. The intensities in which filmmakers showed at Exploding are measured and could indicate a democratic approach to a pre-canonic formation. The proportion of women to men allows us to measure one aspect of accessibility and compare it to mainstream film production.

Content analysis can be defined as a research technique that makes inferences from the identification of objective characteristics within a text. These characteristics can most simply be measured in terms of quantities. Later researchers, such as Krippendorff (1980) put more emphasis on the contexts within which inferences are drawn.

Since the Sixties content analysis has not become as ubiquitous a research method as the questionnaire or focus group, which may be due to a lack of agreement on standard methodologies, which has meant that results from different studies were not comparable. The main reasons that content analysis is useful are:

* The act of measurement is unobtrusive and is unlikely to act as a force that will influence the subject of study.

* As the method acts on documents from the past, which are unlikely to change, the cultural indicators derived in such a way can be checked and are likely to constitute reliable empirical data.

* Data collected in this systematic way is persuasive and difficult to refute as it is easily replicable.

On the other hand the necessary data reduction can destroy nuance and complexity. The imposition of standard measures and the production of averages flattens difference and obscures the value of the singular. The idiosyncratic may be argued to be particularly important in creativity and innovation. And although the process of measurement may be unobtrusive, the presentation and interpretation of results can still be made to appear favourable to a preconceived thesis.

Both these criticisms are valid only for poor content analysis that is not self-critical of the limits of its own unitisation and not supplemented with more qualitative methods. The key question is whether the units counted give a valid measure of the concept that the researcher associates with them.

> Equal counting is a practical simplification that content analysts believe works well in most circumstances, but reality is probably much more complicated.
>
> Webber, 1991, p72

Although such standardisation is necessary it is important to note the implications of variations in value. In my analysis of the films shown, each film is valued as one unit in spite of a wide variation in the types of films and the impact that they have. Whilst the reduction of a film work to a unit value of one is obviously a crude mechanism it seems to produce results which are useful if the limitations of unitisation are kept in mind.

Inferences derived from such totalling must not only be internally valid but must also be tested within the wider context in which 'the text' exists. It is often these wider inferences that are more significant but also more vulnerable to normative reductions. This sort of analysis must entail a qualitative vigilance to ensure that the objectivity of the method does not obliterate the value or diversity of its subject.

If the above limitations are borne in mind content analysis could be particularly useful in the study of art collectives in that it is suited to the analysis of a large amount of data that is inevitably thrown up by a large group or 'movement'.

Exploding Cinema: attendance, works and gender

Three aspects of Exploding Cinema have been investigated using this methodology:

1. Attendance at meetings (1992 - 1997) has been tracked to give a dynamic picture of the involvement of various people within the collective. It will be argued that this gives the best objective indication of the general influence of particular individuals in the collective, creating a model that can be used as the basis of discussion in an area that is often emotionally charged. This is based on recording the attendance at meetings as recorded in the minute books.

2. All the works shown at Exploding Cinema from 1992 to 1999 have already been recorded in a catalogue of film-makers and the films they showed, which has been extracted from the surviving show programmes. From this list of data I extracted those filmmakers who have shown most works and whose work has been given repeat screenings. This shows those who are most energetic in contributing to the main programme. I also argue that this correlates with a process of canon formation. This tentative canon formation is then tested and expanded to include selected makers with one or two films on the list by reference to three further sources (The Vacuum compilation video and two European tour selections from 1994 and 1995). The implications of such a construction are then briefly discussed.

3. The proportion of men to women both showing and taking part in the collective is also examined and discussed in relation to the open access policy of the group. It would be unrealistic to expect an open access policy to compensate for the inequalities within society, but at least it provides an objective measure against which these issues can be examined, discussed and challenged.

In each case I will first enter into a discussion of the units of measurement, or unitisation and the most likely sources of error.

The following quantitative assessments give us some insight into the influence of any individual, canon formation and gender inequality and access. All of these are key issues for any collective of cultural producers. Conclusions have been checked against the oral memories of the present collective and others.

A draft of this content analysis of collective membership was circulated to the Exploding Cinema collective. The feedback produced a number of minor corrections, which I will discuss later, but no major challenges to the main personnel.

Attendance at meetings

In a small collective the attendance at meetings is an indicator of the power any person has in the organisation. Of course there are other factors such as eloquence, persuasiveness, force of personality but attendance is the most basic form of democratic power in a non-hierarchical collective. Meetings are the only fora at which formal decisions can be made by vote. Presence at meetings is a key point at which future actions may be decided. Power and ownership are also closely related. Where ownership is not defined by external constraints or inner legislation it tends to operate by force of occupation and work done.

The data also provides a simple fairly objective record of who was in the collective over time.

Background: There is only one formal post within Exploding Cinema that does not rotate from show to show, this is the role of treasurer. The post of treasurer is held over periods of a year or more. The other posts in the Exploding Cinema are only held for the period in which a show is prepared. A chair and secretary are elected for each meeting from amongst the attendees. There is no elected leader although length of service and work put in does inevitably have some influence. Other forms of organisation with a committee structure can be more efficient but less democratic. In Exploding Cinema attendance and behaviour at meetings is the forum in which decisions are forged. It is also a place where collective relations can become heated, where differences can become evident, although not always explicitly articulated.

It is at meetings that shows are organised and jobs are allocated. These jobs result directly in the form of the shows. It is usually at meetings that loans of equipment, or the conditions of such loans, and other general policies are decided.

Method: The units measured are simply the names as recorded at the head of meetings minutes from 1992 to 1997. These are tabulated per year. The two problems with this unitisation are that:

Every attendance is not recorded at every meeting leading to inevitable omissions.

Full names are usually not recorded leading to ambiguity in some cases.

In each year until 1997 the number of meetings with attendance records is remarkably constant at about 50% (see summary table A). In 1997, when I began my research as a participant observer, 16 out of 17 meetings had attendance records (including two meetings estimated on records of those named as speaking). This new attention to recording attendance may have been an effect of this study, a simple example of how the process of research might begin to change the subject of research. In this case it over-weighs attendance in the post 1997 period in the totalling of numbers.

It is also likely that many early meetings especially would not have been minuted. No minutes exist for 1991 and only three meetings are minuted before the 5th July 1992. Although there were apparently very regular meetings every Sunday in early 1992 I have yet to find any record of them. The existing records do amount to a reasonable sample, apart from that first year until mid July 1992, and the names recorded do accord with people's memories and other records.

The figures recorded are only an indication of attendance. It is possible that someone attended who took the job of minute taker and consistently didn't take an attendance record. This scenario could lead to a regular member of the collective not appearing in the tables. It seems unlikely there are any such errors as any major omissions are likely to have become apparent from people's memories, in response to my circulation of the draft. It should be remembered that the figures are significant in a relative way. I assume that people more active are more likely to be recorded so errors are more likely with those on the margins. It is this desensitising to margins that is one of the objections to content analysis.

In fact it is just as likely that visitors who were not active in the collective could be named in minutes and so appear in these records. To guard against this names had to be recorded more than once to be tabulated in the year tables. The summary table records only those who have at least four attendances recorded and so is a record of only those most active members. Taking into account omissions due to non-recording and other errors it is *just possible* that a person could have attended as many as 6 - 8 meetings without appearing in the summary tables.

The second source of possible error is the ambiguity of first names recorded. After cross checking there is still some ambiguity about the names Roz, Andy and Mick. There was a Roz Grainger and Roz Gilchrist from 1993 to 1995 currently recorded as attending nine meetings in total. A 'Mick' confuses the attendance of the better known Michael Faralley in 1994. Andy Smith and Andy Johnson who both seem to have joined in Spring 1995 are also conflated, recording six attendances in 1995 and 1996 between them.

In addition to these sources of error there are possible inaccuracies due to: the minute takers not picking up on people who regularly come late or who pop out to the toilet; and my own 'coder fatigue' whilst recording this data from the minute books. The main victims of these errors seem to have been Rob Stanley who joined September 1993 but was unrecorded in my data although noted by Duncan Reekie as an active member and Anne Cooper, remembered as an 'intermittent member', who is unrecorded.

In spite of all these sources of possible error the results do seem to be the best that can be done to empirically track collective membership and seems to be accurate for those most active in meetings after mid 1992.

Results: With a little help from other sources the results can also be turned into a simple narrative: The early collective before minuted records included: Stephen Houston, Kathy Gibbs, Duncan Reekie, Danny Holman, Jenny Marr, Anne Marie Barlow, Anthony Kopieki, Laura Hudson, Suzanne Currid, Jennet Thomas, Lorelei Lisowsky, William Thomas and Lepke B.

Some time early in 1992 Anne Barlow and Laura Hudson left and about May, Jenny Marr and Donal Ruane joined. As the year progressed the group grew with the addition of Londie H, Andre Stitt, Mark Pawson, Katia Rossini, John Carr and Tara Babel. By October meetings were regularly being attended by an average of eight people with about 20 people in the collective, about 12 of who were active.

Over the next year, 1993, the collective grew to have about 30 members of whom 19 or so were active. In this year Paul Tarrago, Colette Rouhier and Caroline Kennedy all joined and are seen to be active, forming the kernel of the collective that survived the split of 1994 along with the founding members Jenet Thomas and Duncan Reekie. Other notable additions this year were Ghisli Bergman and Rosalind Grainger who later left to form their own group *Films That make you go Hmmm* in 1996. Throughout 1994 meetings were large often having 9 to 15 people. By the middle of 1994 this had settled down to about 8 to 10 per main meeting.

1994 saw arguments split the collective, as detailed above, resulting in Donal Ruane, Anthony Kopieki, Suzanne Currid, Andy Lowe, Rob Stanley and Jenny Marr leaving the group. The total collective membership gradually declined and it can be seen that a core collective was putting in most of the hours in meetings along with Ghisli Bergman and Danny Holman. the collective officially split after an arduous run of fifteen shows at the Union Tavern on Camberwell New Road. It reformed in October 1994 but many of the names signed to the new agreement in the minute book at this meeting are unfortunately illegible.

1995 begins with about ten in the collective and this new collective now has a stable core which maintains about this number through 1996 and 1997. 1995 meetings were attended by an average of six people although at least two meetings had eleven people. Notable new members this year were Fiona Lord, James Stevens, Sheik and Andy Johnson.

The 1996 collective had about seven key members and meetings were attended by four to seven people. In some ways a low point of membership. But it was also the year that the independent film groups, that had been springing up all over London in the wake of Exploding Cinema, came together to put on the first Volcano! festival. The Volcano coalition seems to have taken up a fair amount of the Exploding Cinema Collective's productive energy from 1996 to 1998. For half of the year the energy of the collective now seems directed to this greater collective enterprise resulting in fewer shows.

In 1997 I joined the collective with German artist Thomas Zagrozek and Australian Sandra. Attendance at meetings went up from six to eight and there were up to nine key members.

In 1998 the total number of meetings went down from fifteen in 1997 to eleven. Sandra went to college and stopped attending meetings although she still occasionally helped out at shows. Paul Motel had joined the group at the end of 1998 and was a regular during 1999 providing the groups transport with his old short wheelbase LandRover. Three new women separately came to two or three meetings in 1998. These were Kirsten, Vanessa and Boot. Caroline Kennedy, the only member to live in North London, was only recorded attending three meetings in 1998, and only one in 1999, although she maintained a strong presence at the shows.

In 1999 Colette Rouhier dropped out to have a sabbatical after doing an enormous amount of work in 1998. Duncan managed to continue to attend as much as anybody in spite of doing a Ph.D. in Falmouth. Damon Herd joined in 1998 and soon became an active member taking charge of the web site.

Interpretation: The charts show the size of the collective, the intensities of attendance at meetings and even how these two factors might correlate to the number of shows produced (see Summary Table B). The advantage of a collective of artists over an individual or small group of two or three is based to a large part on the simple resource of labour power. As already noted, a show requires an active crew of at least six and preferably eight or more people. The charts show the kind of hours that people are putting into the meetings and we can assume this is an index of the general creative energy of the operations as a whole. Of course to be very effective this labour has to be concerted. A large collective is also a resource in the number of personal connections to the wider society. These connections help find films as well as an audience to populate the shows, helping to build a vibrant orally networked base. A larger collective has advantages in being able to distribute publicity by hand with ease as the collective tends to be dispersed over a wide area in terms of the location of their homes, jobs and leisure activities. A large collective is also likely to make inter-group communication and agreement more difficult in some areas. The minimum number necessary to crew an event may define the optimum size of the core collective.

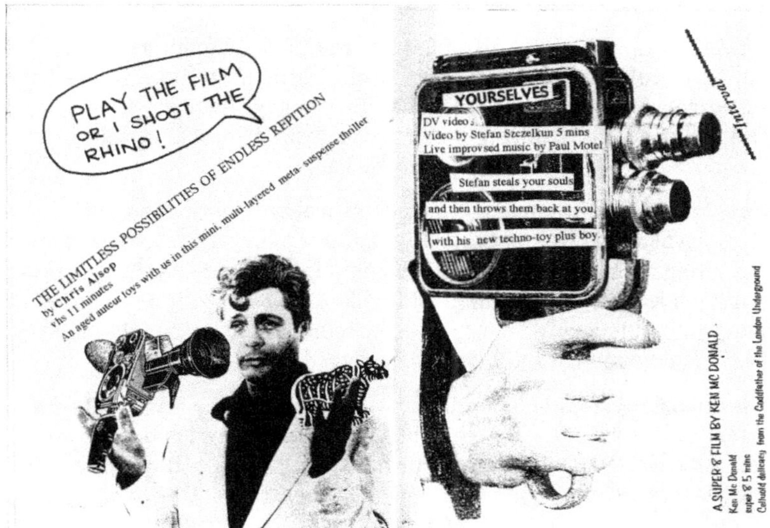

Programme 27 - 8 - 99

The attendance at meetings does seem to accurately record those who were most influential and predict the rise of the core collective that I experienced from the time they join. (see Summary Table A p.106). They are soon putting in more hours in meetings than anyone else. Duncan and Jennet have been there since 1991 - Paul, Colette and Caroline join in 1993. This commitment along with the personal liaisons that arise (two couples - Duncan and Colette, Jennet and Paul) give rise to the core group that can survive the emotional implosion that seems to be almost inevitable in large non-hierarchical open collectives.

The errors of such a content analysis are likely to effect those on the margins of collective activity. At least it is clear how the figures have been derived. Of course the influence of some of those on the margins, who do not attend many meeting, can be considerable. James Stevens is an example of such a person who through his commercial work can act as a modest resource provider, outside the mainstream institutions. Amongst other things he has supported the Exploding Cinema web site as a service provider, funded the first Vacuum and provided event space at his pioneering Thameside cyberclub *Backspace*. His influence is greater than would show up with this particular form of analysis, although it is an atypical sort of influence.

As I have said the fundamental problem of content analysis is data reduction, which is likely to affect the kind of representations that might result from this method if used on its own. As the positive nature of any open collective is its rich inclusivity a historicising representation should perhaps celebrate this. The problem with a reductive analysis is that certain people's contributions become invisible and the emphasis is on those who have an abundance of energy and commitment. It is difficult to see how this problem can be solved without a greater awareness of the need for thorough documentation amongst the collective from the beginning. Self consciousness and pedantic paperwork is probably not consistent with the spontaneous excitement that gives an emergent collective energy and in fact Exploding Cinema may be relatively ordered with its minute books, programme format and website.

A benefit of producing a historical record of a contemporary group is that this analysis can be circulated as a draft amongst the participants. In a sense it will only become 'historical fact' when it is published or the key members are dead and many of the primary materials available now may be lost. Historical certainty or the illusion of it, can more easily be achieved in retrospect.

Conclusion: This method gives an empirical basis for a representation of who was part of the Exploding Cinema Collective and when they were active beginning in July 1992. Assuming the minute books will be publicly archived this should constitute a verifiable historical record. The resulting tables also allow analysis of the flows of individual and sub-group influence within the organisation. There are yearly tables for 1992 through 1997. The Summary Tables A and B cover 1992 - 1999.

Fifty two people recorded at least two meetings since mid 1992 when records started. Twenty two of these were women. At least twenty nine people took a substantial role, being recorded for more than four meetings, which could imply eight or more actual attendances in the period before 1997 when only 50% of meetings had attendance records. (see Summary Table A).

This does show the impressive scale of involvement which Exploding Cinema generated. The numbers represent a significant cultural reach into the population. It also indicates the individuals who were most influential although somewhat masking the range of influence of those who entered the Exploding arena for a short period or who shunned meetings.

Although there are areas of error there is no better method of deriving this data. The margins of error are not excessive and were reduced by further external checks.

Intensities of Work Shown

Introduction: In this content analysis I count and tabulate the people that have shown the most works in Exploding Cinema 1992 - 1997. This will show both the number of different works shown and repeat showings of the same work. The hypothesis is that these filmmakers are most significant, at least in part, by reason of their commitment to repeated showings at Exploding Cinema.

Any broader movement of cultural producers is remembered, or represented historically, by a number of works selected as exemplary from all that were produced. This selection is often known as a canon. A certain paradox is that a canon usually refers to a past historical formation decided through the mediation of a critical apparatus. As this programme of research is active in making historical representations the study of such intensities may contribute to what we may call a pre-canonic formation. This is a set or pattern of works that would be offered up to the broader social processes of legitimation. Canon formation is assumed to be part of a broader hegemonic struggle and is not as predictable or fixed a process as we might assume.

Background and context: Canon formation in commercial cinema is something that is a struggle between an intellectual group of critics, who are ideally independent of the film industry, and the broad paying publics, which may either be a broad popular or a narrow cult following. In spite of the reference to the primacy of 'the judgement of the audience' by Exploding Cinema, their judgement can only contribute to the canonisation process in the limited form of spontaneous applause as the films are not usually available as commodities through any form of distribution. Prior to a show the audience did not even know what movies they are coming to see, as they were not mentioned on the publicity. Nor did the audience register its evaluation of the works in any formal or measured way. There was only the spontaneous applause followed by a general buzz of comment. This may be followed by an individual approach if the filmmaker is present. On 8th October 2001 the Exploding Cinema showed a 22 minute video called 'The North Sea Circle' directed by *Richard Coldman* with *Alexander Gorlizki*. This film was warmly received by the audience. Afterwards Jenet Thomas forwarded two emails to me as I knew Richard and she didn't have his number. These validating enquiries were passed on to Richard.

Other film group organisers, who are regularly in the Exploding Cinema audience, will pick up 'favourites' to show in their own venues. So although the 'audience decides', according to Exploding Cinema rhetoric, these judgements are, with few exceptions, in the ephemeral form of oral discourse and memory. Generally there has been an absence of any critical writing.

There are the occasional films that create an almost tangible effect in the whole crowd watching - perhaps the mutual recognition of a film which captures a new form of representation, not yet seen in mainstream media or which validates the subculture of the audience in a new way. These moments are occasionally documented. An example is the *Dead Dog* film by Victoria Kirkwood, which is discussed by Duncan and Donal in *Loo How's* 1994 documentary.

Apart from the intensity of production measured by this content analysis there are some other processes which contribute to what I have called a pre-canon formation. These are two: selections for tour and the selection for a compilation video.

<u>The Tour selections.</u> Two European tours in 1994 and 1995 have lists which are not derived from open access contributions in the same way that the regular shows are. Many of the films are selected favourites from the past year or so. These are useful in

indicating some of the collective's favourites, even if the actual tours would have a limited direct influence.

<u>The Vacuum compilation video (1996)</u>. Clearly a compilation video is a selective mechanism in a pre-canon formation. It is currently one of the only sources to which people might go to find works that were shown at Exploding Cinema. This is a selection made by the collective sub-group that put together Vacuum.

Method: I made an alphabetical list of the approximately 650 filmmakers with the films they had shown at Exploding Cinema from 1992 to June 1998. This list included the cryptic details that were listed in the show programmes. The few shows without programmes will not have the films shown listed, so this is not a complete list of all films shown. It may in fact also contain a few films that were listed but not shown.

I then selected the filmmakers who had shown more than three films, subtracted all the people who had been collective members and re-listed them in order of the number of works shown. This was complicated by the repeat showings of films. Assuming that repeats are due to popularity I have indicated the number of repeat showings in brackets. I assumed that the fine ordering of the final listing would not be significant, it would be more like a broad net in which would be caught the most active filmmakers showing at Exploding Cinema.

This list can be seen as a pre-canonic selection which has been chosen by an index of the makers commitment to showing work at Exploding Cinema, rather than because of any supposed aesthetic superiority. This approach to canon formation is sympathetic with the Exploding Cinema ethic of open inclusivity. Dates were also included so that the rough period over which the filmmakers were active in Exploding is made clear.

Before giving the results I will consider some unitisation problems. There is an assumption that making many films shows a commitment to the process and to the underground context. A weakness of this assumption is of reducing all films to a unitary value. For instance, I have not taken a film's length into account. This gives an advantage to people who make many short films. Steven Houston, the founder of Exploding Cinema in 1991, is perhaps the main victim of these shortcomings, compounded by the lack of early records when he was active. Records which do exist record him showing just one film, but that was 30 minutes duration and could have been a major work which took years to make.

The film-works list left out performance, which is an important part of the unique ethos of an Exploding Cinema show. However, performances were listed if they clearly included an element of projection. In this way Duncan Reekie, who has produced a long series of spoken work with slide performances, scores highly with content that was, in the main, not moving pictures. Other exclusions are the loops and other decor. If the loops had counted as 'films' then Caroline Kennedy would have scored relatively higher as she is an enthusiastic maker of loops. (There is a video of loops included in my Youtube archive of Exploding Cinema documentary video)

Results: Filmmakers who showed most films 1992 - 98 (who were not in the collective):

(+N) *indicates repeat showings*

George Barber	15 (+4)	1992/98
Andrew Copeman	15 (+5)	1992/95
Arthur Lager	11 (+5)	1994/98
Alan Dein	10 (+3)	1992/95
Mark Video	7 (+4)	1992/95
Dick Jewel	6 (+4)	1992/93
Andrew Kotting	6 (+2)	1992/98
Ken McDonald	7	1992/93
Paul Murray	5 (+4)	1992/93
John Coffey	6	1995/98
Martin Hedley	4 (+4)	1992/95
Lovely Movies	6	1994/98
Nick G.Smith	6	1992/95
David Leister	5	1992/98
Gordon Mason	5	1993/95
Paul Synott	5	1993/95
Pascael Baes	4	1992
James de Carteret	4	1994/5
David Fanning	4	1995/98
Halloween Society	4	1993/96
Rob Ryan	4	1995/97
Small World	4	1995
Victoria Kirkwood	3 (+4)	1993/95
Guy Edmonds	3 (+2)	1995/98
Michelle Gallipeau	3 (+3)	1992/94

Sixty four filmmakers had shown three or more films from 1992 to June 1998 (Counting groups as one). Twenty one of these had produced just three films and a further twenty two had been or are members of the collective. A further twenty-three names of filmmakers who had shown two films, or whose films had been shown repeatedly, were added by cross-reference with Vacuum and the two tour lists. Of these only two had been members of the collective. Vacuum yielded two, the 1995 tour list seventeen and the 1994 tour list a further eight. This implies about eighty-seven filmmakers who should be considered as significant in this period by reason of their commitment to this showing format.

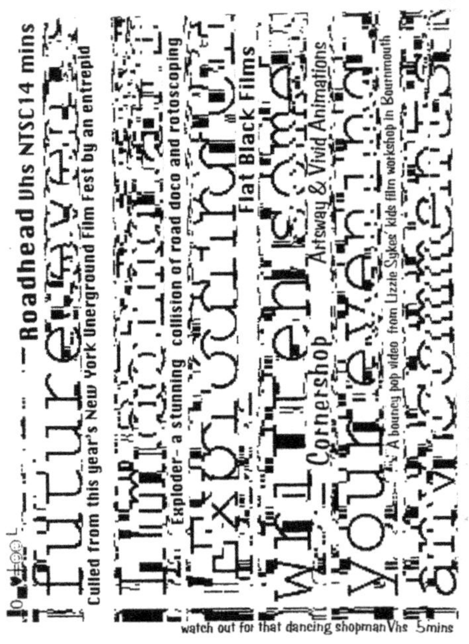

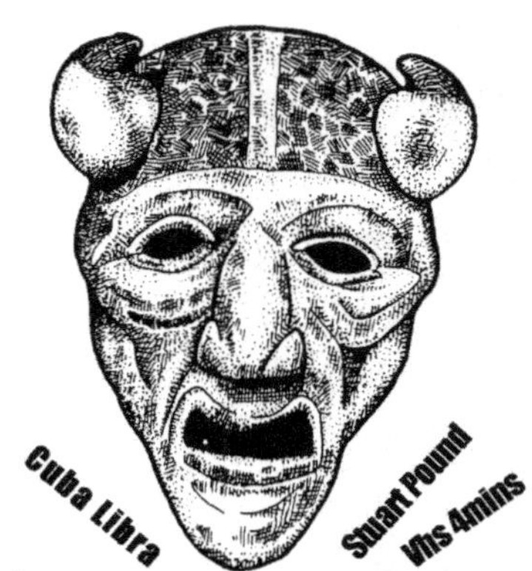

Stuart has been making experimental films for decades but this is his first time at Exploding! This is re-processed remixed found footage from a very familiar advert...

Last Night Meant Nothing
Paul Tarragó   Vhs 20 mins
rich and complex, made on super 8 this is Paul's biggest one to date..from the man that bought you such gems as"Stay in a friendly country" and "How to make a squirrel happy"

Programme 20 - 5 - 99

Analysis & Interpretation: The future understanding of any broad collective phenomena, which produces a great mass of materials, must be mediated through a selection of material. It is only the participants who have experienced a wide range of works. Because they are not archived no-one else can have this experience. A canon, for my purposes, is defined as a selection of typical materials, which convey some, or most of the important or memorable qualities of a broad phenomenon. Of course the word canon also has a meaning of 'all that was best' from a particular genre, period or movement and there is perhaps an element of this in the selections made for *Vacuum* and the tour lists. Further a canon has a connotation of arising from a process of validation by authoritative critics, curators or historians. The lack of literary response to the films shown, helps to focus our attention on the fact that the critical response to over 1000 films by hundreds of people over six years has been oral. And the effects of these works have been disseminated through an oral culture. We can only talk of a critical discourse if this can be theorised as an almost entirely oral phenomena. But this oral response is difficult to track, especially in retrospect. Few traces are left by such an organic social process.

Much of what has been shown at Exploding Cinema is already lost to posterity unless a large amount of funding was found for this purpose in the next few years. Super 8 films in particular often exist in a single copy which is vulnerable. Some collections of show copies, mostly on VHS, were kept by both the older Exploding collective members and other film group organisers. But as far as I know these are not catalogued and have come about by a process of attrition rather than by an organised process of acquisition.

These are often films that are left uncollected by filmmakers - a process that does not favour the more organised filmmaker who supplies a return envelop or collects her film in person at the screening. If archiving is to be attempted an important issue is to decide what is most important to collect. The lists of the most frequently shown filmmakers, largely derived from objective data, may be a useful part of such a debate.

The energy that people put in is largely sustained through inner drives to communicate. At best this is a deeply perceived need to give form to something, which is otherwise not being adequately expressed. Such creative urges underlie the most vibrant and useful productions of culture. Of course such needs may also be incoherent or driven by neurosis and may drive filmmakers to repeat cliches, and encourage those who are drawn by romantic notions of being an artist or filmmaker. But this 'noise' should not deafen us to the importance such phenomena as crucial well-springs of culture.

The historical value of these films is not just to be seen in the production of a few art stars, or the technical or aesthetic innovations that spin off, but is rather in the general discourse generated that is part of culture's continual processes of renewal. This is a discourse whose value is in its autonomy from the vested interests of power and money. How, then, can a historical representation be derived from the process of apparently dissipated oral critical discourse?

> The more we seek after origins the more social creativity becomes obscured and the more the movements of a living culture are negated by the canon.
>
> Howard Slater, 2000

These processes of communication in which people produce 'statements', from which agreements on cultural commonalities and symbols are reached by informal oral communications, underpin the spheres of meaning and value that comprise our social realities.

Conclusion: In some ways the whole idea of an orderly canon appears antithetical to the anarcho-democratic 'open access' ethos of Exploding Cinema. But this may be to misunderstand the idea of non-selection, which is to 'let the audience decide'. This shouldn't imply that the audience and the collective members couldn't still have their own aesthetic judgement. There are still standards but these are seen to be dynamic, in flux and resisting the closure that a formal imposed canon implies. Any future consideration of this body of work must surely search out the singular films that impressed, as well as those filmmakers who showed a commitment to this forum.

A canon is assumed to be the best of an era but it may be that getting canonised is less a pure competition of aesthetic quality and more a power struggle. There is also a large element of commitment, perseverance and getting to know the right people. The character of an era may well be better reflected by this crude charting of intensities than by the more esoteric process of critical filtering and gate keeping.

Canon formation could be part of a rational and open discourse rather than be formed through the selection of a few experts. There is no reason why such specialists could not inform the debate. But even with a more rational canon formation there is the danger that a narrow obsession with canonised works will obscure the inclusive quality of Exploding Cinemas programming. A major part of the aesthetic pleasure of an Exploding Cinema experience is being an active part of a collective synaesthesia, rather than in discovering a great work by an individual artist. It is, at best, a dynamic collage of light, performance, ad hoc technology and camaraderie. At times its appears to either career along like a charabanc full of drunken day-trippers, or sometimes only to be rattling monotonously through a banal videoscape.

Whilst it is important to value all artists, a reasoned selection may be a useful or even necessary tool to understand and appreciate the work of an era.

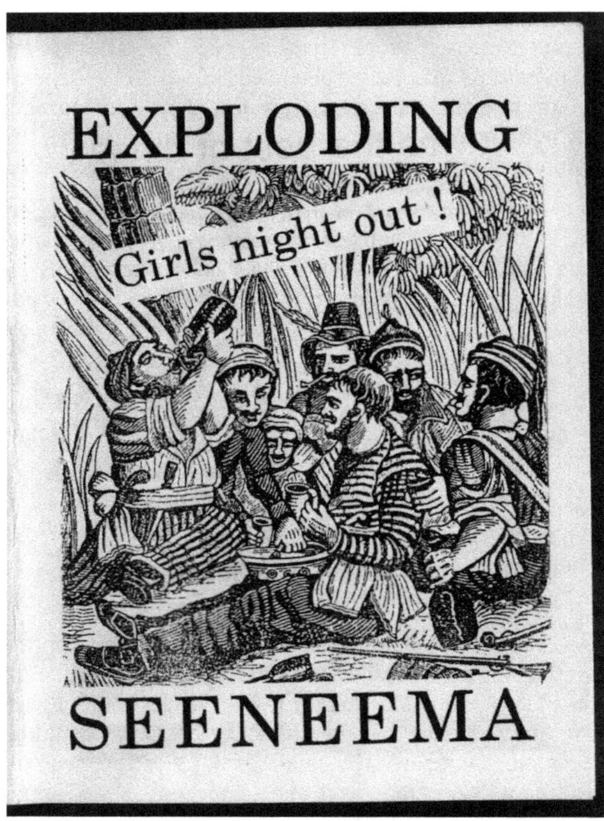

Programme 14 - 3 - 98

Numbers of Women

Introduction: I tracked the number of women who showed work and those who were part of the collective, making a comparison with the proportion of women in other parts of the film industry. This may reveal if the open access policy of Exploding Cinema has any practical effect in making film production more accessible to women.

Method: Numbers of filmmakers who have shown in Exploding Cinema since 1992, who have female names were counted and compared with those with male names. This ratio was also calculated through my intensity tables. I.e. for the filmmakers showing most work at Exploding Cinema. These figures were compared with figures supplied by Women in Film & TV (UK). The relative number of women in the collective was also tracked over time.

Unitisation: A number of names cannot be gendered for various reasons such as: no first name supplied; foreign names and others of unknown gendering; ambiguous names (e.g. Sam), group names. However the percentage of names which is uncountable or ambiguous seems to be less than 15%. It is also well-known that women can sometimes use a male alias to avoid discrimination or pre-judgement. I have not found any guidance on this question but I will assume the number is too low to be significant in this case. (Note from 2021 - I realise things have changed considerably since this was written in 2002.)

These figures do not account the average length of male films compared with female. Each film work is taken to be of similar average value. This may not be tenable as one of the most fundamental material effects of sexism is the lower average wages, and less money that women have, and so we might assume there will be less funds to make self-funded longer films. On the other hand Exploding Cinema has a bias towards low-cost short films so it could be a relatively good environment for women. I will assume, for now that these two considerations cancel each other out. Finally, it is possible that more women work in groups and so avoid being counted.

With a list of 643 filmmakers and 1039 works shown in Exploding Cinema between 1992 - 1997 the sample is large enough to make major anomalies statistically unlikely.

Results:

a. Filmmakers.

Overall the number of women who have shown: 197

Men 353

Ambiguous or opaque 93

A ration of about 4:7 in favour of men.

Women filmmakers were 35% of gendered total.

The unknowns were 14% of the total, which in view of the discussion above could give a slight bonus to women, but not enough to effect the ratio when rounded to single figures.

b. Works shown.

The number of works by women: 295

men: 607

ambiguous or opaque: 136

A ratio of about 1:2 in favour of male authored works. Women's films were 32% of gendered total.

	1991	1992	1993	1994	1995	1996	1997	1998	1999	
Duncan Reekie		9	11	9	7.5	6.5	15	11	10	79
Anthony Kopieki		9	7	4	-	-	-	-	-	20
Kathy Gibbs		8	9	-	-	-	-	-	-	17
Donal Runne		8	6	2	-	-	-	-	-	16
Susanne Currid		8	8	-	-	-	-	-	-	16
Jenny Marr		5	5	-	-	-	-	-	-	10
William Thomas		4	3	-	-	-	-	-	-	7
Katia Rossini		4	9	2	-	-	-	-	-	15
Danny Holman		3	6	6	1	-	-	-	-	16
Jenet Thomas		3	8	9	6	8.5	14.5	12	10	71
John Carr		3	8	-	-	-	-	-	-	11
Mark Pawson		2	2	3	-	-	-	-	-	7
Andre Stitt ?		3	?	2	-	-	-	-	-	5
Lepke B		1	6.5	3	-	-	-	-	-	10.5
Paul Tarrago			11	4	7	6.5	14	10	9	61.5
Andy Lowe			5	3	-	-	-	-	-	8
Colette Rouhier			4	8	8.5	9	14.5	11	1	56
Ghisli Bergman			3	6	4	-	-	-	-	14
Roz Grainger			2	4	3	-	-	-	-	9
Caroline Kennedy			1	8	4.5	6	9.5	3	1	29
Silvy da Silva				4	3	-	-	-	-	7
Robyn Conway				4	-	-	-	-	-	4
James Stevens				3	3	-	-	-	-	6
Sheik					3	2	1	-	-	6
Andy J (+ S ?)					3?	3?	-	-	-	6
Stefan Szczelkun							15	11	10	36
Thomas Zagrozek							13	9	10	32
Sandra							7.5	-	-	7.5
Paul Motel								1	6	7
Damon Herd									3	3
PERSONNEL		13	19	17	12	7	9	8	9	

Amongst the sixty four filmmakers who showed more than two works at Exploding Cinema between 1992 - 1997, Sixteen or 25% were women (compared with 35% of the gendered total). Giving these a weighting for number of films shown and repeats, the percentage is 27% (compared with 32% of the total gendered works shown.)

c. Meeting attendance. The total number of meetings attendances recorded by the most dedicated collective members:

In 1992 female /male ratio was 28/39 or: 41% female

1993   73/68   51%

1992 month	?	?	?	4	5	7	8	10	10	10	11	11	12		
date				5	7	16	2	4	18	25	8	22	6		
Susanne Currid				x	x	x	o	x	x	x	x	o	x		8
Danny Holman				x	o	o	x	o	o	o	x	o	o		3
Janet Thomas				x	o	x	x	o	o	o	o	o	o		3
Cathy Gibbs				x	K	x	o	x	x	x	o	x	K		8
Steven Houston				x	o	o	o	o	o	o	o	x	o		2
Duncan Rockie				x	x	x	x	x	x	x	x	o	x		9
Sophia				x	o	o	o	o	o	o	o	o	o		1
Anthony Kopicki				x	x	x	o	x	x	x	x	x	x		9
Jenny Marr					x	o	o	o	x	x	x	o	x		5
Donal Ruane					x	x	x	x	o	x	x	x	x		8
Londie H						x	x	o	o	o	o	o	o		2
Lepke B						x	o	o	o	o	o	o	o		1
William Thomas						x	o	o	x	o	o	x	x		4
Andre Stutt							x	o	o	o	o	x	x		3
Mark Pawson								x	x	o	o	o	o		2
Katia Rossini									x	o	x	x	x		4
John C									x	x	x	o	o		3
Tara Babel												x	x		2
Debbie ?															
ATTENDANCE	?	?	?	8	5	9	6	6	9	7	8	8	9		

NOTE. 1. The following tables include everyone recorded as having atttended more than one meeting in 2 consecutive years or more than 3 meetings over 3 years. As only 50% of meetings have attendance records it is possible that someone could have attended 3 or 4 meetings or more without being recorded. For this reason the tables are only a guide and do not claim to be complete.

1994	35/47	42%
1995	25/28	47%
1996	23/18	56%
1997	46/58	44%

This list includes a total of 28 people of whom 10 were women.

Analysis & interpretation: The figures show clearly that women are 35% of the filmmakers shown, but average 47% of the collective in number. The steady core of the

1993 month	1	1	3	4	4	5	5	5	6	6	8	10	10		
date	24	31	20	18	25	5	16	23	1	27	22	[?]	31		
Susanne Currid	X	X	X	X	O	X	O	X	O	X	O	X	O		8
Danny Holman	X	O	X	O	O	O	O	X	X	O	X	X	O		6
Janet Thomas	X	X	X	X	X	X	O	O	O	X	O	X	O		8
Cathy Gibbs	X	X	O	K	K	O	O	X	X	K	O	K	K		9
Duncan Reekie	X	X	O	X	X	O	X	X	X	X	X	X	X		11
Anthony Kopicki	X	X	O	O	X	O	O	X	O	X	O	X	X		7
Jenny Marr	X	X	O	X	X	X	O	O	O	O	O	O	O		5
Donal Ruane	X	O	O	O	X	O	O	X	O	O	X	X	O		5
Lepke B	A	X	O	X	X	O	X	X	O	X	O	O	O		6.5
William Thomas	X	X	O	O	X	O	O	O	O	O	O	O	O		3
Andre Stitt	O	O	O	O	O	O	O	O	O	O	O	O	O		+
Mark Pawson	O	O	O	O	O	O	O	O	O	O	O	X	X		2
Kate Rossire	X	X	X	X	X	O	O	X	O	X	X	X	O		9
John Carr	X	X	?	X	X	X	O	X	O	O	O	O	O		7
Tara Babel	A	O	O	O	O	O	O	O	O	O	O	O	O		0.5
Paul Tarrago	X	X	X	X	X	X	O	X	X	X	O	X	X		11
Andy Lowe			X	O	O	X	X	O	O	O	O	X	X		5
Jorg (sp?)			X	O	X	O	O	O	O	O	O	O	O		2
Stephanos					X	O	O	X	X	O	O	O	O		3
Michael Faralley						X	O	O	O	X	O	O	O		2
Colette Roubser							X	O	O	O	X	X	X		4
Ron Briefl									X	O	O	O	X		2
Roz Granger											X	X	O		2
Ghada Bergman											X	X	X		3
Kerry Sharp											X	O	O		1
Robyn Conway											X	O	X		2
Silvy da Silva												X	X		2
Caroline Kennedy													X		1
Rob Stanley													?		+
Attendance	13	11	8	9	13	7	4	11	6	9	9	15	12		27

collective in the four years 1995 to 1998 has been three women and two men. Also the attendances at meetings show women claiming around 50% of meetings attended. This means that, on average, the women were putting in more meeting hours. Or, put another way, the women were more consistent in coming to meetings. This could suggest an equal power balance in the collective in spite of the numerical advantage of the men.

In terms of works shown, women's works were 32% of the gendered total but when we look at the people showing more than two films with Exploding Cinema the percentage

1994 month	4	4	5	5	7	9	10	11	11	11	12	
date	21	26	23	24	27	8	20	1	9	20	7	
Danny Helman	X	X	X	X	O	O	O	X	O	O	X	6
Janet Thomas	X	X	X	X	O	X	X	X	X	O	X	9
Duncan Reekie	X	O	X	X	X	X	X	X	O	X	X	9
Anthony Kopicki	X	X	X	O	O	X	O	O	O	O	O	4
Donal Ruane	O	X	?	O	O	O	O	O	O	O	O	2
Lepke B	O	O	X	X	X	O	O	O	O	O	O	3
Mark Pawson	O	O	X	O	O	X	O	O	O	O	X	3
Andre Stitt	O	X	O	X	O	O	O	O	O	O	O	2
Katia Rossini	O	O	O	O	O	X	O	X	O	O	O	2
Paul Tarrago	O	X	O	O	O	X	X	O	O	O	X	3
Andy Lowe	O	X	X	O	O	X	O	O	O	O	O	3
Michael Faralley	X	O	X	O	O	O	O	O	O	O	O	2
Colette Rouhier	O	X	X	X	X	O	X	X	X	X	O	8
Rez Grainger	O	X	O	O	O	X	O	O	O	X	X	4
Ghishi Bergman	O	X	O	X	O	X	O	X	O	X	X	6
Kerry Sharp	O	O	O	O	O	O	?	X	O	O	O	2
Robyn Conway	X	O	X	X	X	O	O	O	O	O	O	4
Silvy da Silva	O	X	O	X	O	O	O	O	X	O	X	4
Caroline Kennedy	X	X	X	X	X	O	X	X	O	X	O	8
Fiona Lord	X	O	?	X	X	O	O	O	O	O	O	4
Dennis	X	O	O	O	O	X	O	O	O	O	O	2
Mick (see above?)			X	O	X	X	O	O	O	O	O	3
Tosh				X	X	O	?	O	O	O	O	3
James Stevens							X	X	O	O	X	3
Kerry							?	X	O	O	O	2
Anne Buis							x	O	O	x	O	2
ATTENDANCE	9	12	14	12	8	11	10	10	3	6	9	

of works drops to 27%. This difference could be within the error factor we might expect, but probably indicates that at the more intense end of production women are beginning to drop out. This fall is sharper when we look at the numbers of filmmakers in the intensity list above where there are only 25% of women in the most productive sixty four film makers compared with being 35% of the total filmmakers shown.

But how does this compare to women in the professional industry? *Insync*, the house magazine of Women in Film & TV (autumn 1996) had an article by Helen Baehr

1995 month	1	2	3	4	6	7	8	10	11		
date	15	26	12	9	28	22	3	8	6		
Danny Holman	O	X	O	O	O	O	O	O	O		1
Jenet Thomas	X	X	X	O	O	X	X	O	X		6
Duncan Reekie	X	X	X	X	O	X	A	X	X		7.5
Donal Ruane	O	X	?	O	O	O	O	O	O		2
Paul Tarrago	X	X	X	O	X	X	X	O	X		7
Colette Rouhier	X	X	X	X	X	X	A	X	X		8.5
Roz Grainger	O	X	O	X	O	X	O	O	O		3
Ghisli Bergman	X	X	O	X	O	X	O	O	O		4
Silvy da Silva	O	O	O	O	O	X	X	X	O		3
Caroline Kennedy	O	X	X	O	O	X	A	O	X		4.5
Fiona Lord	X	X	O	O	O	O	A	X	O		3.5
James Stevens	O	X	X	O	O	X	O	O	?		4
Juliette Buccanous					X	X	O	O	O		2
Sheik						X	X	X	O		3
Andy Johnson (?)							X	X	X		3
Attendance	6	1	7	4	3	1	5	6	6		

reporting that there was no legal obligation for equal opportunity reporting in the Independent sector. However a report she quotes, without reference, commissioned by the European Commission does give some figures:

> Men occupied the greater share of the senior production jobs, accounting for 63% of executive producers and 76% of directors.

(Insync, Autumn 1996, p5)

Seeing these as a positive value of 37% women executive producers and 24% directors these figure roughly parallel those in Exploding Cinema. Women moving from the underground into mainstream independent production can expect about the same gender ratio as they experienced in the underground. However, figures for the public funded sector from 1993 show:

> The BBC1 had the highest proportion of women in credits: 24% compared to 18%

1996 month	1	1	2	2	3	5	7	7	10		
date	14	29	11	25	10	12	7	23	29		
Jenet Thomas	×	×	^	×	×	×	×	×	×		8.5
Duncan Reekie	×	o	×	^	×	×	×	o	×		6.5
Paul Tarrago	×	o	^	×	×	×	×	×	×		7.5
Colette Roulner	×	×	×	×	×	×	×	×	×		9
Silvy da Silva	^	o	o	o	o	o	o	o	o		0.5
Caroline Kennedy	×	o	^	^	×	×	o	×	×		6
Andy Johnson (or S?)	×	×	^	o	×	o	o	o	o		3.5
Fiona Lord	×	o	o	o	o	o	o	o	o		1
Teresa	×	×	^	^	o	o	o	o	o		3
Sheik		×	×	o	o	o	o	o	o		2
Steve			×	o	o	×	o	o	o		2
Anke					×	×	o	o	o		2
Attendance	8	5	4	3	7	7	4	4	5		

in BBC2 and Channel 4 and just 17% in ITV.

(Her Point of View, BECTU, 1993, p18)

This would show the situation in Exploding Cinema in a more favourable light, showing a 50% improvement on the best of these figures. (More up-to-date figures were not available - 2000). The fact that women put equal hours into running the collective (in meetings at least) could be interpreted to show that women have an equal interest in film production even though they end up authoring less. Put more militantly the women are doing more administration and less authoring!

This might indicate that perhaps the underground doesn't effectively give better access for women than the mainstream does. Of course the direction and production of feature films is still almost entirely male dominated. It may be unrealistic to compare this high finance operation with underground filmmaking.

1997 month	2	2	4	4	5	5	6	6	6	7	8	8	9	9	10	10	
date	9	23	6	20	11	26	2	9	28	7	4	14	15	25	10	20	
Janet Thomas	X	X	X	X	X	X	X	X	X	X	X	O	X	A	X	X	14.5
Duncan Reekie	X	X	X	X	X	X	X	X	X	X	X	X	O	X	X	X	15
Paul Tarrago	X	X	X	X	X	X	X	O	X	X	X	O	X	X	X	X	14
Colette Roubier	X	X	X	X	X	O	X	X	X	X	X	X	X	X	?	X	15
Caroline Kennedy	O	O	O	O	X	O	X	X	X	X	X	X	O	A	X	X	9.5
Sheik	O	O	O	O	O	O	O	O	X	O	O	O	O	O	O	O	1
Thomas Zagrozek	X	X	O	X	X	O	O	X	X	X	X	X	X	X	X	X	13
Stefan Szczelkun	X	X	X	X	X	X	X	O	X	X	X	X	X	X	X	X	15
Sandra					X	O	X	O	X	X	X	X	X	A	O	O	7.5
Vanessa														X	O	O	1
Attendance	6	6	5	6	8	4	7	5	9	8	8	6	6	6	6	7	

Meetings /Attendances Summary Table B

	1992	1993	1994	1995	1996	1997	1998	1999
TOTAL MEETINGS	20	26	21	20	17	17	15	12
MEETING with attendance records in minute books.	10	13	11	9	9	16	13	11
% of attendances recorded	50%	50%	52%	45%	52%	94%	86%	91%
Main Shows (+ = other event)	15	21	17	11+3	5+6	6+3	4+1	6+2
Regular meeting atttendees	13	18	17	11	7	8	7	7

Conclusion: This is a very quick analysis of a complex situation. It may be unrealistic to expect that a micro culture can make a difference to something as deeply and broadly embedded as sexism. But it does suggest that on the most functional level open access without positive discrimination may not be able to dramatically change the basic social patterns of exclusion. The underground as a subculture still seems to be imbued with machismo, be it an 'alternative' machismo.

The situation is, if anything, worse for black and disabled filmmakers. There were no black members of the collective during the period of my participation and very often venues of shows are not accessible to people in wheelchairs. This situation is simply

Films shown by Collective Members most active in meetings 1992 - 1999

	1991	1992	1993	1994	1995	1996	1997	1998	1999	Total
Duncan Reekie		6	8	4	6	3	3	1	1	32 (+10)
Anthony Kopicki		8	6	3						17 (+5)
Kathy Gibbs		1	1							?
Donal Ruane		6	4	2						12 (+5)
Susanne Currid		4	5	3	1					13 (+4)
Jenny Marr		4	5	(2)						11 (+2)
William Thomas		-	-							-
Katia Rossini		1	2	-						3
Danny Holman		2	-	1	-					3 (+2)
Janet Thomas		3	3	3	7	2	4	2	2	26 (+12)
John Carr		3	2							5
Mark Pawson		-	-	-						-
Andre Stitt ?		7	1	2						10 (+4)
Lepke B		4	2	4						10
Paul Tarrago		(1)	2	2	5	2	4	2	2	15 (+8)
Andy Lowe		-	-	-						music
Colette Rouhier		(1)	2	3	3	1	2	1	1	12 (+5)
Kerry Sharp			2	4	(2)	(1)	(1)	(1)		11
Ghishi Bergman			1	4	-					5
Roz Grainger			1	2	-					3
Caroline Kennedy			1	3	2	-	1	-		7
Silvy da Silva					-	2				2
Robyn Conway					-					-
James Stevens					-	-				-
Fiona Lord					(3)	.	.			3
Sheik						1	-	-		1
Andy J (+ S ?)						3	-			3
Stefan Szczelkun				(1)	-	-	(1)	1	2	2	7
Thomas Zagrozek						(1)	-	1	-	-	2 (+2)
Sandra								-			-
Paul Motel									-	-	music
Damon Herd										2	2

NOTES: Kerri Sharp and Fiona Lord were collective members who did not show up in the attendance summary but do register with more than one film in the films register. (n) = Films shown without collective attendance record. - = collective attendance with no film record. (+n) in Total indicates repeat showings.

not as easy to measure empirically as the counting of gendered names. Class is of course even more difficult to measure in this way.

A more optimistic conclusion may be that in the seven years covered by my study more than 200 women made and showed more that 300 short films - a considerable body of women's work that deserves more attention.

Chapter 6

The Exploding programmes

Before considering an analysis of the Exploding Cinema imagery, I need firstly, to consider the historical precedents of the programme format itself, and secondly, to introduce the particular semiotic methodologies I have used. I will then make a classification of the subject matter of the imagery as a whole and discuss the possible meanings of repeating imagery. A few of the subject areas are discussed in general, before selecting four page openings for an in-depth semiotic analysis. Semiotic analysis requires careful contextualisation if it is not to atomise meaning.

All the regular Exploding Cinema shows have had a small A6 size photocopied booklet programme, which is given to every member of the audience as part of the admission cost. There were more than seventy shows from 1992 until the end of 1999 and the Exploding Cinema collective has a unique collection of nearly every programme. These highly illustrated booklets are an important trace in the study of Exploding Cinema as they are the only consistent record left from the actual shows. Most of the programmes were created as a result of group activity. As each person in the collective contributed to the making of these images an analysis of them should provide insight into the group's visual precepts. The rough paste-up zine style of the programmes with their rich background collages and minimal film descriptors stayed remarkably stable throughout the nine years period studied here.

Printed by photocopy they have followed a consistent format which is usually sixteen pages in length but occasionally twenty four pages with self-cover. A typical format:

Page 1 - A cover image with headline caption.

Page 2 - An introduction, which is often wry or whimsical.

Page 3 - List of films shown (title, filmmaker, duration, film stock)

Page 4 to 13 - Collage background with film titles roughly cut and pasted on top, with the addition of a caption or occasionally more detailed information on the film or film-maker.

Page 14 to 15 - Addenda that might include short texts, adverts, etc.

Page 16 - Back cover graphic

A 16-page edition of the programme requires just 2 sheets of A4 to be photocopied on both sides and guillotined in half. The collation and stapling is then done by hand on the day of the show by any collective members or volunteers that are not busy putting the show up. The unit cost of a 16-page programme was about 12 pence. Usually an edition of 150 to 200 was printed depending on the size of the venue. These usually all go by the end of the evening.

The importance of the programmes is brought into relief by the fact that they are, as I have said, the sole surviving trace of each show. In this present study I am interested in how the programmes communicate a collective mindset that in turn reflects a set of values which may be part of a broader sub-culture of which Exploding Cinema is a part.

There is no other available record that comes close to recording the collective ethos. The loops and decor slides used in shows are not done by the whole group although they do have a certain stylistic unity. The posters also tend to be authored by fewer people. So it is the collectively made programmes that describe the democratic ethos most incisively.

The audience rarely discards their pocket-sized programmes at the venue and we can only imagine that many of them are still to be found on domestic bookshelves. People who have found particular significance or inspiration at an event are more likely to have kept them as an aide memoir and souvenir.

The graphic content of the booklets is perhaps given scant attention. Literally intended as a 'background', the images are selected by the participants from a box of cuttings. People might also bring along images. The images as a whole are a visual aspect of the shared mythology of a heterogeneous culture within which Exploding Cinema exists.

The collaged images may be seen as a blip of the collective sub-conscious reified at a moment of time - a slip of the collective tongues, a meeting place of influences from Dada and Eisenstein, to popular traditions. The typography, captions and introductory prose signify the informal, the homemade but artful, the sometimes cantankerous or absurd. The simple format is a container that is both diverse and informal.

This informality allows the content to slip and slide from the artless to the aesthetic and insightful. It allows people to meet and play with scissors, old magazines and glue, for a creative evening together without agonising over a unified design. The results could not be produced by mainstream institutions. A professional designer can rarely be so loose - could not leave so many rough edges. Professional standards would trim all the loose ends and probably use a computer throughout, resulting in the kind of product we are all used to from the ICA, the LUX or most other major arts organisations. The Exploding programmes allow individual voices, poems, or rants to be included at a moments notice without being subject to any editing. If you are present you can include just about whatever you like, so the booklets display a kind of naïve spontaneity.

The booklets are in this way collective artworks in their own right. Although slight they are, like punk fanzines, redolent with authenticity.

> Saying whatever's on your mind, unbeholden to corporate sponsors, puritan censors, or professional standards of argument and design, being yourself and expressing your real thoughts and real feelings - these are what zinesters consider authentic.
>
> Duncombe 1997 p33

This is what gives them a higher modality than the slick programmes of the establishment, at least to those people attuned to the underground reversal of the normative codes of distinction.

An Exploding Cinema programme goes beyond the site of the event and outlasts it. It evokes the memory of an event whilst it stays in the possession of a witness. If we could map the locations of all those old programmes on domestic bookshelves across London it would map those networks of which Exploding Cinema events are but a temporary node. These are networks of discourse and friendship in the most organic sense.

Every page of the more than seventy programmes (1992 - 1998) was scanned so they can be digitally archived in the future. I was initially hoping that they could provide illustrations to my proposed commentary and analysis. But an important dimension was lost in the scanning process. Was it the slight splay of the untrimmed, hand-folded pages that I missed? Was it the inevitable degradation of a copy? Probably both of these things. The tactile quality of the Xerox and wire staple binding is more important than I had at first realised. What was lost most of all, by extracting the page graphics, was the numinous and historical presence of the 'book'. The tenuous link to the ancient codex frame was broken by tearing the image from its tactile micro context.

The Chapbook: A historical perspective

The codex was first taken up by the early Christians to distinguish their sacred texts from the parent religion. The Torah is, we must remember, a scroll. In this form the codex, reproduced by monastic orders with a painstaking process of hand-copying, became the repository of the Word of God - of sacred knowledge. This format of flat pages attached along one edge was to become an advantage when 1400 years later printing with moveable type was to revolutionise the production of multiple copies and with it a profound shift in Western knowledge from the sacred to the secular. The book form is at the core of Western civilisation and carries its past as a profound cultural icon. Even an edition as slight as the Exploding Cinema programme will carry echoes of this cultural heritage. The authority that the tome conveys can have its parodic form, its reversal. The chapbook and pamphlet always sought to undermine this symbolic authority and provide a rickety bridge between the gentlemen of letters and the uncouth oral realm of popular culture.

One of the first mass publications was the eighteenth century chapbook. The dimensions, pagination, lack of separate cover, use of illustration and colloquial style all give the programmes a close affinity with the chapbook. Chapbooks sold for a penny or less and contained songs, verses, histories, jokes, riddles, sermons, dream interpretations and fairytales often illustrated with woodcuts. This was the literature that many of the South London radicals of the 1790s would have been raised on. They are likely to have been passed on or exchanged at Free 'n' Easies or meetings of debating societies, such as the London Corresponding Society. As I have noted these meetings would have happened in similar rooms, at the back of public houses, to those used by Exploding Cinema. Such traditions of independent media were known to members of the radical publishing network of the late Sixties and early Seventies - the Underground Press and the network of radical bookshops.

In the late Seventies the punk ethos of D.I.Y. and the introduction of cheap photocopiers gave rise to the fanzine. This 'zine' format quickly proliferated into other areas. Typically these consisted of several sheets of A4 copied both sides, which were folded and stapled to give an A5 booklet. The layout of these productions was typified by a rough cut 'n' paste style, which showed little respect for perpendicular layout or conventions of correct spelling. You didn't even need a typewriter to publish and be damned.

The introduction of photocopier technology allowed a zine to be published in print runs of just two or three - so virtually no capital outlay was needed. They became the most accessible publishing form in the history of printed matter. Their rough-hewn aesthetic carried connotations of freedom and access to the media. In the Mid-Eighties zines proliferated amongst football fans and had a widespread influence.

> The importance of fanzines cannot be overstressed, both from the purely enjoyment side of giving the fans a good laugh, their role in developing grass roots consciousness in football and tackling issue that effect all fans, such as I.D. cards, racism, sexism, property developers, the safety and comfort of fans and the impact of the Taylor Report.

Richard Turner 1990 p81

The Exploding Cinema programme belongs to this tradition of radical publishing. Before going on to analyse the programmes as a whole, and a few examples in detail, I will critically examine the conceptual tools available for such an analysis of visual communication.

Semiotic Analysis: An Introduction

In the late C19th the eccentric US philosopher C.S. Pierce had proposed a study of 'semiotics'. Soon after this the Swiss linguist Ferdinand de Saussure was giving his influential lectures at Geneva University in which he proposed a general study of meaning and the sign, which he proposed to call 'semiology'. The students who attended these lectures went on to occupy chairs in prestigious universities across Europe just as visual media were exploding, driven by burgeoning consumerism.

Semiotics is the study of the life and meaning of signs in societies. It can focus on verbal language or signs in other media. Signs consist of a sensory form and a mental concept that is evoked by it, (the signifier and signified). This duality refers to something else, that may or may not have a concrete existence - it might be an idea.

Signs are interconnected in our mind by all kinds of associations. These associations might be personal but more often they are shared by people who have a culture in common. Only rarely are they universal - the association of red with high temperature, and so danger, being one of the few examples of a global sign. By studying the free associations that arise in our minds when we perceive a particular stimulus we can begin to map its meaning within a particular cultural context.

Saussure's ideas did not gain widespread currency until a series of magazine articles were published by Roland Barthes in the Fifties. These essays were collected together as *Mythologies* and first published in Paris in 1957. They explored the complex layers of meanings carried by apparently insignificant features of everyday life and popular culture. Barthes continued to develop his theory that was mainly concerned with iconography.

A central problem in linguistics seems to be the older idea of language as an abstract and inert object, rather than as the dynamic result of an ongoing transformational social process. Saussurian semiotics had assumed that a systematic and coherent theory of all meaning could be found.

> It stresses system and product, rather than speakers and writers or other participants in semiotic activity as connected and inter*acting* in a variety of ways

in concrete social contexts. It attributes power to meaning rather than meaning to power.

Hodge & Kress 1988 p1

Robert Hodge and Gunther Kress go on to elaborate on MAK Halliday's 'social semiotic' method (1978). This uses a basic communications model, that of the message which travels from its point of production by way of a medium to its point of reception. All three of these elements are then contextualised. These (social) contexts carry higher level messages or texts, which they called logonomic. These modulate the meaning of the message giving inflections like irony, which may even reverse the denotated meaning.

> Logonomic systems imply a theory of society, an epistemology and a theory of social modalities. Logonomic systems like ideological complexes reflect contradictions and conflicts in the social formations.

Hodge & Kress 1988 p5

The theory of society, which they work with, is one, which recognises that there are dominant discourses that may induce a variety of discourses of resistance. This seems to be a semiotic method that would be appropriate for a study of the Exploding Cinema and its context of an 'underground' culture. Gunther Kress then teamed up with Theo Van Leeuwen to produce a theory of the social semiotics of visual design. I have used their dynamic model to examine a typical set of images from the Exploding Cinema programmes.

The seventy surviving illustrated programmes produced by the Exploding Cinema are full of collaged imagery onto which individual film details are pasted. By studying this background imagery we may get some insight into the world of mythopoetic values that the Exploding Cinema collective inhabits. Each image is chosen to convey something and produce a discourse both between collective members and between the collective and the wider public who attend shows.

I was skeptical that semiotics had delivered much more than a series of helpful concepts in relation to the much promised 'science' of visual meaning before finding the work of Gunther Kress and his collaborators who focused on the uncovering of a grammar of the visual. They also have a vision of a contemporary expansion of visual communication that is independent of the literary, and threatening to overtake it. They suggest that our understanding of this contemporary visual grammar is hampered by the inertia of the vested interests of the literary establishment. In literate cultures graphics are "not treated as either the expressions of, or accessible to means of reading based on, articulated, rational and social meanings." (Kress & Van Leeuwen 1996 p20)

I will now examine the different approaches of Roland Barthes and Kress and Van Leeuwen to the analysis of visual meaning.

The Lexical Semiotics of Roland Barthes

In his book 'Image, Music Text' Barthes starts by differentiating between denoted and connoted meanings. The denoted meanings of an image are our perceived reality. But before we can know this, "the discontinuous world of symbols plunges into the story of the denoted scene as though into a lustral bath of innocence." Barthes (1977)

118

The connotative meanings, which are at least partly constructed by the treatment of the image, are the sum of responses to the meanings of the image, what I prefer to call the associations. All these responses are historically derived and culturally specific.

Barthes reviews the main procedures by which connotations are achieved, with the photographic image in mind.

a. 'Trick effects', which could apply to collage as well.

b. 'Pose', which is the gestural language of the humans and animals depicted.

c. 'Objects', these are the elements of a lexicon of signifying units. He hints that these are 'constituted into a syntax', but we have to wait until Kress and Van Leeuwen in 1996 to find out what this syntax might be.

d. 'Photogenia', which is the treatment of objects with regard to such things as lighting, contrast, focus, printing.

e. 'Aestheticism'. which is any references to past Art, particularly the established canon.

f. 'Syntax', is not the syntax within the image but rather the syntax between a sequence of images, which Barthes suggests is particularly good as a source of comedy.

Barthes discusses the relation of images to words. The caption is said to quicken connotation. It guides and locates our reading through 'the floating chain of signifiers'. This he says gives 'anchorage'. Another effect achieved is that of 'relay', the hinting at what might have gone before or might follow the image. I would add that context can of course act in a similar way on an image implying a preferred reading.

The reader then brings their own specific knowledge to bear, which may be practical, national, cultural or aesthetic. This set of knowledges, from which we make sense of the world, can be called idiolects. Widespread domains of idiolect are known as ideologies.

However, the paradigmatic condensation at the level of connotations is ordered and constrained not just by the idiolect of the reader but by a visual syntax. Barthes does not make any hypothesis of what a non-verbal or visual syntax might be. A sequence of images can borrow verbal syntagmatic relations, but if we look for syntagmatic relations within the two dimensional picture plane we need a new approach, which Barthes does not provide.

A third level of meaning is posited by Barthes. What we have talked of so far he sees as the 'obvious'. The third level he calls the 'obtuse'. It is the zones of meaning that are produced from the relations of signs, from the oscillation between two possible readings, or from a 'spasm of the signifier'. It is the meaning of a *movement* of semiosis. These obtuse meanings contribute to, often unnamable, atmosphere, quality and emotion-value.

Such obtuse meanings may be produced in montages, like those that comprise much of the Exploding programme imagery, from the space that produces a tension between two or more parts.

Kress and Van Leeuwen's Grammar of Visual Design.

Gunther Kress had already begun to open his ideas of a social semiotic to visual communications in the late Eighties.

Discourse is a site where meaning plays between participants in a semiotic exchange, whether this is speech or dialogue, comic or film, ritual or game.

Hodge & Kress 1988 p182

As I have said, Kress then teamed up with Theo Van Leeuwen to develop the basics of a visual semiotic in the book *Reading Images: The Grammar of Visual Design* (1996). Previous references to visual language simply used 'language' as an analogy; *Reading Images* is the first thesis to propose a visual grammar. They point out that a grammar, understood as an inventory of observed regularities, is a means of representation, not just a setting down of rules of normative correctness. The implication of this, which they hint at but do not explore, is that visual design is capable of argument and so could be a media of rational discourse. More radically, they suggest the dominance of the literary should not lead us to conclude that the visual domain is inherently dependent on the linguistic.

The historical dominance of the literary in the West often goes unchallenged. Our knowledge is primarily mediated in this form. Oral cultures, which are outside of this knowledge, benefit from a wider conscious use of our senses and especially the optical senses. Different media have different areas of facility. Oral media, are for instance advantaged in the communication of affective content.

Kress and Van Leeuwen suggest a concept of the 'semiotic landscape'. This has boundaries, a history, specific features, and landmarks. It is comprised of institutions, social groups and time periods.

Some of the main features of their theory of visual grammar include:

Narrative in visual representations:

In order to make a proposition in purely visual media, a vector is needed. A vector is a line, or implied line, that suggests direction. The geometrics of such vector directed sequences of signs are themselves sources of meaning. On the crudest level a rectilinear visual proposition suggests science/ modernity whilst circular or curving vectors the organic or nature.

These vectors relate to the track our eye follows when looking at a picture. Lack of a clear 'reading path' can lead to unease or ambiguity. A complete lack of reading paths may impose a solely paradigmatic reading: considering each sign separately.

Modality:

Modality is the reliability, veracity and authority of an image. We immediately prioritise an image by the modality markers which are embedded within it. In the West high modality is signified by the broad category of realism, when it is equated with truth. In other cultures it might be the sacred. Markers of realism may be such things as detail (especially background detail), depth, quality of material, illumination, colour and craft skill.

> Visual modality rests on culturally and historically determined standards of what is real and what is not, and not of the objective correspondence of the visual image to a reality defined in some ways independently of it.

Kress and Van Leeuwen, 1996, p168

Complex, abstract, esoteric, dissonant or innovatory relations between modality markers may in themselves give a high modality to a work of art.

I would also like to suggest that modality is also conveyed by the 'authenticity' of unmediated and direct expression. The collages of the Exploding Cinema programmes are such expressions - they show an alternate reality that undermines the authority of either glossy realism or of the functional minimalism of blueprints.

Composition

Composition provides an overarching logic of integration through the symbolic meanings of relative position, weight and framing.

1a. **Left and right** denote the 'given' and the 'new'. E.g. A Television interviewer typically sits on the left whilst the guest sits on the right. A broad convention in the West that probably relates to our custom of reading left to right. The eye tends to start at the left of an image and move right. In a triptych the central panel is often the mediator between left and right and so between 'given' and 'new'.

1b. **Head and foot,** or top and bottom, denote ideal and real: promise and product; the emotive and the practical.

1c. **The centre** is the place of the divine ruler, of harmony and symmetry. In Western art and graphic design the use of a geometrically centred image is usually considered naive.

2. **Weight** includes a consideration of relative size, focus, contrast and foregrounding. The relative weightings of these aspects of the image have a centre of gravity, which either balances or gives a dynamic to the composition.

3. **Framing** may be explicit or be implied by line breaks in the image. Lack of framing suggests a group identity to the 'participants' whilst framing unitises or individuates. Although not discussed by Kress & Van Leeuwen framing may be also be implied in the alignments of participants.

Books of images provide sequences in time and should be subject to considerations of rhythm. I have not taken my analysis that far and have only considered single pages as an introduction to the study of this rich interpretative method.

Kress and Van Leeuwen have provided a toolkit for visual analysis that I used, along with some of Barthes ideas, to analyses a selection of page openings from the Exploding Cinema programmes.

The Imagery in the booklets (1992 to 1998)

As I have noted the images that form the background to the majority of pages in the Exploding Cinema programmes are typically made by anyone in the collective who attends the special booklet meetings. These images will be analysed in two ways:

a. First the whole output of some 1000 illustrated pages (from seventy programmes) will be analysed for the overall range of imagery and an ordered classification made. I then analyse this classification itself and discuss a selection of the sub-categories.

b. From this classification four typical double page openings are selected and analysed using a few ideas from the visual grammar of Kress and Van Leeuwen, as summarised above, with help from the indexical strategies of Roland Barthes.

I went through all the booklets giving an intuitive verbal classification to the dominant image on each page. Once a category was established I enumerated further examples in that category. Two months later this process was repeated and revisions made.

Table 1. A Preliminary Draft Classification of Programme Imagery

ANIMALS (Excluding insects)	23	
INSECTS	24	
CAPITALISM	15	
BEAUTY	6	
CHILDHOOD /FAMILY	4	
COMIX	16	
DRUGS	8	
EARLY FILM /S8	19	(Incl. Amateur film/photo)
EATING	5	
FEMALE POWER	8	
FILM STARS	18	
MONSTER /HORROR	18	
ORAL CULTURES	17	
POLITICAL	17	
SEXUALITIES	7	
SKELETAL	2	
OUTER SPACE	2	

In *The Archeology of Knowledge* Foucault emphasises the potential importance of the apparently idiosyncratic, and the dangers of the normative in ironing over difference, I decided to go back to my initial categories and organise them in meta-categories.

> In relation to a history of ideas that attempts to melt contradictions in the semi-nocturnal unity of an overall figure, or which attempts to transmute them into a general, abstract, uniform principle of interpretation or explanation, archeology describes the different spaces of dissension.

> Michael Foucault 1969 p152

The reordering resulted in four main headings, in two pairs, which make up a first order of classification (see Table 2). Outer nature and human nature - lifeworld and system. The second order of classification comprises of fifteen headings of which four are further divided into a third order of sub-categories. Oral culture is divided into seven sub-categories and Capitalism into five, gender and mainstream cinema are divided into two sub-categories each.

Table 2. Classification of Imagery

OUTER NATURE(47)	Insects(24)	
	Other Animals(23)	
	Outer Space(2)	
HUMAN NATURE(19)	Beauty(6)	
	Eating(5)	
	Childhood /Family(4)	
	Skeletal(2)	
LIFEWORLD(92)	Early film /Amateur/S8(19)	
	Radical politics(17)	
	Oral cultures(17)	
		Circus(5
		DIY (2)
		Pirates (2)
		Popular culture (2)
		Seasonal (2)
		Tribal (2)
		Youth culture(2)
	Comix(16)	
	Gender(15)	
		Female Power(8)
		Sexualities(7)
	Drugs(8)	
SYSTEM(51)		
	Mainstream Cinema(36)	
		Horror(18)
		Film Stars(18)
	Capitalism(15)	
		Commodities(5)
		Mass media(3)
		Motors(3)
	Military(2)	
		WW2 (2)

With reference to Kress and Leeuwen's visual grammar as summarised above, I will start by making a semiotic analysis of this table before going on to comment on four subject groups and finally choosing just four page openings for detailed analysis.

If we apply the syntax of 'Left/Right is Given/New' then the 'given' is the broad historical divisions of nature and culture and system/ lifeworld. On the right is a category of social actions positioned as the new.

Overlaying this is the syntax of top/bottom that creates a dynamic between the ideal and the real. Circus is ideal and WWII real within the new. On the left-hand side outer nature and human nature is ideal opposed by the system as real.

This reading reverses a normative version in which we might expect the mainstream or system to be idealised at the top (head denoting the rational) and nature and the body to be in the lower area, or foot of the page, onto which the mainstream imposes its civilising order.

The second order of classification mediates between the given and the new (left and right). This mediation only relates to Oral Cultures, Gender, Mainstream Cinema and Capitalism, which alone contain further groups on the right. Here, in the zone of mediation, it is the resistance, offered by oral cultures and women, that is 'ideal' and capitalism is represented through its mainstream cinema, that is the 'real'.

The horizontality of the classification suggests a flow of processes from established categories to the social flux of action. The modality of the diagram is conveyed by its lack of colour and apparent scientificity. The implied diagonal from top/left to bottom /right suggest a vector which goes from nature to war. The downward direction suggesting an inevitability, which I would not consciously wish to subscribe to, but which may reflect a fear of the consequences of the present world order.

Iconographic comments on selected image groups

I have selected four groups Animals, Circus, Comix and Horror film. The Animals subject areas is selected because it is by far the largest group of images. Circus and Comics are areas which illustrate Exploding Cinema's allegiance to popular culture. Horror is part of this allegiance but is also an inferior mainstream form with which there is much sympathy. Pages pertaining to these themes will then be analysed in more detail.

Images of Animals, including insects: With at least 47 pages with animal images this is the most recurrent theme in the programme images.

Augustine and Aquinas followed Paul in denying the Hebrew bible's injunction of kindness towards animals. Descartes went further, theorising them as without feeling or souls and even Kant followed this Christian line. Jeremy Bentham was the first person to argue for the interests of animals in Western ethics at the end of the Eighteenth century. But it was not until Peter Singer's book in the mid 1970's that this issue was seriously debated and the traditional Christian position reappraised. This was also the first philosophical debate to give rise to a popular movement.

> Is it not crystal clear, then, comrades, that the evils of this
> life of ours spring from the tyranny of human beings? What then must we do?
> Why, work night and day, body and soul, for the overthrow of the human race!
>
> George Orwell, *Animal Farm*

This should be seen as part of an ecology or environmental movement that arose at the same time and has since become a major political force. Such concerns are at the heart of Western counter cultures.

Animals appeared in folk art, mythology and pagan religion because they were an important part of people's rural lives. They inhabit the pages of Exploding Cinema's programmes for different reasons. They are a symbol of nature, but not of a romantic nature nor of a nature 'red in tooth and claw'. The appearance of so many animals in an urban production is surely a gesture against the historical division of nature /culture or town /country. The animals are often in assertive even avenging postures. They are coinhabitants of the earth with us. We see animals holding cameras and generally being active.

Half the animals depicted are insects with their connotations of individual vulnerability but collective ubiquity and indestructibility. They can also be pests, something that the Exploding Cinema identifies with. Nature is here an antidote to a mainstream cinema, which is a standard bearer for the triumph of technology and cultural artifice.

Images of Circus: The first point is that these are subjects who may have originated in circuses or fairs but also appeared in the urban music-hall.

The circus is the most evocative and extreme form of live popular spectacle. A space of contradictions; the exotic; the captured; a performance on dirt; a living encyclopaedia of wonders; Lions and Tigers; impossible feats; unbelievable skills; foreign smells; shock; danger... And all appearing and disappearing like a mirage. Probably the most extraordinary live sights a European child would ever see.

The clown paints the fixed smile of the courtier on his face. The upper class surrounded themselves with the forced smiley faces of their servants. An illusory happiness (whose real moments of happiness were too coarse and vulgar!). The clowns actions though, are sad even laughable, a satire on the hapless condition of the powerless.

The provenance of Exploding Cinema in such popular forms has already been suggested.

Comics: The preferred reading material of the C20th modern young person was the comic. Comics like the Beano and Eagle, and later Marvel Comics played a regular part in the early lives of many young people in the era in which Exploders grew up. Cheap illustrated publications were not considered serious literature. Comic art was excluded from the art school curriculum as a vulgar artform.

I could go further and say that literary culture was *iconophobic* which goes a long way to explaining the low cultural position of comics and graphic novels. Whilst teaching on a pre-diploma course in Colchester in the early Nineties I had to ask students to remove comic art from their portfolio, however good it was, as it would seriously jeopardise their chances of getting onto a degree course at the prestigious London College of Printing.

Apart from its widespread influence on most of our childhoods, the comic was a significant part of the underground culture of the Sixties in specifically adult forms. A good example is Robert Crumb who provided a loving satire of hippy street life, with its incessant dope smoking and other inane behaviour, which is still widely read. The exclusion of the comic from the literature of the establishment was perversely, a positive qualification for an underground cultural form.

There was something of a revival of non-commercial comic culture in the 1980's with a focus on women comic artists such as Carol Swain, comics as a form of artist's book, and self-organised alternative comic conventions.

> There may be a future - or very ancient past truth in these derisory, vulgar, foolish, dialogical forms of consumer subculture.

Roland Barthes, 1977, p66

The comic frame both captures the moment - often the peak of action or depletion but accompanies this with a mimetic text which transverses time. A text in which the frozen characters speak to each other or philosophise to themselves. The frame is activated in its stillness by this text which transports us beyond the images. This transcendence of the image produces a set of what Barthes called obtuse meanings. The quality of comics lies not only in their writing or graphic skill but more importantly from meaning implied in the space between the frames, in the tension between the graphic and the literary. A form that has many parallels with film.

The Horror genre: Although long established in cinema the growth of the horror film as a genre, only took-off in the 1950s. The first drive-in cinema opened in 1933 but they didn't really become commonplace until car ownership became commonplace in the wake of the Second World War. By 1956 there were over 400 which were earning 25% of the total cinema box office. The audiences were mainly young and this encouraged the film industry to begin to make films tailored to this market. These were either rock music films like *Jailhouse Rock* (1957) or horror films. The classic of the period, *I Married a Monster from Outer Space*, was made in 1958.

> Their emphasis on spectacle implicitly recognised that the audience might have other things to do than just watch the film.

Richard Maltby, 1994

Effective horror films would actually make the audience sweat, shake and scream with a mixture of thrill and terror, and cling onto each other. This excitement went into a darker and more visceral area of emotion than the kinaesthetic thrills of musicals or the teeth-grinding tension of thrillers. It reached for the substance of nightmare and darkness. And as nightmares are illusions, the horror film is closer to its referent than the convention of realism that dominated respectable cinema. This innate vulgarity did not allow them to be considered as serious cinema. As a genre they had a minority or 'cult' following and stayed irrevocably low-budget.

Within the genre standards did evolve and classics were recognised. George Romero's *Night of the Living Dead* made in 1968 on a low budget was one such. *The Texas Chainsaw Massacre* (1974), which has only got a British certificate in its uncut version some twenty five years after it was made, is another. Wes Craven's *Scream* (1996) showed the genre finally becoming accepted within the mainstream.

Not that horror is a subject that appears much in the films shown at Exploding Cinema. It is more its outsider status as a low-budget cult genre and the visceral quality of its aesthetic that makes it a reference point in the programme imagery.

Semiotic analysis of images from the programmes

I suggest you look for meaning in the programme spreads yourself, before reading my interpretation.

1. <u>9th November 1996, pages 6/7</u>

A round Renaissance balloon is threatened by an extinct fossil skull that bears down on it. If the balloon is the imagination which presages the technological society, which itself is rising. So although the balloon looks vulnerable, it is the wild animal, however fierce in countenance, that is to be the victim. The balloon is a temporary 'goal' which leads upwards to the signs on the top right facing page, which are other late medieval characters. A bald monk toasts the rise of technology, which, ironically, is shifting the control of knowledge away from the monasteries. His head is bowed before the inevitable rise of a secular materialist knowledge but his downward gaze may suggest superiority. The vector of his gaze leads our reading path to an aristocratic hawk, which looks on, proudly from its branch. It has survived an earlier transition from hunting to agriculture and will, in Britain at least, survive the transition to capitalism.

The 'new' pinnacle of technological success is ironised in the lower half of the right-hand page. A television set in the place the hawks droppings might land. A TV family with a 'background' which is reduced to banal horizontal lines, look away passively from their settee to an exuberant woman on the screen. Are they any more powerful than the little frog on the left-hand page, which looks up from its corner?

The two pages are unified by a complex grammar of vectors, which guide our reading. The text has little relation to the images, although it is difficult to avoid the top left heading 'Life in this Society' as an 'anchor'. The computer generated typography is in a Fifties hand-lettered style which makes an ironic connection to the monks implied function as scribe and the birth of the TV nation.

2. <u>8th July 1995, pages 4/5</u>

Two vertical compositions face each other across the page spread. On the left is a vulgar form of high art, on the right a high form of popular art. Both share a surreal representation with Freudian resonances of anxiety. At the top of the left-hand vertical,

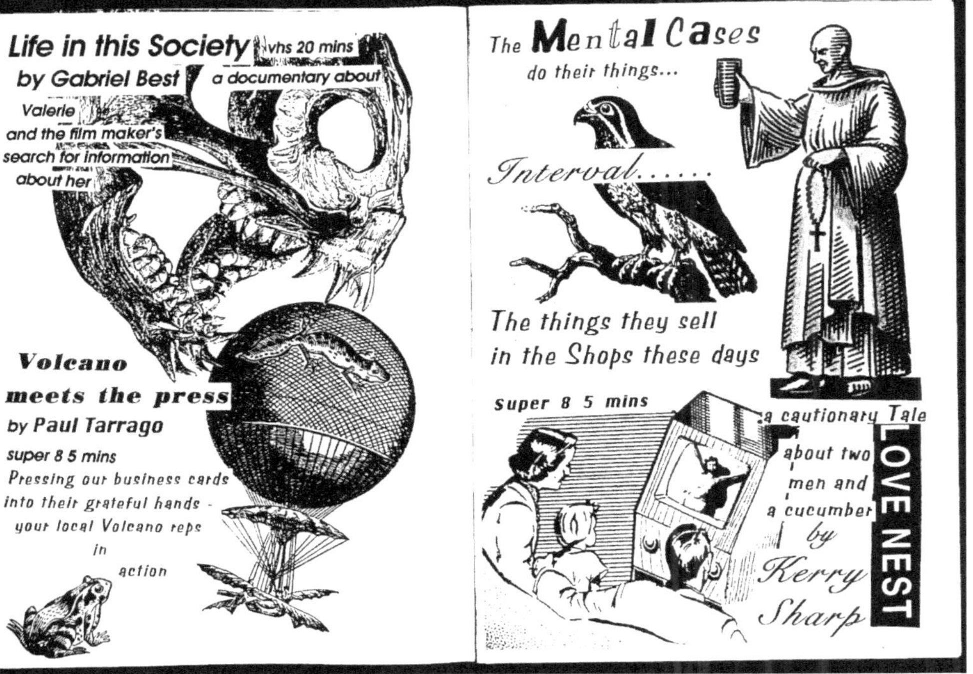

the naked girl bears a smile, which masks her resignation. Lower down an open-mouthed vulva screams 'reality' as ants carry their huge eggs threateningly towards each mouth. On the top of the right-hand vertical is a domestic 'kitty' cat' at the bottom a wildly prancing zebra carrying the column of tumblers - The domestic as ideal and the wild as real.

On the left-hand page, the status quo of high art is represented by the visual disturbance of Op Art and the mental disturbance of Surrealism. On the left hope for renewal is to be found in popular art, represented as the three old fashioned acrobats. Here is an example of the reversed grammar that is common in underground visuals.

The captions work closely with the images: choking; County Girls; Jaunt; LOVE IS DEAD; which all seems to illustrate the images - in another reversal of the normative.

Between the two parallel verticals there is produced a spine of obtuse tension as our minds oscillate between the two meanings and their reversals. We are again reminded of Barthes' third, obtuse, level of meaning and the need for an active audience not weighed down with aesthetic baggage.

3. <u>9th May 1998, pages 4/5</u>

No collage is used on these pages. Two contrasting iconic images face each other. On the left a photograph with a dark background, on the right a classic image from Marvel comics. The 'given', two women wearing only fishnet tights, are locked in a passionate embrace. The 'new' is the violent ejection of The Thing, a dark hairy creature, by a vast

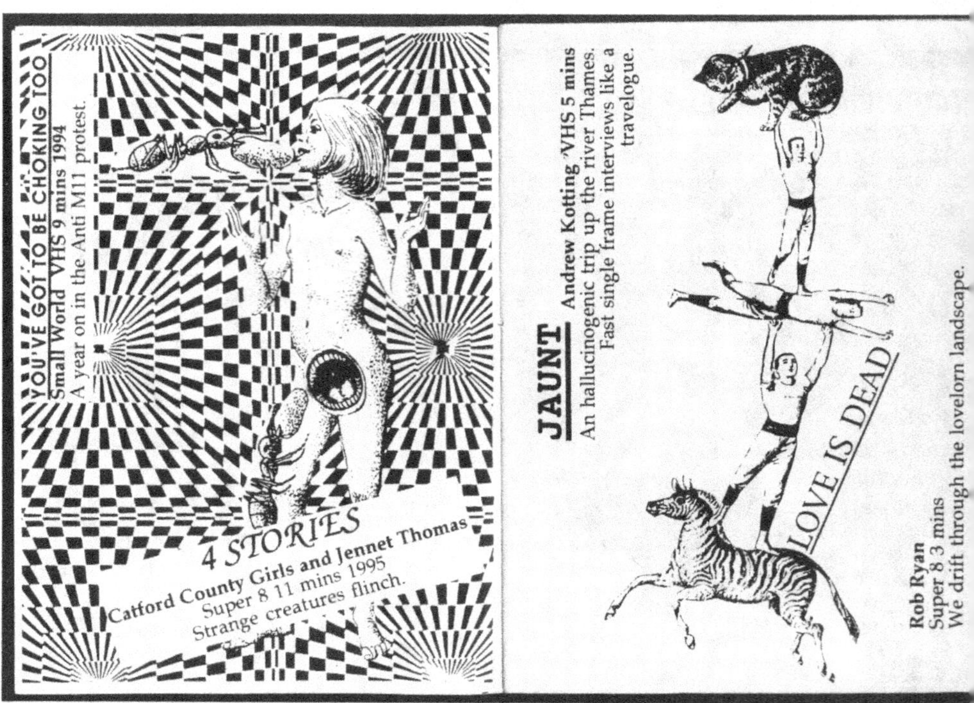

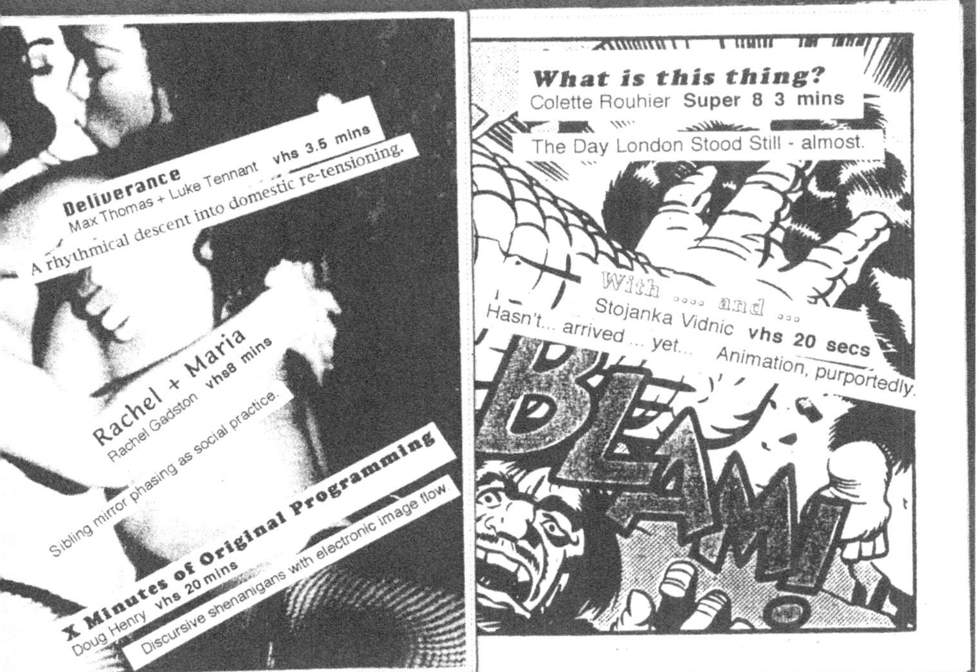

9th May 1998

scaly arm (The Hulk?).

A strong vector of meaning transverses both pages from top left to bottom right - BLAM! The implied source of this vector is the open mouthed kissing of the women. A movement from the emotive to a useful confrontation. Does this connote a powerful downward rejection of machismo, powered by women being together? Or is it a consequence of forbidden love - a violent expulsion to the margins, with its implied moral uncertainty?

Again an oscillation of meanings provokes a challenging uncertainty. The words 'deliverance', 'Rachel + Maria', 'X minutes', and the phrase 'What is this thing?', all seem to lubricate the action and anchor the reading above.

4. <u>17th April 1993, pages 10/11</u>
In the next page opening the hairy face of Freddy Krueger fills the screen with a terrifying grimace. His rough gouged face looks down and meets the readers gaze head on. The centre being the place of the divine ruler, according to Kress and Van Leeuwen. A divinity that is here ousted by a good god's primal negative. The tilt of the head creates a diagonal vector across the eyes, which leads us across the spine to the picture on the right.

Here a contrasting scene of apparent classical repose shows a woman braiding the hair of a naked girl with silky skin. The girl looks around and out towards us, her anxious gaze turned towards an apple, which hovers in the lower foreground. She stands on a vector from Krueger's threatening mouth. Below her feet are steps leading down to a lower level - which is in heavy shadow.

Freddy's face is unframed. In contrast the two women are framed by dark marble and stone. On the left a modern icon of horror, on the right an icon of classical repose. Horror arises from our subconscious, from the underground, to challenge the detachment of the classics as a veil covering abuse. Civilisation is a mask for oppression. The classical scene represents an ennobling civilisation with a sense of its foundation, but the appearance of Freddy produces 'a spasm of the signifier' which displaces the benign façade that is given by the classics. His intuitive cry of outrage displaces the rationalisation of desire.

The obtuse level of meaning unsettles the normative reading. The text adds to this sense, perhaps even anchoring meanings and syntax too firmly.

Semiotic Analysis - Conclusion

The range of concerns expressed by the collective amounts to a dissection of the counter culture as it refracted through the prism of the Exploding Cinema collective. The four aspects of this taxonomy selected for further discussion uncover aspects of the collective mind-set not detailed in other parts of the thesis.

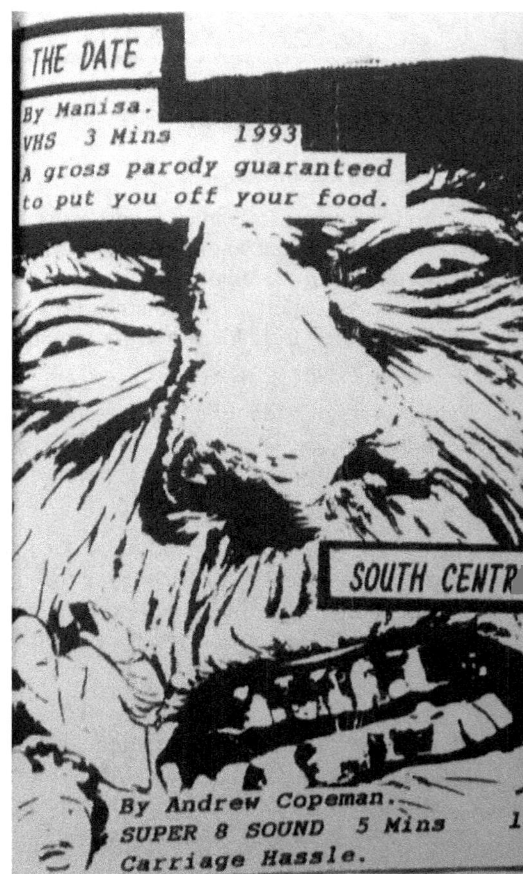

17th April 1993

In spite of its scientific pretensions semiotic analysis is still an artform that bears the subjectivity of its author. It is rational to the extent of being systematic, theoretically considerate, and so to a degree transparent in method. With this in mind I hesitate to 'prove' things about the group subconscious of Exploding Cinema by this partial analysis - I have no doubt different interpretations could be made.

What such an analysis does signal is that a sympathetic in-depth reading of Exploding Cinema activities is possible. It is the representation of this aesthetic depth that is my primary aim rather than any attempt to over-determine meaning.

Kress and Van Leeuwen's visual grammar asks the viewer to be active and responsible for the validation of her own reading. An idea that mirrors the Exploding Cinema ethos of an active audience.

postscript

Methodological approaches did have some incongruence with the culture of Exploding. A particular example of this was Duncan's performed satire on Semiotics.

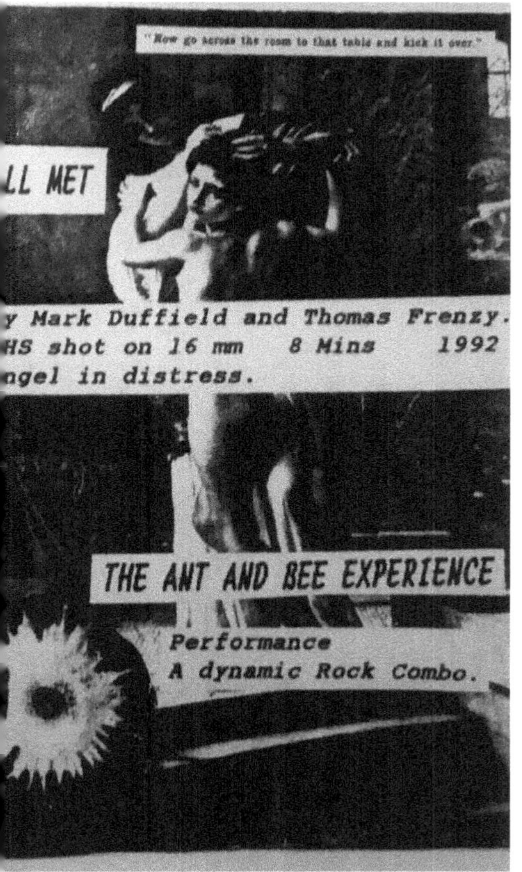

Chapter 7

Participant Observation: open access, independence, and identity

This chapter focuses on three issues: Exploding Cinema's ethos of open access; how the group's finances relate to their independence; and some issues of group identity. My main source of information are the logbooks I compiled in the two years I was a member of the collective. I will start by considering ethnographic methodology in general.

I joined the Exploding Cinema slightly before the period of the research began at the beginning of 1997 as a way of ascertaining that such a project was feasible. I then took part in the collective as an active member and researcher keeping a log of my activity from November 1997 to December 1999. This meant attending meetings, helping to make the programmes and setting up shows. I doubt if a non-contributing member could have been put up with for very long - in such a small group there is usually a need for 'all hands on deck'. The other members were aware of my research and were in agreement with the general aims of my thesis, however I did not seem to have a special position as an 'observer' within the group. Although people did occasionally joke about me scribbling in my black books, mostly I was seen as a fellow artist/activist. After December 1999 I stayed part of the group but without keeping a regular logbook. In fact for the first half of 2000 there were only three shows and relatively little activity.

I recorded my observations in the most classic literary mode of ethnography - by writing up regularly soon after meetings, shows or other events and when thoughts about the group and its latest activities was fresh in my mind. When I compiled the logs I deliberately included other activities I saw as relevant contexts both to me as artist and researcher and to the Exploding Cinema.

I did also record a few still photographs and some documentary video footage of shows. A series of formal interviews with each member of the collective is written up in a separate chapter framed by the practices of Oral History.

Introduction to Ethnographic Method

Daniel Miller has suggested that, at least within common Western cultures, the main skill that may be required of the ethnographer is the ability to drink! This is because much ethnographic material comes by way of gossip, so you need to be able to hang out and get on with people, which in the West often includes drinking alcohol. This was certainly true with Exploding Cinema and there is a sense that the reward of getting through a meeting is a drink down the pub. However, you also need to write up what is heard and observed on a regular basis, something which may not easily follow a session of drinking.

Miller pointed out that the methodology of participant observation was in practice highly pragmatic. A researcher should, 'use whatever works well'. He emphasised just one crucial critical principle - there is invariably a difference in what people say and what they do. People are, for instance, often concerned with normative appearances in social settings whereas individually they may admit to being, or may be observed as being, more idiosyncratic.

An important consideration is in gaining the trust of a group and achieving an empathy with them. This entails seeing the world from their point of view. This typically takes at least a year and the tradition in anthropology points to a minimum period of 18 months of fieldwork research. This also has the advantage that all seasonal cycles of activity are likely to be witnessed after there has been a period for the observer to settle within the group.

As with all methodologies there are advantages and problems associated with this research. If we are aware of the limitations of the methodology in relation to its subject we are likely to be more aware of the partial nature of the knowledge that results. I will consider these under the following sub-heads.

> a) The effects of the intrusion of the research programme.
>
> b) Subject positions and cultural differences between the participant observer and the subjects being studied.
>
> c) The cultural and historical baggage and technical limitations carried by the methods of observation and recording.
>
> d) Interpretation of data.
>
> e) Ethics.

A Short Historical Introduction to Ethnography

Observation of a phenomenon within the context within which it occurs is one of the most basic methods of empirical research. When the study is of a group of humans this methodology is usually known as ethnography. If the observer becomes a part of the group in some way the methodology is called participant observation.

Ethnography was first used in the mid C19th and came to mean the scientific description of contemporary human societies and their cultures with an increasing emphasis on culture. The participant observer records what s/he observes on a regular basis. This record is then used as the basic source of data from which knowledge about this group and its activities is constructed.

There have been three paradigm shifts in the history of anthropology. The classic first period was in the context of Nineteenth century imperialism. Fieldwork was usually undertaken by untrained colonial officials who sent their observations to armchair scholars who studied these reports at their desks. The subjects of study were the 'other' to the codes of Western civilisation. The field-workers usually based their reports on interviews with 'informants' rather than by being participants in the society that they were studying.

As colonialism collapsed in the Mid-Twentieth century and sociology established the usefulness of rigorous studies of Western populations, ethnography came to be used in the West's homelands. People were still studied as isolated and static groups, who were outsiders to the civilised culture within which the professional discipline of anthropology was based. But a participant observation was increasingly used.

Then in the 1980s there were a series of major intellectual challenges to the methods and conceptual frameworks of anthropology. The first may be represented by Eric R. Wolf's book 'Europe and the People Without History', which was published in 1982. This book showed that the vast majority of human societies and groups were not isolated from waves of influence that resonated across the globe from the earliest times. No group could be adequately studied as an isolated phenomenon that was fixed in its behaviour. All humans groups were a dynamic part of global forces. Wolf pointed out that between 1670 and 1760 the Iroquois tribe was demanding scarlet and blue dyed cloth from the Stroudwater Valley of Gloucester in England. This was one of the first areas 'in which English weavers lost their autonomy and became hired factory hands' (Wolf 1982 p.4). After a lengthy analysis of the forces of global history he concluded that human cultures were more interconnected than they had appeared to be:

> We can no longer think of societies as isolated self-maintaining systems. Nor can we imagine cultures as integrated totalities in which each part contributes to the maintenance of an organised, autonomous, and enduring whole. There are only cultural sets of practices and ideas, put into play by determinate human actors under determinate circumstances. In the course of action, these cultural sets are forever assembled, dismantled and reassembled.
>
> Eric R. Wolf, 1982 p391

The next major challenge surfaced with the publication of a collection of papers under the title 'Writing Culture: the poetry and politics of ethnography', which was edited by James Clifford and G. Marcus. Published in 1986 this challenged the scientific model that had been applied to ethnography. Whilst science was good for a study of *things*, it was shown to be of limited use in the study of interactions between different cultural subjectivities. The subjective dimension suddenly surged to the fore. Culture was seen as composed of dynamic and contested codes, and in these contests the poetic and political were inseparable. Science was a product of culture rather than standing above it. The literary interpenetrated with the academic, and writing about culture was always political and ethical. Cultures so described had been as much invented as simply described by the written form. This last point was first made by Hayden White in his celebrated essay 'The Fictions of Factual Representation'.

> The process of fusing events, whether imaginary or real, into a comprehensible totality capable of serving as the object of representation is a poetic process. Here the historians must utilise precisely the same tropological strategies, the same modalities of representing relationships in words, that the poet or novelist uses.
>
> Hayden White 1985 p125

This led to a more self-consciously narrative based ethnography, which emphasised variety and idiosyncrasy rather than a norm established with statistical data or imposed from preconceptions. It accepted the literary aspect of the writing-up process, which was freed of an often pedantic pseudo-scientific style. This was in the context of more extreme challenges to the idea of a unitary subject, coming from an emergent post modernist theory. Identity was no longer seen as a fixed single entity but a complex phenomenon that shifted and changed with context.

Nonetheless, certain aspects of the scientific model were still useful. The power of a generalisation that can be deduced from a representative sample, is too useful to be completely undermined by the critique of positivism: as is the use of an explicit methodology which can be repeated to allow later verification of, or challenge to, the conclusions reached. It is important that any methodology can be accountable rather than claiming an arbitrary authority.

Thinking critically about this methodology

a) The Effects of Intrusion

My method of research was an active one. As an active group member I inevitably contributed to changes that took place in the group. The most noticeable things that changed during my period of study were technical and financial. Having bought a video projector and Public Address system, the expenses for each show were reduced by around £100, which makes for more income or the possibility of smaller audiences. There are a few ways in which my participation could be seen to have contributed to a new direction within the group, or in which I challenged the groups modus operandi, or came into conflict with members of the collective. This seemed to be due to the differences between my own art practice and the established practices of the collective. As previously mentoned, when we did the 'roof show' in Peckham I built some substantial structures with timber that was freely available near to the site. This needed to be hauled five storeys up the outside of the factory on ropes - an arduous task especially as the weather was very hot at that time. Later there were complaints from the older collective who saw this as being in conflict with the Exploding Cinema style of operation which, it was said, was about projecting images rather than building actual structures. 'We are into theatrical illusion - not architectural construction' (Duncan Reekie).

Another example occurred at the AGM in December 1999 where Duncan Reekie presented a written proposal that aimed to confront the film establishment and become the basis of a petition. This proposal suggested a new basis for funding film production. Its main aim was to end the state sponsored production funding for short film and to redistribute that money to a decentralised circuit of autonomous centres for exhibition and distribution.

This seemed idealistic to me and I argued against it. A radical democratisation of film funding seemed unrealistic outside of a much broader cultural critique. I also argued that a programme of change that would find wide support would need to arise from a prolonged process of open debates rather than be prescribed. Others in the group were not so vocal in their opposition as me but they were also not enthusiastically supportive of the petition. Nothing more seemed to come of it. Did I contribute to the demise of this initiative? Could it have evolved in practice and, even if apparently impractical in its early formulation, still have provoked a useful debate on how film was funded? Did this intrusive criticism unwittingly dampen a revolutionary spark? After all, radical innovations are likely not to arise in the most reasonable of guises.

The extent to which researchers can invalidate their research by changing the object of their study is a complex theoretical debate that there is not space to go into here. It is also possible that the publishing of the history of a group which has had a lack of recognition, can contribute to the subsequent demise of the group. Such groups may be hanging on waiting for such a recognition in order to feel their project is completed. I believe that documentation does have this meaning, often providing a sign of a project's completion. (In this case Exploding Cinema has continued for 20 years since my research was completed.) What Michael Agar calls the 'professional distance/ personal involvement paradox' cannot perhaps be theoretically resolved in favour of one position or another - it is rather a point of ongoing critical awareness for both sides.

This chapter tends to a viewpoint borne out of personal involvement. The possible error that could have arisen from this bias was offset with as much methodological rigour as possible within my strategy of triangulated methodologies.

b) Subject Positions, Cultural Difference and Authority
The question of being aware of the cultural framework and political interests from which researchers makes choices as to what to record, and that colour the interpretations they make, is part of a reflexive approach to research. The idea of a completely objective viewpoint is hardly tenable any more within the social sciences and humanities. The antidote to this myth is to make the level of objectivity apparent through methodological transparency and to be honest about the spin that may have been given to material. Michael Agar argues that a clear distinction between the subjectivity of an ethnographer and a subject of study is no longer possible - the world is too culturally interpenetrated. An example is an isolated tribe who watch the 'Discovery' satellite TV channel. But the position of the researcher is also a part of a claim to authority. There is the claim to speak an informed truth about a particular people that is socially validated by academic institutions, journals and learned rituals. The PhD itself is part of a series of rituals that can help confer such authority.

My subject position as an artist committed to collaborative working, with experience of around ten cultural collectives clearly motivates my research and leavens my research with experience. On the other hand I am aware how my own preferred practice occasionally clashes with the Exploding Cinema formula. Here are some more examples: I prefer to work in a more site-specific way relating to the locality; I prefer a less brash and more thematically unified style of décor; and also I would prefer such a group to be more mutually supportive around the making of work, rather than being focussed mainly on shows.

These sort of differences lead at times to a certain tone of discontent in my account which if taken a face value, would not be consistent with my role as 'detached' observer. At the same time I'm aware that any member of the group will have such 'moans' and that my own are probably not unique. Because of my background, my experience is the experience of a collective member even if I am also a researcher. To have retained a cool distance would have been to miss the frustrations and discords that are integral to collective working.

c) Recording Methods
The ways in which ethnographic observations are recorded have cultural and historical baggage and technical limitations. There has been considerable debate about the effect of literary traditions on the anthropological logbook. Writing, being relatively slow, is said to make the logbook entries more reflective. But what does this mean? It is about translating the fullness of the reality experienced into written form. This means making an apparently complete transcription of an oral world, in which not all experiences are even spoken about, into a literary form. Usually field notes are meant to be directed to the concrete and be exhaustively detailed. However, my log notes are more of a

recording of thoughts, relations and observations of people's opinions.

Of course even participant observer research is limited in what it can reveal with the resources available. I was aware that even with such a small group, short period of observation and relatively small cultural area of influence, the groups activity was much more complex and wide-ranging than my study could encompass or represent.

d) Interpretation of Data

There must be other interpretations that could be made from my logbooks. As an example, people often showed an interest in the dynamics of collective group working. Why do collectives work well or fall apart? This is not something that I have analysed here, but my notebooks might be of interest to someone who was attempting to make such an analysis in the future.

The application of third party theory as a method of interpretation of ethnographic data was seen as politically suspect (Agar, 1996 p.420) It is better that ethnographic data is 'theory generating'. Theory generated from the subjects themselves on their own terms, is less likely to impose the values of one culture on another. It should even use their own words, expressions and ideas but not be bound by them.

In this case many members of Exploding Cinema are capable of expressing their position at least as well as me and often do. Often this is done in a style closer to the underground idiom. The point in this case is not my skill at writing but more basically the will to pull the complex whole together in a form that meets the demands of a particular epistemic formation.

What do I want to claim for the work? Not a generalisation about the way collectives work but rather a generalisation about the value of such collective cultural production within a wider democratic culture. The participant observation was about generating an account that was able to come to grips with complex social relations on a level that was emotionally connected, in a way that would be missing from more detached quantified methods like content analysis.

As I have noted one of the main points of guidance given to ethnographic practice is to pay attention to the difference between what people *say* and what people *do*. This can be extended to the gap between the documented representations of their activity and what they actually did. The logbooks can serve to fill gaps left by the group's own self-documentation or to act as checks on these types of representation.

> For historians seeking to 'explain' the 'facts' of the French Revolution, the decline and fall of the Roman Empire, the effects of slavery on American society, or the meaning of the Russian Revolution, what is at issue is not, 'What are the facts?' but rather, how are the facts to be described in order to sanction one mode of explaining them rather than another.
>
> Hayden White, 1986, p. 134

e) Ethics:

One has a responsibility to the relationships formed. This is conventionally realised by allowing the subjects access to the draft report with a 'right of reply'. In practice I have found that reading long academic texts is burdensome to most people, especially when they are offered in draft form, and is not an adequate solution to this question of ethical responsibility.

The central ethical question may be as to whether the PhD ritual offers up vulnerable subjects as sacrificial victims of knowledge - a knowledge that would then be used by the state to better control such groups. In the light of the theoretical discussion of the social pathologies produced by the systemic invasion of the lifeworld (not included in this version), we might take this seriously. If the authority of this theory carries enough weight - and a PhD study is a part of this systemic weighting - then all I can offer as a defence is that the object I produce will not be a palatable or reductive representation but rather one that resists closure and is *quaquaversal* (A neologism from the radical art collective: Exploding Galaxy meaning to move outwards in all directions at once).

Analysis of the main themes of the log books

The first job is to search for categories and patterns. I read through the 360 pages of my notes in the three A4 logbooks. Each topic or theme that emerged was noted and the relevant page number recorded under that heading. Of course these are bound to be mainly themes that I imposed from the last three years of study but I am also aware that new patterns may emerge from this sort of data collection. Thirteen of these headings which I had noted did not get further entries. Eight of them had eight to thirty pages with relevant material. Some of the headings, like 'contexts', were too broad and needed further sub-division. On the other hand, some of the unique categories could be moved together under a more general heading. In the end it was themes that were key to Exploding Cinema and that had not been covered by other aspects of the research, which I chose to write up and present here.

In the end I focused on three key themes: open access, the practicalities of financial independence, and identity formation. Other logbook material has already been used in the narrative history chapter. In fact data generated by being a participant observer inevitably infuses all the research thinking and writing.

a) Open Access - Ethos and Reality

Open access for filmmakers does not seem to lead to an influx of pornography, racism or other abusive materials that could cause offence in an open setting.

The North American underground broke taboos and relied on forbidden fruit for some of its appeal. The Kino Kulture venue in London tended to sometimes show such 'transgressive' material. This sort of material is not ideally suited to an show open to all ages and it rarely appears on the Exploding Cinema screen. There is no explicit policy or guidelines on what is not acceptable; filmmakers just do not seem to offer material they themselves seem to perceive as unsuitable.

This principle also applies to material that is not extreme in any sense. Much Video Art, especially that of a durational nature, which is increasingly popular on the contemporary gallery scene is unsuitable for a seated evening audience and does not often get sent in.

This is my experience of doing the programming for the second roof show in Peckham in 1998, derived from logbook notes:

> 'I phoned people on the database and hauled in a few filmmakers who had shown at Exploding Cinema in the past. Then more works were passed on to me from Colette who is the main number for information on the flyers.' (Log 2 p.153)

The point is - who responds to the open access invitation? The films shown seem to be made by: collective members; their friends; people who show regularly; people who get in touch through our web presence; students; established film-makers in other fields who've made something that isn't destined for the mainstream. By this account the reality of open access programming relies on the organic contacts that surround the programmer, the collective and the event itself as an ongoing institution - in that order.

I suppose the policy of no selection might not be viable with a well-funded festival in a prestige venue that widely advertised 'no selection'. It might then get flooded with material. No-selection with Exploding Cinema is in the context of a localised network with the natural quantitative limits of human friendship. In that you can only maintain significant relationships with a limited number of people. There are other forms of inertia that can limit the number of people wanting to show work. A passage from my logbook:

> 'A woman friend of Ian's who works on TV, was pissed off with the lack of inventiveness on TV and so she got together with friends and made her own programme. I suggested she should show it at Exploding but she said 'it wasn't our style'. I suggested we didn't have a style because we show whatever is given to us. She persisted that her group were into 'high production values'. I just repeated that didn't exclude her. But it seems that for her Exploding Cinema presented a context of retro, low production values *as an aesthetic* - which can help maintain the divide that it critiques.' (Log 2 p.167)

It should be emphasised here that works with the highest production values have often been shown and have seemed to co-exist happily with rough-cut home produced material.

A selection of sorts is made for tours, which fall outside of the main format. Although I was told that anyone who phoned up wanting to show a film in the period before a tour would be included on the basis of the slogan 'Selection but no rejection'.

The programmes of the smaller gigs are selected by whoever is organising them or whoever takes the initiative. This is an account of a less organised small event at the Anarchist Bookfair, October 1999:

> 'One of the collective had said we didn't need to make a programme of films to show but then just set up and showed his own programme of videos from 2.30 until 5.00pm. This was disconcerting as Damon, Stuart Pound and myself had brought along videos but didn't have a say.' (Log 3 p.340)

It is not easy to influence the collective to do things which are not already within its normative practices. Opposition is often not vocalised and is felt only in the form of a mute resistance, often only expressed as pronounced lack of enthusiasm. The normative style of Exploding Cinema decor has a brash retro pop/ camp style based on collections of slides made by the core collective. The style of decor does provide an upbeat atmosphere for a variety show and it would take quite a lot of energy to introduce something different. I would almost feel that the identity of Exploding Cinema was being challenged. Perhaps it is not suprising that an inertia surrounds the specifics of the 'décor' once it has been established as the house style.

When a new person joins they tacitly accept a set of ongoing practices some of which are highly specific, although their fixity may be invisible to those that have been engaged with them for years. In practice it is the core group that tend to maintain the house style. Do they in this way exert a kind of covert semiotic ownership?

> 'The inner group is embedded in a wider friendship network which comes to shows and embraces the core group but not the newer members, who can never attain the (sub)cultural capital of the founding members.' (Log 1 p.86)

> 'Exploding Cinema is open to all as long as you are determined, tough, energetic and not looking for a group that cares about you. You've got to be self-contained, able to take put-downs or people throwing wobblies, and the usual underground collective shit.' (Log 2 p.177)

This is not a criticism of the core collective who in fact demonstrate enormous generosity, putting much voluntary work in whilst they were subsisting on the lowest of incomes. My point is just to compare the reality of the collective practice with the ideals of open access and peerness.

There are also advantages to be got by newcomers from this existing network as well as from the wider position that Exploding Cinema's reputation has built up in the USA and Germany. New members are quite welcome to use this network to their own advantage, although few seem to. It should also be remembered that Exploding Cinema did nurture the groups who came together as the Volcano Festival from 1996.

b) Finances and Independence

One of the main differences between Exploding Cinema and the state sponsored short film agencies is that it is independent and run by voluntary labour. It is financed simply through door takings at its main shows and receives no other sponsorship or grant funding. During the period of my participant observation the financial situation changed considerably.

a) When I joined at the beginning of 1997 there was a One-2-One mobile phone which was mainly kept by one of the collective, and although the calls were free the monthly standing charge was a drain on the finances, especially during periods in which few shows were being put on. Its usefulness in the run-up to a show seemed out of proportion to its ongoing costs. When I finally got to have use of it, it seemed obsolete and almost useless, as the batteries only allowed about half an hour of actual mobile use. Of course to the keeper of the 'phone, connected to the mains and free in the evening and at weekends, it was a good 'perk'. And it must be noted that this person worked very hard for Exploding. This vested interest meant that there was considerable resistance to getting rid of the 'phone. This finally did happen in May 1998 after months of discussion.

b) We had to hire a video projector for each show. We got this mainly from James Stevens at £25 a time, although sometimes we had to pay £50. The purchase of a second video projector was the biggest capital expenditure that Exploding Cinema made requiring a surplus of almost £2000 in the bank. The first projector had been bought in 1993. As has been discussed after the group split up in October 1994 there were bad feelings about the projector, and a year later the projector was 'repossessed' by people from the faction that had left. This experience left some traumatic memories attached to the ownership of such equipment for the core collective and this may have accounted for the slowness with which a second projector was purchased.

In 1998 a powerful second-hand projector was offered by James Stevens and was paid for in stages. James was given the final £500 cash during the second roof show on 15th August 1998. Owning a projector meant that £50 less income needed to be earned from each show.

A major technical breakdown in the sound at the Union Tavern on 1st April 1999 made it clear that a spare bulb for the video projector (an expensive item at over £200) was a necessary purchase, as a broken projector bulb would have brought the whole show to a halt. Did reducing risk of breakdown take a certain edge off the show? Previously Exploding Cinema would celebrate its ramshackle quality as being part of its low-budget makeshift aesthetic. Better equipment made the show appear to be 'more professional'. Could this be the thin end of a process of economic rationalisation?

This is another instance of something I supported in the group because it seemed like 'common sense', but could have lead to a change of style which moved it away from its original character and appeal.

c) A sound system was often hired in. When I first joined, sound was regularly provided and set up by a Japanese artist called Taka for a fee of £50 which included an amplifier and speakers, although transport often had to be supplied by Exploding Cinema. Debate on the purchase of an amplifier and speakers was a hot topic but the decision was only taken after the disastrous breakdown of the sound in April 1999. A new sound system was purchased in May 1999.

d) The ticket price was a regular topic of debate when I first joined the collective. The issue of whether there should be a concessionary rate was also controversial. A meeting of the 7th July 1997 agreed a £4 with £3 concessionary rate, but in the event everyone paid £3 as it is uncool to demand documentation. By 1998 the door price had been raised from £3 concession to a flat rate of £4 which led to some ugly arguments at the door. A few people argued that by not having a concession rate and raising prices the Exploding Cinema was selling out by excluding those on Social Security Benefits. Most of the collective felt that Exploding Cinema should not be part of the money system or exclude people because of high door prices. This had a symbolic resonance because of the association of the group with the poorest lumpen sections of the population that tend to comprise the counter culture. This was another dimension of the open access ideology. On the other hand the price hike was simply in line with an inflationary drop in the value of the pound since 1992.

These four changes brought an improvement to the financial stability of the group, but may have altered the image of the Exploding Cinema. Overheads were drastically reduced by as much as £150 per show and the door price hike brought in an extra £100 or so (per 100 paying audience). This made the financial basis of the group much more healthy and stable but at the same time introduced other pressures. The obvious result is that there is more to spend and this puts pressure on the democratic framework.

It seems that there is an unspoken tension between the ownership that accrues from having created and maintained an organisation on a voluntary basis for many years and the democratic constitution which gives each member, including new members, an equal say and vote. This investment of large amounts of ones life unpaid also speaks of a deep commitment which newer members do not, and perhaps cannot, attain. People need a sense that the funds they have helped to generate have been spent in ways they agree with. If there are little or no surpluses this problem cannot arise. Conversely a hand-to-mouth existence also bring its stresses.

In spite of these considerations, a strong financial situation is essential to the ongoing survival of the Exploding Cinema and is the main thing to guarantee its ongoing independence. Its very persistence as an organisation that has defied financial realities for more than eight years, fuels its influence. Almost everyone associated with alternative culture has heard of Exploding Cinema and its influence had spread to USA with the help of the website and a few visits by individuals from the collective.

> Thankyou for sending the Volcano programme. Thank God people still have the courage and tenacity, will and verve to organise no budget events.

Letter from Marshal Anderson in Scotland (1-10-1998).

These questions of economics link to the slogan of 'No-Budget film making' which has been used to promote the idea of open access to film making from the beginning of Exploding Cinema. A £10 Super 8 camera from a car boot sale and a £10 role of process-paid film is all a person needs to express themselves on film. But by the end of 1998 the film establishment had hijacked the 'No-Budget' label and with their access to the mass media made it mean something different. *Shooting Gallery* on Channel 4 had Cathy Burke, the working class everywoman for the Nineties, endorsing the new definition which included films made for 'just a few' thousand pounds.

c) Observations on group identity

'Colette said that the Exploding Cinema had a 'personality" - implying that its formula should be conserved. (Log 1 p.65)

As I have noted there is inertia in the group that maintains this characteristic 'formula'. The 'personality' of Exploding Cinema has evolved out of the early collective and is clearly successful in the sense of attracting a regular audience. For those who were there early on and active in creating this formula, the 'personality' must feel profoundly owned and a part of their past. Adherence to this formula is not spelled out in the Collective Agreement and is not a stated requirement of membership although it is perhaps self-evident after experiencing a two or three shows. However, even the core members do become weary of the formulaic nature. Colette's expressed reason for having a sabbatical from the Exploding Cinema was that it was all 'getting too predictable'.

Paul Tarrago has said he doesn't believe that there is a British underground. Later Duncan expressed a similar sentiment. In spite of the recent activity by London film groups there is no alternative national or international circuit for films to be disseminated through, as there was in the Sixties. On the other hand, there is a 'counter culture' and Exploding Cinema is seen to be part of it.

The Exploding Cinema's inclusion in the book *Cultures of Resistance*, published in London in 2000, put Exploding Cinema alongside a whole range of other manifestations of oppositional culture that showed together in the festival of the same name in Tower Bridge Road in December 1999. It described itself as: "A coming together of artists, activists, musicians, sound-systems, filmmakers, chefs, performers."

Exploding Cinema takes part in a diffuse network of oppositional communications. In addition to the events themselves, it is the style of publicity and programmes that give Exploding Cinema symbolic membership of a wider counterculture.

> 'In underground terms the best publicity is a lot of obscure, well designed and witty but cheaply printed flyers pinned up on all sorts of obscure notice boards, given out at key meeting places and mailed out to a network of regulars. Hipsters pride themselves in being able to spot such stuff amongst the plethora of highly coloured attention grabbing commercial advertising'. (Log 3 p.317)

Conclusion

We can see that Exploding Cinema gets its identity firstly from its style of décor and presentation, which relates to the aesthetics of popular art rather than those of high art. Secondly, its identity is associated with a wider counter culture. This counter culture has a limited support for creativity which is a lower priority than politics or lifestyle and direct action campaigns. This means that there are no formal avenues for the distribution and showing of movie material.

Financial independence is a key feature of the Exploding Cinema. It is this independence from funding that allows it to put on spectacular shows attracting large audiences whilst allowing the most direct access for filmmakers to show their work. There are those who would prefer a lower door price and less professionalism and those who would like a context of higher production values to showcase their work. Open access is mainly about allowing any filmmaker to show work without submitting to a selection procedure. This ideal in reality favours those closer to the collective. Certain forces seem to prevent Exploding Cinema being swamped by the open invitation to show 'anything' not least of which is the self-selection of filmmakers themselves. Policies such as open access also have a polemical value as slogans.

Open access is also be applied to the collective membership, as anyone in the audience is invited to join. By having a low door price and unpretentious venues the shows are accessible to those on low incomes. Participant observation allows these policies to be seen in practice over a long period and a wide variety of venues.

Chapter 8

Oral Histories: biographies of the collective

I will introduce oral history as a methodology. This is followed by a discussion of the six interviews with collective members made in the autumn of 1999. This is under three headings: covering matters of ethnic identity; educational and class backgrounds; and cultural influences. Relations between these life experiences and the broader historical provenances of the group are noted.

Oral History Methodology

> I was only seven when she (my great-grandmother) died and most of her stories came to me through other family members. They taught me when I came to consider them much later, to treat so called 'oral history' with care. As stories and anecdotes they were lively and interesting, as were the stories passed on by other branches of the family - stories of seafaring under sail and of the theatre and music hall. But as factual or descriptive accounts they lost and gained much in the telling.
>
> Dorothy Thompson, 1993 p5

Is this what is meant by oral history? If a person takes note of the stories told by their grandmother are they an Oral Historian? Dorothy Thompson's great grandmother's stories were told to her by other family members. They were not direct memories of experiences but memories of the stories that they had heard from her grandmother. To construct an oral history, in the academic sense of the word, it is preferable to record a person talking about the past that they themselves experienced. What Dorothy Thompson is talking about is the story of the past that is passed down to us through oral culture. A clear distinction needs to be maintained between the two meanings of oral history. Clearly someone talking about their own experience has a certain immediacy and veracity that a secondary account does not.

So someone relating their memory of what someone else said is clearly a lot less reliable than a direct memory of what they themselves experienced. With memories of secondhand stories we enter an area of hear-say and eventually of myth - which is in itself interesting but which we can usefully differentiate from accounts of actual experiences. Even directly related memories of things experienced constitute evidence that should not be asserted as historical fact without a rigorous checking against other sources.

Oral cultures may be defined as being all those cultures in which the written form does not play a central role. The performative is central in oral cultures. The word is not just spoken but accompanied by a veritable flux of expressive forms. Oral communication occurs in forms which include tonal variation, volume modulation, velocity and rhythm as well as gesture, posture, facial expression and expression of emotion - it is a multi-sensory performance medium. This is in addition to the musical characteristics which are unique to spoken language like jingling combinations and regional rhythms. I have already made the point that Exploding Cinema is embedded in oral culture. It is therefore important to understand oral culture if we are to fully appreciate the communicative dynamics of cultural arenas like Exploding Cinema.

For the purposes of this methodology we should note that whilst written and printed documents, such as the programmes, may be more accurate at fixing events in a precise chronology, oral accounts might tell us more about the dynamics and emotional force of experience that actually motivates and gives qualitative content to social history. Both sources of data have their uses in making sense of the past and there is no reason why these uses cannot be complimentary.

Quite apart from the formal differences whole areas of human life have gone unrecorded in written documents and are accessible *only* through the verbal reports of witnesses. This information can be quite utilitarian; such as how an obsolete tool was made and used. Or it can be more subjective information, such the experience of war. This subjective information may not be simple to transcribe as much of its value may be contained in the non-verbal aspect of oral communication, as described above, rather than in words alone.

The oral history interview differs from the journalistic interview in that it should ideally not be driven by the agenda of the interviewer. It should be the interviewee that decides on the priorities of their testimony. Oral history is ideally interviewee led.

The History of Oral History

How and why oral history came to differentiate itself as a distinct area of study from mainstream history is important to understand oral history as a distinct methodology.

After WWII the expansion of higher education meant that thousands of lower-class people entered tertiary education of the first time and began to notice the absence of their own ancestors in the history books. The hegemonic controls of the literary elite were also being challenged by the insistent demands of the new mass communications markets. Historians such as G.D.H. Cole and H.L. Beales, radicals from the Thirties, founded *The Society for the Study of Labour History* and for the first time the history of common people began to be studied in earnest and without condescension, by historians such as Edward and Dorothy Thompson.

By the mid-Sixties a new lower-class intelligentsia had started to ask radical questions about the lack of primary sources from which a more democratic history could be constructed. Quoting Dorothy Thompson again;

> The wealthy and educated insiders had left many records. Not only in the mass of material concerned with government and high politics, but in the literature, in the records of legal cases, property transactions, in personal journals and correspondence, and in every kind of document from wills to laundry lists. The poor had no muniment rooms and seldom entered any records on their own terms. They appear as servants, criminals, recipients of charity or as turbulent or obedient subjects.
>
> Dorothy Thompson, 1993 p16

It was in the heady atmosphere of the Sixties cultural revolts that Oral History arose to fill this void. It was Paul Thompson from one of the new universities that made the first large scale oral history programme in Britain in which 459 Edwardians born between 1872 and 1906 were interviewed about their family and work. Published in 1975 as *The Edwardians*.

This work was aided by a technological advance… the portable cassette tape recorder.

The first oral history tape recording had been made in the 1930s as part of the US New Deal Federal Writers Project but cumbersome early equipment limited its use. The advent of cheap hi-fidelity mobile sound recording allowed the oral to be archived as evidence, so the most compelling argument against the use of oral sources in the construction of history began to evaporate.

Oral History, was like a radical movement at first. It was a power surge from the bottom of society to make knowledge of ourselves visible. Our consciousness of who we are as humans is allowed to encompass a wider, more inclusive view into the past.

Since then, oral testimony has informed many history programmes on television and has had a huge influence on documentaries. A good example is Stephen Peet's 'Yesterdays Witness', the world's first oral history TV series, which he produced and directed from 1969 to 1980. "We made over 80 programmes for this series." Stephen Peet (CV/self information flyer, 1999). There are now several institution based archives in London: The Imperial War Museum, The National Sound Archive at the British Library, the BBC Sound Archive and The Museum of London are amongst the largest.

Thinking critically about this methodology

Many witnesses may suppress traumatic memories. The full emotional force of a person's experience is not usually available outside of the special conditions of regular therapeutic counselling. This is a limitation of my interviews. In spite of this, some very personal and emotionally charged information is revealed. Again, it should be emphasised that the reductive nature of transcription does tend to mute the emotional charge of oral statements.

Apart from the suppression of trauma, another problem with oral testimony is the vagaries of distant memories. For instance, it is very common for people to telescope two similar events into one. Even the two world wars were commonly mixed up by people who had lived through both of them. This was true of the Exploding history when I was asking about the early continental tours. I was not able to get a coherent account of the second tour to Germany. The more dramatic, recent and repeated an experience, the more likely it is to be remembered clearly. Even relatively recent events are not available without the right triggers. Asking the right question can gain access to a flood of vivid memories which in another context might not be accessible. But even written documents are dependent on the vagaries of memory and as Alessandro Portelli points out; "What is written is first experienced or seen, and is subject to distortions even before it is set down on paper." (History Workshop Journal 12 1981)

The process of oral history can be a medium of social and personal change in itself. Even something as simple as asking someone to tell you their life story can allow them the space to re-appraise their lives, sometimes in profound ways. Being part of the rituals of a more formal history making process can validate the worth of a person's life - perhaps at a time when little else does. Oral history in old peoples' homes has been noticed to have a profoundly therapeutic effect. This has led to a cross-over in practice with clinical psychology which is now an area of practice often known as Reminiscence work. As the population of elderly people grows the value of these processes may become increasingly important.

But the recording process can also lead to unexpected closure. Recording an account of an experience can give it a sense of completion. This is even more likely if the record is published. I feared that a published validation of the efforts of the Exploding Cinema Collective might make it seem less urgent to keep asserting the live event. Twenty years later this worry of mine is no longer valid, if it ever was.

As I have said, the limitation of research into the past using Oral History is the life-span of the population under study. Now that tape archives, such as the excellent resources offered by the Imperial War Museum, are established, it will be increasingly possible to listen to people who died before we were born. It must be admitted that cassette tapes are a tedious form of primary source, being impossible to flick through in the way you can a book. This constitutes a real limitation to their use compared with records on paper. The advanced search facilities of digital recordings have gone some way to solving this problem and promise to make oral recordings an important component of future knowledges.

Oral History offers the possibility of a more diverse or consensual history whose emphasis is not so much the hard - cold - dry - facts but more the warm, moist, emotional aspects of human experience. The existence of diverse, non-linear digital archives, based on a democratic process of recording oral testimony is something that would make the historicising of social relations on a wide scale more feasible. My aim with the current interviews is less ambitious. It is simply to see what influences in peoples lives led them to join Exploding Cinema and once there, how these earlier experiences might have contributed to shaping the cultural activity.

The interviews with the Exploding Cinema collective were recorded on DVCAM video in people's homes from August to December 1999. Interviews were made with Thomas Zagrosek, Colette Rouhier, Paul Tarrago, Jenet Thomas and Duncan Reekie in their own homes. Caroline Kennedy was interviewed during an event at the Anarchist Bookfair in October. The forty minute interviews were divided into two halves. For the first twenty minutes I asked people to tell their life story with some emphasis on their first experiences of film and art. There was then the possibility of a short break followed by a twenty minute interview which asked for their most memorable experiences of Exploding Shows and whatever else they wanted to say about their time with Exploding Cinema.

I had made an earlier Hi8 video recording of Duncan Reekie talking about the early history of the Exploding Cinema and his own life in 1996. So I started the new interview by asking him further information about one aspect of his family history which had a direct link with performance. The rest of the interview was a discussion of theoretical issues with regard to the historicisation of Exploding Cinema.

The audio was then transferred to standard audio cassette tape and professionally transcribed. The transcriptions were checked against the tapes. VHS viewing copies and electronic files of the transcription were sent to each of the interviewees.

Print-outs of the transcriptions were then used to construct an edited script that foregrounds what key aspects of the life histories of these collective members. I edited the transcripts under three headings: Where they are from; What their early influences were; How they came to join Exploding Cinema. I wanted to show how people's backgrounds have an influence on present cultural formations. Or to put in general terms, how present formations arise in part from the subjective experiences of actors and those of their ancestors.

It would no doubt be better to view this material on video than read the edited transcript. The sound and image on video inevitably gives a richer and more vivid representation compared to the transcripts and allows us to grasp the performative quality of oral communication.

The Interviews

We need to be able to see what kind of people brought Exploding Cinema into being and committed seven or eight unpaid years of their lives to maintaining it. As we shall see the historical precedents ascribed to the Exploding Cinema can be evidenced as part of the formative experiences of key members of the collective. These stories vividly illustrate historical influences that are otherwise academic. Whether in Jenet's description of a family slide show or Colette's accounting of going to drive-in cinemas in Cape Town.

This set of interviews records the Exploding Cinema collective at one point in its history after I had joined it. It does put an emphasis on the core members at a particular time and of course this is only a partial representation. This problem of reduction is integral to all historicisation but is particularly problematic with the large open collectives or networks in which I am interested. It can only be justified by the argument that a partial view is better than none and that this is just the beginning of a process which others can add to.

In spite of their higher education and being to some degree a part of the 'expert' film world, I hope the interviews show how much of the core members formative experience was of popular and oral cultural forms.

An examination of the content of the interviews. brought an unexpected viewpoint to the surface. Firstly, it was notable that the group was in fact multicultural having a wider range of ethnic backgrounds than I had been aware of. Secondly, in relation to the oral nature of the Exploding discourse, it was interesting to note each person's educational and class backgrounds. Thirdly, their cultural influences often relate to aspects of the Exploding Cinema format and echo the provenances discussed earlier in this thesis to a remarkable degree.

Ethnic Backgrounds

The ethnic backgrounds of the collective included an Australian, an East German first generation immigrant, a South African Turk, someone with a Jewish background, a second generation Spaniard, and myself as a second generation Pole. In fact Jenet Thomas was the only person with two English Parents in the group interviewed. Such a list does not really do justice to the complexity of these influences. Extracts from the interviews give this picture more fully:

Well my parents are Germans but my grandparents are from the border between Austria and Yugoslavia - Slovenia, which is now Ljubljana. (TZ)

I was born in Perth, Western Australia … I came over here when I was about fifteen for a holiday and never went back. (CK)

My mother was raised in South Africa in Durban… Then met my father… they met in Turkey, and they never went back to South Africa really until I was born.

When my mum fell pregnant with me, my grandparents had to come over and see her through the pregnancy. They tried to get my father to marry my mother and my father said no, 'I never intended to marry her, I need to marry a Turkish woman'. So my mum said, 'Fuck you!' And the whole family went, 'Fuck you!' And she stormed back to South Africa with me, and so I was raised (in) Cape Town. (CR)

It gave me a slightly arrogant feeling of feeling different from my contemporaries in that my dad was Spanish… My parents split up when I was about eleven and so family life was a bit disrupted in some ways. My dad was having to work a lot to support us, and over time he developed a drink problem. So he stopped reading so much and spent more or less most of his free time asleep. It was a pretty uninspiring home life in my adolescence. (PT)

From my experience with the collective 'Bigos, artists of Polish origin' it is clear how the immigrant experience of displacement makes cultural adaptation an important issue. Although it is difficult to track the precise influence this background of migration onto Exploding Cinema without much further research, it is possible to surmise some general dynamics. The immigrant has to face a huge cultural displacement. A negotiation happens between a new host culture and the original ethnic identity as the immigrant culture assimilates to a greater or lesser degree. Often the host country tries to enforce its mores and to subdue the foreign culture in a process of cultural subjugation. The maintenance of a cultural integrity by the immigrants and their children often requires considerable self-invention and creativity. People who are undergoing such changes would seem to be natural candidates for the more experimental and marginal areas of cultural production.

The shared experience of displacement and cultural otherness may also help in terms of group cohesion. It is certainly not a conscious issue in the day to day running of the group and doesn't seem to feature in the logbook notes. It is very much a background feature, which has only come to prominence through these interviews.

Educational and Class Backgrounds

Everyone in the collective of this time had been through higher education and several taught part-time in further or higher education. The class backgrounds were generally in the area of lower middle class. This category can include people whose working class parents had worked their way up the 'ladder' to middle class jobs (e.g. Jenet and Paul).

My mother's father was a painter and decorator and in the war… I don't know if my grandmother had a job, but anyway, they were respectable working class. I know he had to go up ladders a lot, my grandad… My dad's father was a clerk for Imperial Tobacco and… I think his father was a cobbler and he kind of raised himself up by going to evening classes and became a clerk. He worked with Imperial Tobacco and got free tobacco every week until the day he died… My dad's family were a little more posh than my mother's family. They had middle class pretensions whereas my mum's family were ordinary - felt themselves to be ordinary folk. (JT)

My mother told me a couple of days ago, when I asked her about her father being a builder and bricklayer, that he didn't run his own company. His wife, my grandmother, was a housewife. I think she had my mum when she was quite young. She got married when she was about nineteen. On my father's side, my

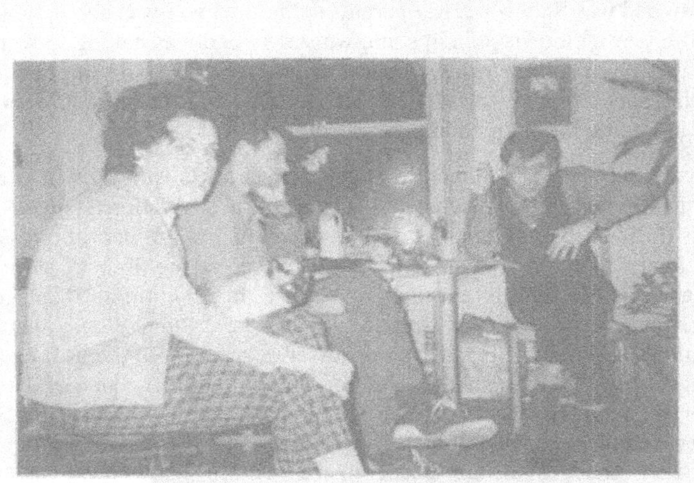

Colette, Thomas and Duncan

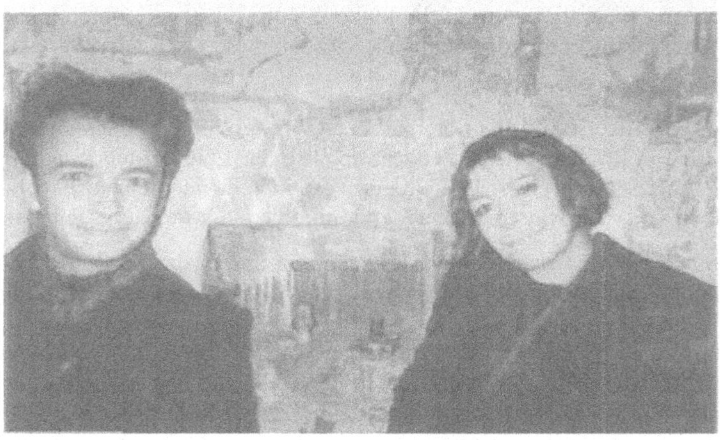

Paul and Jenet

grandad started off as an office boy in the Spanish equivalent of ICI. He worked in that company his whole life and ended up being a director by the end of it. (PT)

Lower middle class can also encompass people who seemed to have a conventional middle class background but whose parents had been relatively poor, (Duncan and Colette), or whose parents were in mixed class marriages, (Duncan and Paul).

> The story is that on my father's side my father was brought up by his grandmother while his mother worked and she was a single mother… She was secretary for the theatre critic of the Daily Herald, the old Labour paper, and through being secretary she'd meet loads of actors… Yeah, six kids in the family and we just kind of ran wild really because there wasn't much you could do with us. And I just used to watch TV all the time. (DR)

The pressures of being raised by a single parent, (Paul and Colette) complicate this picture.

> My mother was a Secretary. And South Africa was really hard, because in South Africa, when you are a single parent, with a child, then you are obviously a whore… So what my mother had to do was put me in boarding school. (CR)

Thomas Zagrosek is the only person with a straightforwardly working class background.

> I just heard yesterday, because my uncle is visiting at the moment, that my grandfather from my father's side was a social democrat who was shovelling coal into a piece of machinery for about 30 years. Apparently he was incredibly well-read, so if you for example visited a place like London then you could ask him where to go, what to do and where to turn left and where to turn right and he could tell you, even (though) he never left his little home town. (Laughing). I was a hairdresser, I was learning the trade as a hairdresser - My choice was of leading a normal life, getting a hairdresser's job, getting my own shop eventually… or going abroad to study art. (TZ)

Caroline's class background is ambiguous (lower middle Australian suburbanite) and shows the difficulty of translating class labels across national boundaries.

By educational achievement we might say the cultural class background tends to be lower middle class but by their economic status the group were all relatively poor with low incomes.

The relevance of this is in relation to the oral nature of Exploding Cinema discourse, and to demonstrate that the collective members, at this point, are not derived from an elite class. I am defining this elite class as those people who are well-read and literary, that sends its children to private schools and then on to the top universities. Working and lower middle class cultures tends to be more or less oral cultures or at least to have an oral provenance. Nonetheless, a certain proportion of these 'lower' classes do go to higher education and absorb, or at least become conversant with the literary codes of the dominant classes.

Although the collective cannot be seen as typical working class with their sometimes middle class parents and tertiary education - they do have a heritage which is working class a generation back. Or their circumstances have meant that they have not grown up enjoying the privileges we associate with a middle class upbringing.

If we assume that cultural influences fade gradually over several generations we can see that the personnel in the collective are in general weaned by 'the masses' rather than the elite. And as such they share and are embedded in that mass culture.

Cultural Influences

The film provenance of Exploding Cinema has been discussed earlier from what might be called a cultural history perspective. With oral history we can gain insight into another form of historical provenance which is embedded in the family histories of the participants. This shows how cultural forms reproduce themselves and are coloured by a collective amalgam of personal experiences as well as being formed from more diffuse cultural forces. The early influences of the Collective were reported as being via books, television, home-movies or slide shows, Saturday morning film clubs and drive-in cinemas.

But one influence stood out as going much further back. This is Duncan Reekie's remarkable family connection with a famous star of the musichall, Little Tich.

> A relative was Little Tich, the Great Little Tich… Little Tich was a very famous comedian and musichall performer whose act consisted of wearing shoes that had very, very long built-up sections at the front. This would allow him to lean forwards slightly and then more, and more, and more, until he was leaning forwards at a completely untenable angle! (*Laughing*) Then he'd be able to stand back up again. And then, the other thing he did was, he would dance on these big shoes and sort of do some very strange dances. And then, he would jump up and stand on them, like almost stilts or something! (DR)

The influence of books was varied and ranged from second-hand non-fiction to hip existential classics of the Sixties (read in the Seventies).

> I lived in the suburbs like all Australians do, and it was very boring. I was reading English comics all the time. I just wanted to be in England all the time… I loved books but my family didn't do any reading at all. I don't know what they did - they are all very shady. I used to like archaeology and science and stuff like that. From an early age I used to go to the library and read loads and loads of non-fiction… The house was full of junk. It is a very nice sort of Sixties house, but it is full of old Victorian rubbish. My dad collected books everywhere, (and old sewing machines and everything), it was just piled high. It was like the Adams Family house. (CK)

> I suppose books were my main influence when I was a kid, rather than film. I read an awful lot of existentialist literature when I was about 16 - 19 that I think had quite an affect of me, I read the Sartre trilogy and lots of Samuel Beckett and Kafka… I read a lot of trash as well, a lot of Tolkein novels. The Tolkein craze was definitely part of that. (JT)

The core collective members were born into the heyday of Television. They were part of the first television generation. By the mid-Sixties to early Seventies television had saturated the population and the content had got beyond the naivety of the Fifties.

> I was always a real TV addict, and films as well really. My parents are quite old,

so I grew up with watching old films with them, and really being immersed in old film culture, and knowing all the names of the actors and actresses from the Thirties onwards, and the directors. I used to like gangster films, and musicals, just anything old. Anything made before 1970 I really like, the same with books. (CK)

I loved Science Fiction things on TV. Things that I really remember are things like *Dr Who*, and *The Tomorrow People*, a slightly spooky children's science fiction series. I was a complete addict for that, both me and my brother. *Lost in Space*, all those things. (JT)

I remember seeing colour television for the first time, being taken to see it by my father and being quite amazed. But we had a black and white one. Things like *Department S* would be a favourite programme of mine - it was very strange. It was like a camp Seventies version of *The X Files*, which was much stranger than The X Files. There was a character in it called Jason King played by Peter Wyngarde, and he then got his own series. There was another very strange programme I used to like called *Ace of Wands* which was about a kind of hippie warlock detective. That was in the Seventies as well, they should revive that. There were a few, very strange attempts to have a counter cultural pulp sort of genre, hippie detectives and things, which were quite interesting. But I used to watch everything. I was very omnivorous... I never thought I was going to be a filmmaker particularly, but I just used to watch TV all the time. (DR)

I have discussed the importance of home movies to underground film in general and as a framework from which to understand the oral cultural frame that surrounds Exploding Cinema. The biographical experiences suggest that 35mm slide shows may have been more ubiquitous than Super 8 film in the Sixties. Another important home media mentioned by Jenet Thomas in her interview is her dad's experiments with a reel to reel audio 'tape recorder'. The experiences of both, reveal important similarities with the Exploding Cinema format. From the ever present whirring of the projector to the audience interjections and close connection with the subject matter on screen. Of course 35mm slides became the main materials of the distinctive Exploding Cinema décor.

It would be like a family get together with about fifteen or eighteen people. A lot of the events would be embarrassing moments with the children, and everyone would scream with laughter. My brother being forced to hold a chicken by my dad and crying was always a favourite. But I think it is the darkened room, whirly projectors, sort of thing - and the breaking, snapping, smoke coming out, that sort of thing, which is very much like the Exploding Cinema really, in lots of ways. (CK)

Dad took loads and loads of slides, mostly holiday pictures, from quite an early age... We had very formal, very exciting slide shows, where all the lights would go down. We would have sandwiches and crisps and we would watch ourselves in Lake Windermere or whatever. It was nice and kind of tedious at the same time - it seemed to be the thing you did in those days, and I know a lot of my friends that did that as well. If you didn't have cine-cameras, that is what you did. You made it a bit like a cinema, you put the lights down and you projected the slides. So, yes, I have got a very fond attitude to slides, you know, slide projection and that idea of reliving memories through slides. From about eight, me and my brother had little cameras, and they were Instamatic cameras and we documented everything -

mostly holidays, but also pets. (JT)

Home movies and slides also provided the first experience of film making, both taking pictures whether movie or slide and of course all the different modes of being 'caught' on camera.

My dad used to shoot movies from the 1940s, on Standard 8 and then on Super 8. He was always getting us to come outside and take pictures of us, films of us. Which was a lot of us walking towards the camera all the time. So I grew up with someone who was always taking photos. You could hear him say, 'Walk towards the camera'. And we would say, 'Oh God! Do we have to?' I really hated it… There is a record of all six children doing that, all of us walking towards the camera… But they are just such beautiful (images)! (CK)

Next there were the experiences of watching proper mainstream movies but that were outside of the norm of darkened space and passive seated audience. First there was the common experience of the young person's Saturday morning 'flicks'.

In South Africa we used to go to the Saturday Movie Club every Saturday. We'd see *Flash Gordon* shorts before a feature film, and it was thrilling because our parents would drop us off, and we would go into the cinema. We were about seven or eight, and you would be in… like a sea of kids. And they would all be like wriggling, and wriggling, and they all had sweeties and packets. Then as soon as the lights went down absolute all hell would break loose. Everybody would be screaming at the top of their voices and lollies and things would be flying around. It was thrilling! Then we all settled down and watched Flash Gordon and whatever the Saturday movie was. (CR)

Another form of movie presentation that challenges the dominant cinemas normative mode is the drive-in. The spectacle and informality of drive-ins could have been an influence on Exploding Cinema. I have already noted how the drive-in heralded the new B Movie genres of Horror and Rock in the Fifties.

Drive-ins were a big deal for us every Friday evening. It was like a religious kind of thing. Regularity on Friday evening - get home from school - tidy up the flat. Mum gets home and we all get together and go down to Chicken Lickin' and get our tubs of barbecue chicken and chips, Coca-Cola and then shoot down to the Silver Mine Drive-in. Goodwood was another good drive-in, and there was quite a few…

My favourite one is Silver Mine. You go up this huge mountain range, and then as you get to the top you start curving down like that (gesturing), and then there would be this huge silver screen and all these cars. You could see them, like the lamps going up and down… as they spun into their places. We would drive down into that. Then you would drive around trying to find your mound, and trying to get close to the screen. You would park your car and get this huge clunking cast metal speaker - clunk it on the side of the window and set-up camp. We would go off to play on the swings for a while and then we would have dinner. Then we would go back and play on the swings some more and all the kids would be down at the swings shouting and fighting and carrying on. All the ads would be these huge fucking things going on above your head, and you were like on the swing going whey-hey! It was pretty exciting. I mean you could turn around and see all these cars parked there... and the wonderful smell... The massive canopy (of stars) and also the heat, you know, and the smell of the fast food and popcorn. It was everything that you loved. Hot nights with crickets making their noise in the background. That was a really big experience for me you know, the Drive-In. (CR)

Put these experiences together and you can practically reconstruct an entire Exploding Cinema show from them. The mixture of influences implies the cultural background of the collective was closer to a working or lower middle class cultural experience. The culture of the lower classes cannot be reduced to its stereotypes of popular culture, especially after the opening up of tertiary education and its associated intellectual aspirations to the masses from the Sixties.

In my adolescence I started to watch seasons of Jean Luc Goddard and Bunuel films and my dad was kind of interested in Bunuel because of the Spanish connections. Jean Luc Goddard, yeah, I was so bowled over, because he combines literary interests with all these elements of anthropology and sociology, but with trash genre narratives and just great visual motifs and, so many different influences. He wasn't just like a filmmaker he was like a film maker/ writer/ poster maker, and polemicist. I was just so excited even though I was just watching those things on TV.

Then I started going to art cinemas. The Everyman mostly, also The Scala and The Ritzy and... When I eventually moved to London I would probably be going about twice a week and often one of those visits would be to see a double or a triple bill, so I'd probably go and see about five or six films a week. (PT)

From these early stirrings of interest in film there were still barriers to be crossed before the idea that films could actually be made, rather than simply consumed, was taken in. Not least of these barriers was internalised sexism.

I was always interested in film making, but I was a technophobe... I was quite nervous about filmmaking. I think its definitely a gender thing. My father and brother were the scientists and me and my mother, we didn't change a light bulb, you know what I mean... They did everything. There was a big gender differentiation of technology and I saw film technology and I thought... I was nervous of it. One of the ways that Exploding Cinema was a big inspiration to me was that I saw the way people were fiddling with Super Eight. (JT)

Of course men are also infected with lack of confidence and this may be especially true of lower class men. Experimental film could be a way for the social outsider to see what was possible. Here is Paul Tarrago's first encounter with Maya Deren.

As I left college (doing Spanish) I started going to loads of evening classes. That's where I started seeing a lot of work that I'd only vaguely read about - both experimental and art cinema. Like Maya Deren's film *Meshes of the Afternoon.* The first time I saw that I just thought, 'Wow!' I could see how you could do it, it wasn't unbearably complex, and it wasn't exclusive. Even though it was made about forty-five years before I'd seen it, I could see a way in. I could imagine making it, which was really exciting. I'd read about how she'd made it as well, so that made it even more possible. At the same time I was going to these classes and learning how to operate film equipment and thinking 'Yeah I can do this', so that's how I started making films. But I was kind of quite overwhelmed by the usual thing of self-doubt so I didn't really progress in the way I would have believed that I should have progressed as a film maker. -

My *The Requiem for an Ice Baby* was the first time I actually showed a film I was happy with to an audience - that people liked, and... I was asked back to show it again at the festival thing. (PT)

Another sort of barrier to making art was disillusionment with the art world or the film industry as a context for work.

At college I got a little disillusioned with the art world, with the workings of the art world... The best thing that can happen to you is to become a famous artist. And then you have to deal with all the 'having to sell yourself'. (TZ)

Even, once radical organisations become institutionalised and even unworkable in their later years as Duncan Reekie found:

I learned about the way the film industry worked and the way that the funding organisations worked. And I started to meet a lot of people who were involved in the funding organisations or who were involved in so-called political film making, or oppositional film making, or whatever you want to call it, and independent film making. And I began to become very disenchanted with the whole thing and I began to realise that, if I was going to make political films, then I had to rethink the project, the project had to be totally rethought...

I'd been going round slagging off the (London) Film Co-op for quite a long time on very little evidence and people started to say to me, 'Well, how can you slag off the Filmmakers' Co-op when you don't know anything about it?' So I went and worked voluntarily at the Film Co-op for three or four months and it was just really a miserable experience. I became involved in the Co-op politics and the collective politics, the democratic politics that was going on. And basically it was infighting and horrible personality clashes. And it basically confirmed all my worst prejudices, (which was very gratifying). (DR)

A similar experience of disillusionment can be got from the commercial world as Colette Rouhier found:

I was an Art Director in advertising. I came to London to be an Art Director here. I had done an award winning TV commercial in South Africa, and I had high hopes for myself. Got here, hated it - really hated the scene... It seemed to be really mercenary, in that anything will go... I then got onto the film degree in the Polytechnic in Central London. I started off brilliantly, had a great time in the first year. The second year was not bad. But the third year was a nightmare - a fucking nightmare, everybody was into this ridiculous idea of being the writer or director and so on. You are different to us, because we are 'techies'. And there becomes this rift, this real rift, almost like they had joined a union there and then. And the union wasn't about helping to make films, it was divisive. Where they would be saying 'Where do you want the camera?', 'You didn't give me a shooting script?'. And rather than trying to help the process, it was getting all dysfunctional. And I thought to myself, my God, if this is what the film industry is like, this fucking hierarchy thing, and everybody fucking being brats within the hierarchy, then I really don't want to be there. (CR)

The lived experience of a wide range of dissatisfactions like this makes for a powerful and radical collective drive. The problems that these people had faced were solved by their engagement with Exploding Cinema either by giving them direct access to the most expressive and creative processes of filmmaking or by giving them a platform and collective support from which to be critical of the system that had oppressed them. Of course in the long term the marginalisation of Exploding Cinemas activity gives the long term collective members other challenges in terms of prolonging such activity, whilst their generational peers might be rising through a more conventional career path.

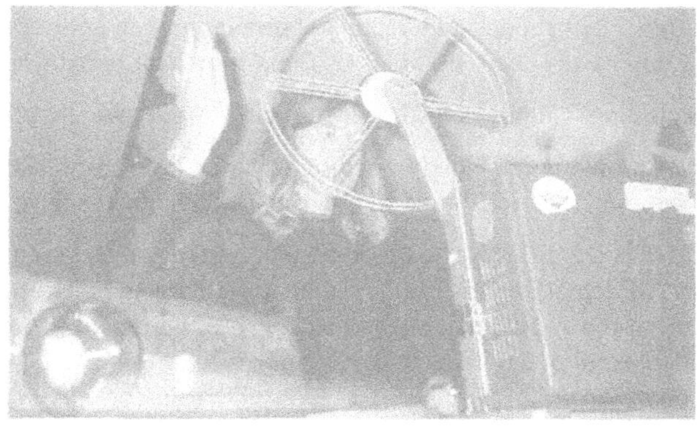

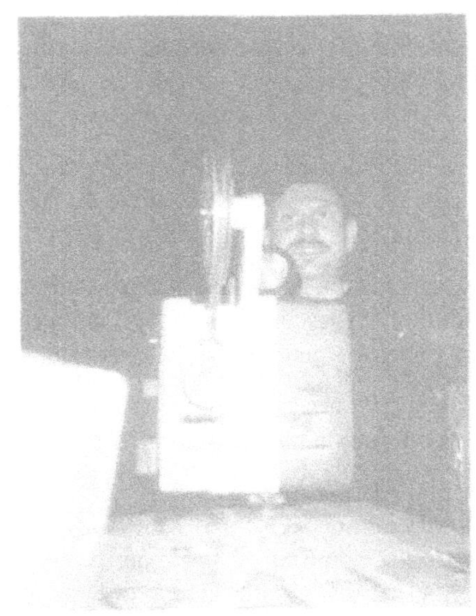

Caroline above
Duncan below

Chapter 9

Concluding with 12 takeaways for discussion

1. That it is possible to make a representation of an artists collective with minimal resources that fulfils the criteria of reputable knowledge.

2. Open artists collectives have values that are at odds with the art world and establishment culture, and even with capitalism itself.

3. That there are problems faced by artists collectives that are mainly interpersonal and it may be possible to find ways to overcome them, or at least survive them better.

4. The Exploding Cinema had, without any state funding, an enormous influence on culture. Just going by the sheer numbers of films shown and artists supported.

5. Perhaps Exploding Cinema isn't the reproducible model we thought i might be.

6. That archives probably are slowly opening up to include more lower class stuff and this research programme contributed to pointing out what was missing in archives.

7. The original thesis put forward a theoretical argument - that for culture to be a constituent part of democracy then it has to be unfettered and open in the way that these independent self-motivated collectives are. Cultural agencies and institutions that are permeable and open themselves, are more likely to be able to nurture the swarming of common cultural values needed to underpin consensii on a continental or global scale.

8. You can make up your mind if you are considering doing similar work on collectives what methodologies might be of use. I've probably bored the general readers silly with my in-depth consideration of research methods.

9. This is a partial object of knowledge… just a beginning. Much more can be done and I hope it will be. eg a whole PhD could be done on the programmes, or the films. And the Exploding Cinema collective from 2001 to 2021.

10. I consider these artists unselfish pioneers. I hope that this book goes some way to recognise and thank all those who contributed their labour to this wonderful counter-culture project. Thirty years of generosity and experiment.

11. My vision is that open collectives might be a form for a future anti-elitist and inclusive working class culture that is fairly funded and resourced, and free of state influence.

12. My main point of criticism is one shared with many forms of working class culture and is intrinsic to their dominated status and alienation from intellectual institutions - the lack of critical apparatus. The problems with setting up such formations are complex but not insurmountable.

The real history of cinema is invisible history. History of friends getting together, doing the thing they love. For us, the cinema is beginning with every new buzz of the projector, every new buzz of our camera. With every new buzz of our cameras, our hearts jump forward my friends.

Jonas Mekas (February 11 1996 American Center Paris)

Progress means: humanity emerges from its spellbound state no longer under the spell of progress as well, itself nature, by becoming aware of its own indigenousness to nature and by halting the master over nature through which nature continues its mastery.

Theodor Adorno, *Progress, The Philosophical Forum* 15.1–2 (Fall–Winter 1983–1984)

'Conscious Evolution Now!'

THE GOAL OF FUNDING FOR THE MEDIA ARTS IS THE MANAGEMENT OF SOCIAL DISSENT

Funding insidiously limits independent thinking. It draws people into a state agenda of non confrontation. It quickly neutralises critical or vulgar thought especially if it has a political edge.

If we all got paid, we'd need a least £1500 per show. The door price would be £15 plus. The group would become a closed shop, as we came to rely on the income. Funding breeds dependency.

In the Sixties and Seventies the underground was visibly different from straight society, now capitalism is hip and the value of autonomy is more difficult to see.

"Those who were chosen in ever fewer numbers for ever larger projects, have become models of self-censorship, self-delusion and commodified self-representation for the aspiring to emulate."
Keith Sanbury, September, 1997

Let the patrons get stuffed! Their funds are stolen from the working class (who produce all wealth and get shit) Refuse the humiliation of begging to be granted our own money.

Deny the state its cultural facade - its pretence of being civilised. Support autonomous cultures.

WHY OPEN COLLECTIVE?

To put on a show like this you need about 8 people minimum. First to get the publicity widely spread... then on the night we have: an MC, projectionist, sound techie, sound person, door persons, decor (slides and loops), programmer, driver and floor manager. There is also work to keep accounts and maintain equipment and website which is often a bit thankless. People come and go but at least one of the current crew has been on the job since early 1992. Others have joined more recently. Some left to form their own group.

In 1998 it was equal genders now we need more women to join. Each show takes around 200 hours of unpaid work using something like 7 slide projectors, 4 - 6 loop film projectors the main video projector and the PA. All this stuff has been bought and is maintained from the price you paid to get in. No Funding.

There are loads we don't have time to do - like write about the movies shown and print a journal, or make an web archive of the over 700 filmmakers that have shown with Exploding since 1992. Being open to new members keeps the old collective on their toes. Our next meeting is on Sunday 13th August...

Join the collective - we need your love.

Appendix 1

Other open collectives - archival activity

After I had defended this thesis at the RCA in 2002 I spent some of the subsequent years working on archiving the other collectives that I had been a part of. This section is to note what was achieved in each case to date.

Portsmouth Artsworkshop (1969-71)

Apparently there were something like 150 arts labs or art workshops in UK inspired to some degree or other by The Arts lab in Drury lane, London. Little has been done to archive Portsmouth Artsworkshop and I had only a very small archive that has survived. But very recently one of my examiners has brought out a book on the main London Art Labs. *London's Arts Labs and the 60s Avant-Garde* by David Curtis, 2020

The Scratch Orchestra (1971-73)

Members of the *Scratch Orchestra* have been good at maintaining contact and celebrating anniversaries which have fed into various archives. Most recently a week long celebration of *The Scratch Orchestra at 50* was held at Morely College. Previously there was a 25 years celebration at the ICA and for the 40th a whole weekend of Scratch programmes and archive recordings on Resonance Radio 104.4 fm and online (36 hours in all. Broadcast on 2 + 3/5/2009).

http://www.spiralcage.com/blog/?p=589

http://www.spiralcage.com/blog/?p=613

http://www.spiralcage.com/blog/?p=637

For my own part I organised a group of original Scratchers and new generation improvisors to workshop and then perform two major performances exploring the **Improvisation Rites** from *Nature Study Notes* in 2014 and 2015. The archive of this process was published in a collectively compiled book: *Improvisation Rites: from John Cage's Song books to The Scratch Orchestra Nature Study notes: collective practices 2011 to 2017*. A final group discussion and evaluation were hosted by MayDay Rooms who had previously taken a small archive of my *Scratch Orchestra* ephemera. Our presence on the Mayday Rooms website led to an invitation to lead a performance in Documenta 14 in Athens 2017. Thanks to Anthony Davies.

Search *Scratch Orchestra* on Mixcloud. e.g.

https://www.mixcloud.com/Resonance/scratch-orchestra-50th-anniversary-broadcast-4-january-2020/

New Dance Magazine Collective (1977-79)

This small collective was closely connected to **X6 Dance Space** in Butler Wharf adjacent to Tower Bridge. X6 and New Dance Magazine was recently the subject of investigation and show at Cell Space curated by Rachael Davies. A section of my first video shot on a Portapac was part of that exhibition.

https://www.cellprojects.org/exhibitions/liberation-notes-etc

The International Mail Art Network (1981-1986)

A vast global network that exchanged artworks and organised themed shows has archives in many places. My own effort to archive my small collection did not seem to be a priority. I was one of many thousands of participants, and for a limited period. I did archive mail art in the

National Art Library at the V&A (in the time Simon Ford was a librarian) and in the Tate Library.

The digitised catalogue of one of the projects I initiated is linked to here:

https://monoskop.org/Mail_art

Brixton Artist's Collective (1983-87)

An important large open artist collective running a gallery in Brixton, London. Subsequently spurned by the Art world proper even though many of the people who showed there went on to achieve mainstream success. The main independent archive has been made by Andrew Hurman and is online here.

https://brixton50.co.uk/

I used the resources of my workplace at the Regent Campus of University of Westminster to host and record a day seminar on BAG in 2012 that has been passed on to the Tate Archive. Transcript here:

http://stefan-szczelkun.blogspot.com/2012/05/activating-brixton-art-gallery-1983-86.html

Another archival effort was an event at 198 Gallery which obtained a Heritage Lottery grant to accumulate and workshop material that was subsequently deposited with Tate Archive. My contribution to this was an oral history video (the edit of which is unfortunately no longer in the public realm)

http://brixtoncallingproject.blogspot.com/

Bigos, Artists of Polish Origin (1986-92)

This was an artists exhibiting project I organised with help from Kasia Januszko and others. Archival material is now archived by Tate Archive. Enter the word 'Bigos' into their search box and six pages of entries appear.

https://www.tate.org.uk/art/archive

See also this video: https://youtu.be/LQ41eZUV-Mc

Working Press: books by and about working class artists (1987-97)

This was a project, started with Graham Harwood, which resulted in the publication of 18 books over a ten year period. The University of the Creative Arts, Farnham bought a set of the Working Press publications and also a wide range of contextual pamphlets and other alternative print ephemera of the period. They also took folders of letters and other ephemera generated when I was organising the project. They catalogued all this and then raised money to 'activate' the archive and get some of the students to engage with it. This process ended with a beautifully designed catalogue, which is available as a free ebook.

http://www.thebookroom.net/rise-with-your-class-not-from-it/

Appendix 2

Theory 1 - Cargo Cults to communicative action

Many years before joining Exploding I had been inspired by accounts of the Cargo Cults of Polynesia. I first read about Cargo Cults in Julia Blackburn's book, *The White Men: The first response of aboriginal peoples to the white man*, (1979). This led me to the seminal book by Peter Worsley, *The Trumpet Shall Sound: A study of 'Cargo' cults in Melanesia* (1957) .

> As social tensions build up... action of any kind is a relief. At one level this relief is gained through the performance of large-scale social tasks such as gardening or building Cargo houses... Catharsis is gained from the actions of motor behaviour which spread throughout the community as if by contagion.
>
> Worsley 1957 p249)

These cultures had made an imaginative response to the arrival of the White Man, imitating Western forms, such as cricket or airports, to attract Western wealth or 'cargo'. As we know, the spread of white culture across the world has been highly dominative and destructive of indigenous cultures. It seemed that the people who adopted 'Cargo' strategies had enough flexibility in their 'traditional' cultures to invent rituals of adaptation to these radical changes and that these new rituals and artworks helped them to survive momentous changes. Other societies, which were more rigidly bound to tradition, were often wiped out. To a working class artist in England who was interested in interventionist public art and social change, the Cargo Cults offered an inspiration.

My main insight from this was that culture could act as a set of discourses which could both evaluate changing conditions, re-evaluate persistent problems, and at the same time provide rituals, or therapeutic processes, of adaptation. It was not just individual artworks that were important but the socio-cultural processes within which they occurred.

The other powerful influence in coming to my choice of interpretative framework was that democracy seemed to be the most important and hopeful world trend. Our mass media seems unable to predict or represent this trend which, time after time, seems to surprise us. In the 1970s we had no sense from our daily newspapers that Soviet sponsored state communism in Poland could end. Then, seemingly out of the blue Solidarnosc arose, ten million strong and overturned everyone's expectations, producing an amazingly peaceful transition from totalitarianism to democracy. The end of Apartheid in South Africa had a similar effect. Reading the media we were convinced apartheid would not change 'in our lifetime' and if it did there would be terrible bloodshed. Suddenly, apartheid was breathtakingly consigned to the dustbin of history - again without widespread bloodshed and in a relatively short space of time. How does such a widespread action become current, gain legitimacy and achieve such widespread co-ordination of action? To my mind it can only be through oral culture.

Prior to the American Revolution and the subsequent French Revolution, democracy, as we understand it today, existed nowhere. Now there are democratic states on every continent and region. This tendency towards democracy is one of the central narratives of modernity in spite of current reversals. The question is, did the processes I was involved with, often working with groups of other politically motivated artists, contribute to a wider democratising process? Did our activity 'from below' contribute creative perspectives to the future choices available to humanity?

I had recently studied Michel Foucault's ideas on power and discourse, and Pierre Bourdieu's theories of cultural capital and taste. I then read some lesser-known philosophers of the American tradition, like Richard Shusterman. Shusterman was one of the few philosophers offering a defence of popular culture on the grounds of aesthetics. This process led me to Jurgen Habermas' theories of social communication, which had had little attention from art or cultural theorists. A possible reason is that the form of his arguments, their literary style, do not provide the creative stimulation that artists found in such theorists as Deleuze and Guattari. However, Habermas' project seemed to be most relevant to my concerns. His theory also looked more thorough, comprehensive and coherent than anything comparable. Habermas had been thinking about how we form a rational consensus that provides a secure base for democracy and at the same time expand our conception of democracy, from the very limited power sharing that is achieved by a defining praxis focused on voting and representation, to something that is founded in the 'communicative actions' of everyone in society.

The Theory of Communicative Action was first published in Germany in two volumes in 1981. This theory is profoundly hopeful - it recognises the knowledge and communicative competencies that reside in ordinary discourses - the task of theory is to give these implicit knowledges and processes of communication a theoretical exegesis which would allow them to become centre-staged in our politics. He argues that the potential for transcendent rationality resides in the validity base of everyday speech, rather than just in literary discourses and from here I could see that his epistemic goals are profoundly democratic.

The problem was that Habermas did not take his theory beyond verbal discourse to the sensory arts in any detail. I made a critical summary of his theory, the main objections to it and possible remedies to apply his theory to art work but this writing is considered outside the scope of this book. It is however available on my Blogger blog.

How can processes of collective cultural production, whether Cargo rituals or Exploding Cinema, be shown to be central to the formation of the values that provide a dynamic evaluation of our human condition? Such a theory could legitimate collective cultural action as essential to a more inclusive concept of democracy?

Theory 2 - Cultural Expression and Democratic Consensus

I wanted to choose a particular emphasis on culture's function which was appropriate to frame Exploding Cinema's activity. The non-verbal arts are expressions of the human senses. These works can aim to make a direct relation between human desire, its sensory form of expression and the subsequent proliferation of cultural 'statements' (ie artworks). Verbal language is integrated into this model and I will comment on the social consequences of the development of printing and literary culture and its gradual separation from orality.

So, art expressions make qualitative judgements about aspects of our collective being. Broader cultural processes bring these judgements into a public sphere in which communities of understanding and agreement arise (or not!). These cultural agreements underpin the more formal processes of reaching consensii that are the stuff of democratic politics and legislation.

The idea that the central purpose of culture is the evaluation of the conditions of human existence has gained a widespread intellectual consensus:

> Culture may be thought of as a causal agent that affects the evolutionary process by uniquely human means. For it permits the self-conscious evaluation of human possibilities in the light of a system of values that reflect prevailing ideals about what human life ought to be. Culture is thus an indispensable device for increasing human control over the direction in which our species changes.
>
> Prof. Jaegwon Kim. *The Oxford Companion to Philosophy,*1995, p172

The idea may be found in Raymond Williams' *Culture and Society,* which was first published in 1958.

> The idea of culture is a general reaction to a general and major change in the conditions of our common life. Its basic element is its effort at total qualitative assessment... what it indicates is a process not a conclusion.
>
> Raymond Williams, 1958, p285

The profound scope of culture's function is indicated by the phrase 'total qualitative assessment'. Williams designates this as the 'basic element' of culture. Another idea that Williams articulated is the way the meaning of the word culture goes through a series of historical metamorphoses. From its C17th origin in horticulture, it comes to mean the training of the habits of mind, with a goal of perfection. Then it comes to also indicate a general intellectual state of society and or the 'general body of the arts'. Finally in the C20th it takes on an anthropological meaning of being the totality of a particular group's way of life. The modern concept of culture developed alongside the egalitarian and inclusive concept of democracy that was set alight in Europe by the French Revolution of 1789.

> The idea of culture would be simpler if it had been a response to industrialism alone, but it was also, quite evidently, a response to the new political and social developments, to democracy.
>
> Williams, 1958, p17

I wanted to use culture to mean a field of intellectual and imaginative work, *as well as* culture as a whole way of life. The more specialised experiments and free play that occur in the arts are subject to broader cultural discourses, before the new judgements they suggest are taken up, or ignored, by a wider community.

In their historically institutionalised, professionalised forms the formal state funded arts are clearly separated from most communities in Britain. They cannot, from this position, very easily draw from or offer their results to culture as 'a whole way of life'. For the purposes of arguing for the value of Exploding Cinema as a cultural generator I need to find a method of epistemically refiguring the arts, which allows a more intimate relation of culture to society to be envisioned.

Our species has evolved in an intimate relation with the surface of our planet primarily through our senses, so there is a certain benign eco-logic to the assembly of these senses. The relationship between our bodily senses and the global ecology is clearly benign in the sense that our ancestors survived a million years in these environments. Particular cultures have ascribed importance to different sense receptors for particular advantage, but it may be reasonable to assume that an evolutionary scale of wisdom still clings to the integrated use of the complete set. Creatively playing with all our senses we are most directly in touch with our ecological substrate. It is from this level of engagement that our judgement in relation to our material context must surely arise. Certain senses may be more efficient data carriers, but in terms of our species' evolution every sense must have its necessary part to play. A wise relation to our environment could well entail cultural processes that engage all our senses and all our abilities. Perhaps not all at the same time!

The normative categorisation of art forms does not make their relation to our sense receptors clear. The 'five senses' is a phrase that is commonly used to refer to our spectrum of senses. These five do not include the thermal sense, one of the most crucial to our well-being. The traditional five are composed of multiple sense organs. Each sense flux logically has a means of expression and an art form that arises from it. These art forms, and their combinations, give us the most direct way of connecting our intuitive intelligence with the flux within which we have evolved to live. Freedom of expression and play in each of these sensory art forms should be considered of crucial importance in terms of the most elemental job culture must perform - its effort at total qualitative assessment. I am emphasising the centrality of non-verbal arts to our concept of culture but of course each of the sense art form is modulated with language. Arts whose media is entirely verbal language are one step removed from our direct experience of being in the world. These more abstracted arts are particularly good at providing an overview of the experiences gained through our senses. Whatever non-verbal understandings are reached by our response to the work of artists, they must still be validated by a process that will engage in critical language in one form or another.

The call and response of the combined codes of our sensory apparatus at some point in our evolution gave rise to the meta-code of speech, that could capture all the important symbols from the perceptual cornucopia and reduce them to a unified shorthand system of sounds accompanied by facial expressions and gestural signs. This performative verbal 'language', along with the use of tools, transformed the relation of Homo Sapiens to each other and the rest of nature producing a more complex and reflexive consciousness. The cultures that arise from this form of communication are primarily what I mean by oral cultures.

Writing arose from an amalgam of visual signs and phonetic glyphs. Based on the earliest existing traces it has been suggested that writing allowed contracts to develop, accounts to be kept and bureaucracy to develop to allow the organisation of more complex societies.

Writing stayed as the domain of a minority of monks and aristocrats until the development of printing in Germany in 1450. The manufacture of books by machines gradually shifted the control of knowledge into the secular realm. It also began a shift of knowledge from oral circulation to literary encapsulation which was to have a decisive influence on culture. Before the printed book there had been a technological revolution which had occurred with regard to wind and waterpower. This involved a sophisticated and widespread use of mechanics on a large and dynamic scale. This knowledge was in the main circulating in the oral domain. Another example concerned midwifery. The skill of midwifery was an area of women's knowledge that circulated orally. The literary means by which male doctors ousted the traditional midwives and healers is well-known.

In such areas the book allowed a literary class to encapsulate and develop these knowledges, by increasing the intensity of discourse and quality of systematic thinking that could be brought to bear on any specific issue. But in this process the class that is most literate and who own the means of the production of books, and commodity production in general, also gradually gain control of this new knowledge. This knowledge is the basis of a process in which production is mechanised on an unprecedented scale, making the owners of these industrial manufacturing processes wealthy and so forming a new section of the owning classes.

Rationality and scientific and technological knowledge become associated with the literary sphere and the new class of capitalists. In contrast most oral cultures are represented as an inferior realm associated with the working classes and base sensuality.

Although it is true that the circulation of written studies produced certain new powers and enclosed areas of knowledge that had previously circulated orally, the oral realm is still an essential part of human communications. It seems that the literary discourses have had some trouble in admitting the vital capacities of the oral realm particularly with respect to the processing of culture. It is rapidly becoming apparent that the literary is in fact simply a temporary historical communications medium within the much larger realms of performative oral communications, which itself is embedded in the totality of our trans-sensory coding systems.

If the basic elemental purpose of culture is, as Williams said, to make an ongoing dynamic and total qualitative assessment of our situation then it is largely in the realm of oral culture that these assessments, in their most fluid and mercurial form, are brought to consensus.

Oral communication is not simply the spoken word. Oral communications is essentially performative and the most open of public spheres. It may be informed by written texts, but the culture is in its greatest state of flux when communication is least limited by mediation. A new idea then has the potential to spread through a population like a contagion. When the oral communication is less intense and widespread we might find Walter J. Ong's descriptions of the process as rhapsodic or like weaving or stitching as appropriate.

Culture is essentially a set of meaningful materials and processes held and used in common. A social process of communication by which a consensus, on the symbolic content and value of these materials, is arrived at, is logically necessary. We may assume that if conditions change, then some of these symbols will also change, as the qualitative assessment procedures of culture respond to the new conditions. If a culture does not change in response to changing conditions then it has become rigidified, and that society is in danger of being unable to be responsive to change and to successfully adapt. The survival of a society is then, assured by the collective process of intelligence that has so far supported the successful evolution of humankind.

As all the senses are synthesised in our body leading to action, so the arts must be synthesised by the social body to produce an intelligent cultural response to our environment. Discourses that are contained within narrow media disciplines are of limited use to such a broad response.

The sort of processes which can very quickly produce large scale common responses, happen within the oral realm. However much the process is informed by the newspapers, expert reports or networking on the internet. Humans are highly attuned to the responses of those around them. Our fundamental needs to be social require this on the most fundamental level of communications. We co-ordinate our responses to be able to act in concert and achieve social coherence.

The promotion of 'consensus' is much misunderstood and feared. To some people it seems to suggest either a social homogeneity imposed by a majority or a consensus manufactured by an intellectual elite. Either way it leads to an intolerance of difference and a lack of appreciation of diversity. It seems to imply a process of exclusion which leads to the worst excesses of populist bigotry or colonial oppression.

Such fears can confuse an understanding of culture that is inevitably a process of reaching agreements. We couldn't speak if we hadn't agreed on the meaning of words. These agreements do not have to be wholesale or imposed. They do not necessitate intolerance of those who demure. Sub-cultures form, exist, dissolve and resonate in retrospect. Cultures with a clear identity, in which millions of individuals are active, are nothing if not dynamic, multi-layered, fractious, in much the same way that Foucault has shown that the progress of the discourses of knowledge to be less orderly than our received ideas of rational progress.

> A culture is also a pool of diverse resources, in which traffic passes between the literate and the oral, the superordinate and subordinate, the village and the metropolis; it is an arena of conflictual elements, which require some compelling pressure - as, for example, nationalism or prevalent religious orthodoxy or class consciousness - to take form as a 'system'. And indeed the very term 'culture' with its cosy invocation of consensus may serve to distract attention from social and cultural contradictions, from the fractures and oppositions within the whole.
>
> E.P. Thompson 1991 p6

For a culture to be identifiable, and for communication to be successful, in spite of all the chaos of contending opinions, and noise, there has to be a basic set of agreed signs - as with a spoken language.

The question remains as to *how* this process of qualitative assessment, which is at the centre of cultures purpose, occurs in practice, and what part is played by the play of artists. This essay cannot answer such an ambitious question but it can attempt to further articulate the question, to revive Williams's emphasis on the symbiotic relation of culture and democracy and to propose some fecund ways in which this occurs.

In contemporary Britain small innovating groups or subcultures make actions in public spaces which serve as 'proposals' which can be more or less widely discussed, adapted, and then taken up or ignored. The more free these groups are, of institutional and particularly state institutional framing and guidance, and the more inclusive in membership, the more they can be open to the desires of the wider population, rather than being guided by the needs of the system.

Such groups of independent artists are often not in positions to build and maintain archives, publish knowledge and set up legitimating rituals for their work. They are usually unfunded which also makes it difficult for them to persist with their activity for very long.

There seems to be a simple continuity that can be proposed between the processes of culture and democracy. Both are fundamentally about reaching mutual understanding as a basis on which to co-ordinate our actions.

Culture may be seen as particularly important for the direct evaluation of the environment as experienced through the senses. The results have a performative or material form which can be critically re-evaluated at any time. Democracy can be seen as the reaching for a more linguistically abstracted process of rational argumentation to achieve agreements as a basis for policy and legislation.

There seems little reason to make any hard and fast boundary between these categories; one flows surely into the other. But the separation of culture and democracy, both as objects of knowledge and practices, is a historical fact that has been reified in institutional and material forms. This separation seriously impoverishes democracy and emasculates culture in the process. A consultation document from the Cultural Strategy Partnership for London (December 1999) was pervaded by assumptions of a top-down management of culture which defined culture as a source of wealth and entertainment but almost completely ignore the elemental function of culture as pointed out by Raymond Williams.

This distortion of the purposes of culture puts us in danger. It tries to replace the ability of a people to respond to their conditions with a culturally integrated leadership of managers and experts, whose self-interests are inevitably modulated by their dependence on state funding. Fortunately some people do ignore this and get involved in the independent production of raw cultural responses. Exploding Cinema being a good example.

PROGRAMME

Rabbit Stories	08:00	Sean Conway	2006
Please teach me how to shoot you			
Dear Steven Spielberg	01:48	Michael Heroux	2004
Big Willow Echo Camp	19:00	Stefan Georgiou	2006
The truth and the pleasure	09:00	Stefan Szczelkun	2007
Little Star	05:00	Jennet Thomas	2007
	02:16	Sean Reynard	2001

INTERVAL

Ian Saville, Socialist Magician!

To the tower my love			
November	05:38	Martin J Callanan	2005
Scum of the Earth	25:00	Hito Steyerl	2004
Frank	04:00	Ben Slotover	2007
An Angel in Penge	05:38	Adam McAlavey	2006
	05:00	Duncan Reekie	2007

INTERVAL

Spring 2005			
My Ewld Fella	07:02	Gary Anderson	2005
'Stamps' Episode One of	01:00	Sean Reynard	2001
'The How and Why series'			
Family	05:30	Paul Tarrago	2007
Beast from bombed beach	04:09	Marko Maetamm	2007
Time Variations Var. 1	04:40	Dick Dale	
Home Movie # 1			
Ginger Boy	05:00	Ming-Yu Lee	2006
Chaos	10:00	John Robertson	
	03:45	Khalid Souqbi	2004

Programme 20 - 4 - 2007

Unfunded and unrelenting...
EXPLODING CINEMA IS BACK!

What is an audience?

"Rather than ask, "What is the attitude of a work to the relations of production of its time?" I should like to ask, "What is its position in them"
—Author as Producer, Walter Benjamin

Stranded somewhere between the ironic prankster and the radical idealist, is the artist's persona. An outdated remnant of the avant-garde model of the artist? Are artists still "outsiders"? Is the critical role of the artist curiously incongruent against what is actually a profitable and exclusive professional sector which promotes its entrepreneurial activities on the fetishisation of a mythical past?

Although the artist/audience relation is a testing-ground of social conventions; it is also, equally the successful absorption of these propositions. Artist and audience are integrated within mainstream social, economical and cultural mechanisms. They are more alike and complicit in the roles which they have carved out for each other. The modernist spectator – abused on the basis of presumed incompetence – is dead.

The EXPLODING CINEMA holds OPEN SCREENINGS for a popular audience. We are unfunded and non-profit so we are unable to pay contributors but we do offer an exciting interactive public forum. All profits are used to run screenings and to develop new projects. New members can immediately become involved in running the cinema and developing skills and projects.

To show your films or join the collective,

DON'T HESITATE... CONTACT US NOW!

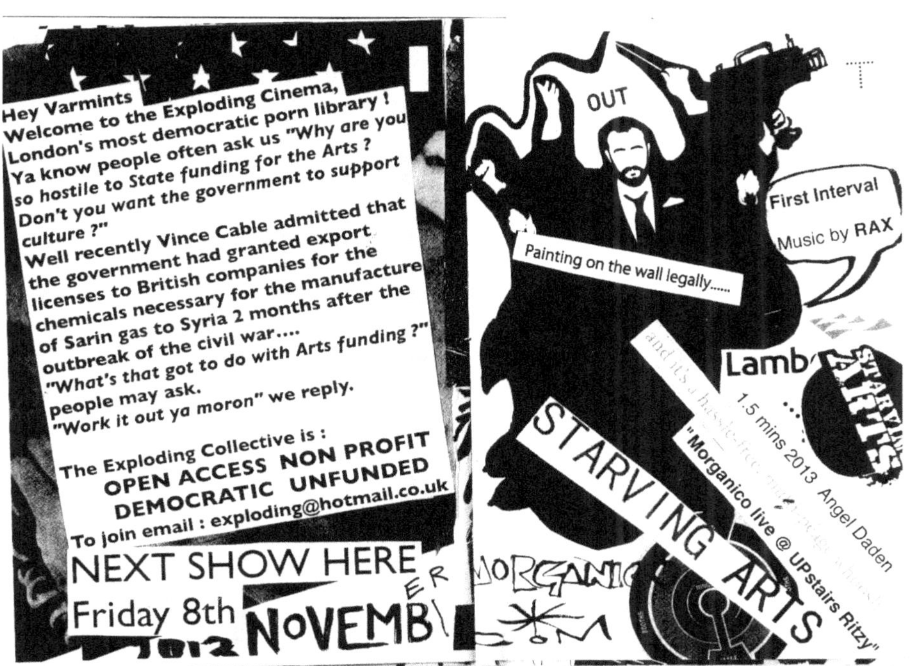

Programme 27 - 9 - 2013

Appendix 3

Research Methodologies and the importance of being reflexive

Research Methods - rational, reflexive, systematic.

Preliminary Thoughts on Reflexivity.

Although each of the methodology chapters has a critical account of that methodology as an introduction, I think it might be useful to make a few remarks about my approach to methodology in general.

In classic academic research, written records, published texts, archived materials and laboratory processes are examined methodically. An account of this examination is then written and published which contains full references to the locations of the sources of information. Ideally the account also implies a critical appraisal of both the authority of the sources of information and the methods of examination. The conceptual frames through which the data produced is evaluated are also, ideally, approached critically. The original materials and texts should be in the public realm so that future researchers (or peer reviewers) can re-examine them to challenge any interpretations made.

Behind this is an idea of *progress* through disciplined discourse, by which the accumulated results - formal Western knowledge - allows us ever deeper and more accurate understandings of the world. This ideal is more difficult to realise the further we get from processes that are defined by laws of mathematics, including those of probability. Even with this limitation, a logical and open method of inquiry has been remarkably productive in transforming our world within a few centuries. However, the millennial optimism which accompanied the first waves of scientific and technological progress has been jaded by the apparent inability of this potent form of rationalism to solve fundamental issues of social justice, environmental degradation and warfare. This disillusionment has led to the underlying assumptions and practices of the European Enlightenment being critically re-assessed in recent years.

My research is made within this historical and cultural context. Subjects deemed worthy of study leave their records in archives. Here they are stored in an orderly way to allow access by scholars and enthusiasts. One clear limit of Western knowledge is defined by what is, and what is not included in these public archives.

There has existed a long controversy between quantitative and qualitative social research methodologies. Quantitative measurement appeared to be objective and scientific while qualitative evaluations were contingent on the subjectivity of the researcher. In recent years this simple opposition has broken down as it has been recognised that even apparently objective data requires subjective selection, interpretation and value judgement. On the other hand qualitative methods such as oral history can access crucial information that may be unavailable in any other way and may also be subjected to rigorous checks to ensure the validity of key data.

The only quantitative method I used was content analysis. The other methods I used can all be seen as qualitative. I have discussed the pros and cons of methods used in the introduction to the relevant chapter.

Reflexivity is key to qualitative research of all kinds. The concept of reflexivity may be a way of bringing qualitative methods to account for themselves in a way that goes some way to satisfy the demands of scientific method. This is generally a matter of questioning how the processes of research and analysis, have an effect on research outcomes. Tim May (1998) saw reflexivity as having two dimensions: the endogenous and the referential. Endogenous reflexivity is the examination of the processes by which communities constitute their social reality. This can refer to a community under study and /or it can refer to the research community itself. For instance - how the objects of academic curiosity are constructed within broader ontological patterns. Referential reflexivity is the study of the relations between the person who engages in the research and the persons or groups who are the focus of that research. Tim May asked whether an expert coming into a situation for a short period with alien motivations can hope to come to a reliable understanding of the lifeworld under study. Peter Worsley (1997) pointed out that communities have their own ontological structures of great subtlety and sophistication and that these 'knowledges' are often not sufficiently appreciated. The researcher runs the risk of imposing ontological structures arbitrarily from their own already dominant culture.

The social sciences have wished to emulate the authority of physical sciences by maintaining a separation of subject and object. This became known as the Positivist model, in which it was believed that a complete knowledge could be gained of human life worlds solely by systematic and objective methods of research. This led to a split in social researches between the Positivists who favoured quantitative methods and those others who used qualitative methods. Since the late 1980's the different values and limitations of each approach have been recognised and are increasingly integrated within research programmes.

Sociologist Pierre Bourdieu (1988) argues that a reflexive practice will help to free intellectuals from 'their illusions - and first of all from the illusion that they do not have any, especially about themselves'. One such illusion he refers to is that academics have 'misplaced beliefs in illusory freedoms'. More prosaically reflexivity might offer the possibility that, in unveiling the determinants that surround any research, we might acquire a relative freedom from such determinants.

In 1971 Alvin Gouldner had pointed out how ethnographers could be seen to be normalising cultural fields, a critique which threatened to reveal the interests behind Western constructions of knowledge and destabilise the dominant worldview. The academic myth of value neutrality was still strong. Gouldner was under no illusions about the inertia that such radical reflexivity would meet. He proposed that the only way forward was for the researcher to become a channel for social change. It was not simply a matter of reforming the research process but a question of 'how to live': "What is needed is a new praxis that transforms the person." (Gouldner, 1971 p494)

The next development in reflexive practice was the feminist critique of epistemology. Sandra Harding (1991) showed how science could carry a male agenda and exclude female concerns. From this it was realised that it was not just the immediate relations between researcher and researched that must be brought into question, but much deeper questions of cultural and class affiliation should to be considered. This argument has led to a call for a democratisation of intellectual discourse. This would mean research that is more accountable, accessible, culturally specific and open to local evaluation. This can lead to a deconstruction of authorial authority on the one hand and to an enthusiasm for methodological heterogeneity on the other. If we take a range of approaches we will be less likely to railroad conclusions within simplistic or preconceived frames. This strategy is known as the 'triangulation' of methodologies and is the strategy I adopted in this research programme.

Reflexivity in this thesis is addressed at various stages. The reports on each research methodology are preceded by a discussion of the strengths and weaknesses of the methodology. In this sense reflexivity is making the methodologies, and the use I make of them, more transparent and accountable. The limitations of the truths they reveal are laid bare.

The precedents of this research, in my experience of artists' collectives in the last twenty years, is now available on the web. These accounts imply that my intellectual frame of mind and indeed my commitment to do this research has been forged out of this experience.

Some answers to the questions of what is represented and what is missed by the archived materials are provided by the use of participant observation and oral interviews. Selections from these research methodologies are also included in the chronological account. As I pointed out in the introduction there is a critical time in the following narrative when I join the collective. From this point in early 1997 the narrative becomes based on my own witness, and the archive materials are infected to some extent, by my presence. This results in a change of narrative style.

Any historical study can take a synchronic and/or diachronic approach. The *diachronic* is a chronological approach - one thing is followed by another - events have consequences, which we can follow with a linear sequence. This generally means picking a narrow path through time, which moulds the resulting representations in various ways. Written narrative has its own tradition that has been traced back to the Hebraic Old Testament and the Greek Iliad. There are certain literary techniques that we might expect in any narrative form, especially those that play with our expectations, which generate tensions and enrich them with digressions. Dramatic high-profile events and personalities that change things are more likely to be recorded than more mundane social processes. This sort of history tends to favour an idea of progress rendered through the eyes of leaders. It gives a representation of history in which change appears to be brought about by great individuals rather than through social agency. A social history is inevitably complex and does not easily submit to the simplifications demanded by a good story. The Exploding Cinema collective is a microcosm of a wider society and even with its limited size it starts to provide the complex interactions that make a simple narrative problematically reductive. Even without the demands of a narrative certain viewpoints, interests, memories and subjectivities become highlighted at the expense of others.

Synchronic history was conceived as providing a detailed cross section of the simultaneous happenings of a particular time. It gives what Clifford Geertz called a 'thick description'. All kinds of unconnected events can make up human experience of a time and place. Even when we want to look at the emergence of something as profound and specific as 'printing with moveable type' we may find that many convergent factors contribute to the point of invention which do not readily lend themselves to a narrative sequence. A synchronic approach allows us to create a picture of life at a time or place, in much finer detail, showing the complexities and essential redundancies. It allows us to include that which is unchanging or mundane but which is essential to character and atmosphere, and so to a fuller understanding. Because it allows more to be included it can be a more democratic approach which can include the texture of lives and processes which are unremarkable by the criteria for inclusion in traditional historical narratives. The unremarkable is also often the typical, that which is held in common.

I first wrote up the archival history of Exploding Cinema in two alternating strands. One focused on the events and venues and was in the most part chronological or 'diachronic'.The other strand mainly concerned themes, like politics and policies, and events like the Volcano Festivals that occur over a period of time. These sections build up a synchronic picture of the group during this period.

Bibliography

In three parts: 1. Books; 2. Articles in Journals, chapters in books, etc; 3. Videos and other media.
<u>Please Note</u>: Books published in London/UK unless noted as elsewhere.

1. BOOKS

ADAIR, Christie. *Women & Dance*, The Macmillan Press 1992

ADONIS, Andrew. & Stephen Pollard. *A Class Act: The myth of Britain's classless society*, Hamish Hamilton 1997

ADORNO, Theodor & Max Horkheimer. *Dialectics of Enlightenment*, Verso 1997 (orig. 1944)

ADORNO, Theodor. *Minima Moralia: reflections from damaged life*, Transl. E.F.N.Jephcott, Verso 1978 (orig. Frankfurt, 1951)

AGAR, Michael H. *The Professional Stranger: an informal introduction to ethnography*, Academic Press, second edition, 1996 (orig. 1980)

ALASUTARI, Perti. *Researching Culture: qualitative method and cultural studies*, Sage 1995 (orig. Finland 1993).

ALCOFF, L. & E.Potter. eds. *Feminist Epistemologies*, Routledge 1993

ALVESSON, Mats & Kaj Skoldberg. *Reflexive Methodology: new vistas for qualitative research*, Sage 2000

ANDERSON, Benedict. *Imagined Communities: Reflections on the origin and spread of nationalism*, Verso 1983

ANON. *Cultures of Resistance*, 2000

ALVESSON, Mats & Kaj Skoldberg. *Reflexive Methodology: new vistas for qualitative research*, Sage 2000

ARBLASTER, Anthony. *Democracy*, second edition, OUP 1996 (orig. 1994)

ARONOWITZ, Stanley. *Dead Artists Live Theories and other cultural problems*, Routledge 1994

BAKER, Houston A. Jr. *Rap and the Academy*, Chicago U.P. 1993

BAILEY, Peter. ed. *Music Hall: The business of pleasure*, OUP, Milton Keynes 1986

BARTHES, Roland. *Image - Music - Text*, Fontana, Glasgow, 1977 (orig. 1961)

BARTHES, Roland. *The Semiotic Challenge*, California U.P., USA 1994

BATTCOCK, Gregory. Ed. *The New American Cinema*, Dutton, New York 1967

BELGRAD, Daniel. *The Culture of Spontaneity, improvisation and the Arts in Postwar America*, Chicago U.P. 1998

BENJAMIN, Walter. *Illuminations*, Transl. Harry Zohn. Fontana 1973-77 (orig. Frankfurt 1955)

BERGER, A.A. *Media Research Techniques*, Sage California 1991

BIGNELL, J. *Media Semiotics: An introduction*, Manchester U.P. 1997

BLACKBURN, Julia. *The White Men: the first response of aboriginal peoples to the white man*, Orbis 1979

BLAUG, Ricardo. *Democracy Real and Ideal: discourse ethics and radical politics*, New York U.P. 1999

BOAL, Augusto. *Legislative Theatre: using performance to make politics*, tranl. Adrian Jackson. Routledge 1998

BOURDIEU, Pierre. *Distinction, a social critique of the Judgement of Taste*, Transl. Richard Nice, Routledge 1984-89 (orig. Paris 1979)

BOURDIEU, Pierre. *Homo Academicus*, Transl. Peter Collier, Stanford U.P. USA (& Polity Press, Cambridge) 1988 (orig. Paris 1984)

BOURDIEU, Pierre. *The Rules of Art, Genesis and structure of the literary field*, Transl. Susan Emamel, Polity Press, Cambridge 1996 (orig. Paris 1992)

BOYES, Georgina. *The Imagined Village: culture ideology and the English Folk Revival*, Manchester U.P. 1993

BOYLE, Deirdre. *Subject to Change: Guerilla television revisited*, Oxford U.P. 1997

BRATTON, J.S. *Music Hall: performance & style*, OUP, Milton Keynes 1986

BREAKWELL, Ian. *Diaries*, Pluto Press 1986

BREAKWELL, Ian & Paul Hammond. eds. *Seeing in the Dark: a compendium of cinemagoing*, Serpents Tail 1990

BRETT, Guy. *Exploding Galaxies: the art of David Medalla*, Kala Press 1995

BREWSTER, Ben & Lea Jacobs. *Theatre to Cinema: stage pictorialism and the early feature film*, Oxford U.P. 1997

BRUYN, Severyn T. The Human *Perspective in Sociology: the methodology of participant observation*, Prentice Hall, USA 1966

BURCH, Noel. *Life to Those Shadows*, British Film Institute 1990.

BURTON, Alan. *The People's Cinema: film and the Co-operative Movement*, National Film Theatre, 1994

CARDEW, Cornelius. *Stockhausen Serves Imperialism*, Latimer, 1974

CAREY, John. *The Intellectuals and the Masses, Pride and Prejudice amongst the Literary Intelligensia 1880 - 1939*, Faber & Faber 1992

CAYGILL, Howard. *The Art of Judgement*, Blackwells 1989

CEPLAIR, Larry & Steven Englund. *The Inquisition in Hollywood: politics in the film community 1930-1960*, Berkeley 1983

CHANAN, Michael. *The Dream that Kicks: The prehistory and early years of cinema in Britain*, Routledge, 2ᵈ edition 1996 (orig. 1980)

CHRISTIE, Ian. *The Last Machine: early cinema and the birth of the modern world*. London: BBC 1994

CLIFFORD, J. *The Predicament of Culture*, Harvard U.P. Boston 1988

CLIFFORD, J. & MARCUS G. Eds. *Writing Culture: The poetics and politics of ethnography*, California U.P. Berkeley 1986

Contemporary Polish Artists in Great Britain, Association of Polish Artists, 1983

CURTIS, Dave. London's Arts Labs and the '60s Avant-Garde, 2020

CURTIS, Dave. *Experimental Cinema*, Studio Vista 1971

CURTIS, Dave. ed. *A Directory of British Film and Video Artists*, Arts Council of England/ University of Luton 1996

CUTTS, Simon & Erica van Horn, *The Artist Publisher: a survey by Coracle Press* 1986

DENIZEN, Norman K. *Interpretive Ethnography*, Sage 1997

DICKSON, Malcolm. ed. *Art With People*, AN Publications, Newcastle, 1995

DIXON, W.W. *Exploding Eye*, S.U.N.Y. 1997

DOCHERTY, David, David Morrison and Michael Tracey, *The Last Picture Show? Britain's changing film audiences*, British Film Institute 1987

DUNCOMBE, Stephen. *Notes from Underground: Zines and the politics of alternative culture*, Verso 1997

DUSINBERG, Deke & A.L. Rees. eds. *Film as Film: Formal experiment in film 1910 - 1975*, Arts Council of GB/ Hayward Gallery 1979

DUSINBERG, Deke. *English Avant Guard Film: an early chronology*, (m/s available at British Film Institute library) c1980s

DWOSKIN, Stephen. *Film Is: The International Free Cinema*, Overlook Press, N.Y. 1975

ECO, Umberto. *A Theory of Semiotics*, Indiana U.P. USA 1976

FANON, Frantz. *The Wretched of the Earth*, Penguin 1967 - 90 (orig. France 1961)

FERRELL, Jeff. *Crimes of Style: urban graffiti and the politics of criminality*, North Eastern U.P. Boston, USA 1996

FINNEGAN, Mary. Psychedelic Suburbia: David Bowie and the Beckenham Arts Lab, 2016

FOUCAULT, Michel. *The Archaeology of Knowledge*, Routledge 1989-97, (orig. Paris 1969)

FRANKEL, Ellen & Paul. eds. *Democracy*, Cambridge U.P. 2000.

FREEMAN, Jo. & Cathy Levine. *Untying the Knot: feminism, anarchism & organisation*, Dark Star/ Rebel Press 1985 (reprints of texts from early 1970s)

GARFINKEL, Harold. *Studies in Ethnomethodology*, Prentice-Hall USA 1967

GEERTZ, Clifford. *The Interpretation of Cultures*, Basic Books N.Y. 1973

GEERTZ, Clifford. *Local Knowledge*, Basic Books N.Y. 1983

GIDALS, Peter. *Structuralist Film*, Routledge 1989

GINSBURG, Carlo. *The Cheese and the Worms: The cosmos of a sixteenth century miller*, Pelican 1980

GOODY, Jack. *The Interface between the Written and the Oral*, Cambridge U.P. 1987 - 93

GOODY, Jack. *Representations and Contradictions: ambivalence towards images, theatre, fiction, relics, sexuality*. Blackwells 1997

GORMAN, Clem. *People Together: a guide to communal living*, Paladin 1975

GREEN, Jonathan. *Days in the Life: Voices from the English Underground 1961 - 1971*, Pimlico 1998 (orig. Heinmann 1988)

GUILLORY, John. *Cultural Capital: the problem of literary canon formation*, Chicago U.P. 1993

GUPTA, Akhil. & James Ferguson. eds. *Culture, Power, Place: explorations in critical anthropology*, Waybe State U.P. Detroit USA 1997

HABERMAS, Jurgen. *The Theory of Communicative Action, Vol. 1, Reason and the Rationalisation of Society*, Transl. Thomas McCarthy, Polity 1986 (orig. Frankfurt 1981)

HABERMAS, Jurgen. *The Theory of Communicative Action, Vol. 2, Lifeworld and system: a critique of Functionalist Reason*, Transl. Thomas McCarthy, Polity 1989 Paperback edition (orig. Frankfurt 1981)

HABERMAS, Jurgen. & Christian Lenhardt. *Moral Consciousness and Communicative Action*, Polity Press 1992

HABERMAS, Jurgen. *The Liberating Power of Symbols: Philosophical Essays*, MIT Press 2001

HAMMERSLEY, M. & P. Atkinson, *Ethnography*, Routledge 1995

HARDING, Colin & Brian Lewis. eds. *Talking Pictures: The popular experience of cinema*, Yorkshire Arts Circus Sheffield 1993

HARDING, Colin & Simon Popple. Eds. *In the Kingdom of Shadows: a companion to early cinema,* Cygnus Arts 1996

HARPER, Sue. & Vincent Porter. *Weeping in the cinema: a reassessment of Mass Observation material,* M.O. Archive, University of Sussex 1995

HALLIDAY, M.A.K. 1978, *Language as Social Semiotic,* Edward Arnold 1978

HAYWARD, Phillip *Culture, Technology and Creativity in the Late Twentieth Century,* John Libbey, Luton, 1991.

HEBDIGE, Dick. *Hiding in the Light: on images and things,* Routledge 1988

HELD JR, John. International Artists Cooperation: Mail Art Shows, 1979 - 1985. Dallas Public Library Texas 1986

HODGE, Robert & Gunther Kress. *Social Semiotics,* Cornell U.P. New York 1988

HOME,Stuart. *The Assault on Culture: Utopian currents from Lettrisme to Class War,* Aporia Press & Unpopular Books 1988

HONDERICH, Ted. ed. *The Oxford Companion to Philosophy,* Oxford U.P. 1995

HUNTER, James Davidson. *Culture Wars: the struggle to define America,* Basic Books N.Y. 1991

JARANDARIE, Khosrow. *Spoken and Written Discourse: a multi-disciplinary perspective,* Ablex Stamford, Connecticut 1999

JAMES, David E. ed. *To Free the Cinema: Jonas Mekas and the New York underground,* Princeton U.P. 1992

JENKINS, Keith. *On 'What is History?': from Carr and Elton to Rorty and White,* Routledge 1995

JONES, Chris & Genevieve Jolliffe, *The Guerilla Film-makers Handbook,* Cassell, 1998 (1996)

JORDAN, Stephanie. *Striding Out: aspects of contemporary and New Dance in Britain,* Dance Books 1992

JOYCE, Patrick. *Class,* Oxford U.P. 1995

KAPLAN, Ann E. *Rocking Around the Clock: music television, postmodernism and consumer culture,* Methuen 1987

KERR CAMERON, David. *The English Fair,* Sutton Publishing 1998

KNIGHT, Julia. *Diverse Practices: a critical reader on British video a*rt, Univ. of Luton/ Arts Council of England 1996

KRESS, Gunther & Theo Van Leeuwen. *Reading Images: The grammar of visual design,* Routledge 1996

KRIPPENDORFF, K. *Content Analysis,* Sage 1990

KUENZLI, Rudolf E. ed. *Dada and Surrealist Film,* MIT Press USA 1996 (orig. 1987)

KULTERMANN, Udo. *Art Events and Happenings,* Transl. John William Gabriel, Mathews, Millar Dunbar 1971.

LAING, Stuart. *Representations of Working Class Life 1951-1964,* Macmillan 1986

LeGRICE, Malcolm. *Abstract Film and Beyond,* Studio Vista 1977

LEVINE, Lawrence W. *Highbrow Lowbrow: The emergence of cultural hierarchy in America,* Harvard U.P. USA 1988

LOW, Rachael & Roger Manvell. *The History of British Film 1896 - 1906,* George Allen & Unwin 1973 (orig. 1948)

MACABE, Colin. *The Eloquence of the Vulgar: Language, cinema and the politics of culture,* British Film Institute 1999

MacDONALD, Richard Lowell. *The Appreciation of Film: The Postwar Film Society Movement and Film Culture in Britain* Exeter Studies in Film History, 2016

MACDONALD, Scott. *A Critical Cinema 2,* California U.P. 1992

MACDONALD, Scott. *Avant Garde Film*, Cambridge U.P. 1993

MACHRELL, Judith. *Out of Line: the story of British New Dance*, Dance Books 1992

MACPHERSON, Don. ed. *Traditions of Independence: British cinema in the thirties*, British Film Institute 1980

MALTBY, Richard. ed. *Popular Culture in the Twentieth Century*, Grange Books 1994 (orig. 1988)

MASON, J. *Qualitative Researching*, Sage 1996

MASSEY, Anne. *The Independent Group: modernism and mass culture in Britain, 1945-59*, Manchester U.P. 1995

MAXFORD, Howard. *The A-Z of Horror Film*, Batsford 1996

McCORQUODALE, Duncan, et al. *Occupational Hazard: Critical Perspectives on Recent British Art*, Black Dog Press Leicester 1997

McGUIGAN, J. *Cultural Populism*, Routledge 1992

McNAMARA, Martha J. and Karan Sheldon, *Amateur Movie Making: aesthetics of the everyday in New England film 1915 - 1960*, Indiana UP 2017

MEKAS, Jonas. *Movie Journal: the rise of the New American Cinema 1959 - 1971*, Collier, N.Y. 1971

MELLENCAMP, Patricia. *Indiscretions - Avant-Guard Film, Video & Feminism*, Indiana U.P. USA 1990

MILLER, Daniel. *Material Culture: and why some things matter*, UCL 1988

MILLER, Daniel. ed. *Shopping*, Routledge 1998

MACEY, David. *The Lives of Michel Foucault*, Hutchinson 1993

MUNT Sally R. ed. *Cultural Studies and the Working Class: subject to change*, Cassell 2000

NUTTAL, Jeff. *Bomb Culture*, MacGibbon and Kee 1968

O'PRAY, Michael. ed. *The British Avant-Garde Film: 1926 - 1995, an anthology of writings*, Univ.of Luton/ Arts Council of England, 1997

PEOPLES, J. & G.Bailey. *Humanity: An introduction to cultural anthropology*, West Publ. Minneapolis St Paul USA 1994

PHILLIPS, Andrea. Ed. *Out of Time: Hull Time Based Arts 1984 to 1998*, H.T.B.A. Hull 1997

PERKS, Robert, *Oral History: talking about the past*, The Historical Association, Kennington, 1995

PERNECZKY, Geza. *The Magazine Network: the trends of alternative art in the light of their periodicals, 1968 - 1988*, Edition Soft Geometry Koln 1993

POSTER, Mark. Cyberdemocracy: internet and the public sphere, in David Porter ed. Internet Culture, Routledge NY 1996

PREVOST, Edwin. *No Sound is Innocent*, Copula, England, 1995

PREZIOSI, Donald. *The Art of Art History: a critical anthology*, Oxford U.P. 1998

REEKIE, Duncan, *Subversion: the definitive history of underground cinema*, Wallflower Press 2007

REES, A.L. *A History of Experimental Film and Video*, British Film Institute 1999

REHG, William. ed. *Insight and Solidarity: discourse and ethics of Jurgen Habermas*, California U.P. 1994

RENAN, Sheldon. *The Underground Film: an introduction to its development in America*, Studio Vista 1968

RICHTER, Hans. *The Struggle for Film: towards a socially responsible cinema*, Transl. Ben Brewster, Wildwood House 1986 (orig. Vienna, 1976)

RITVO, Harriet. *The Platypus and the Mermaid, and Other Figments of the Classifying Imagination,* Harvard U.P. 1997

ROBINSON, David et al. eds. *Encyclopaedia of the Magic Lantern,* The Magic Lantern Society 2000

ROSALDO, R. *Culture and Truth: The remaking of social analysis,* Routledge 1993

ROSCAROLI, Laura and Gwenda Young with Barry Monahan, *Amateur Filmmaking: the home movie, the archive, the web,* Bloomsbury 2014

ROSE, Jonathan. *The Intellectual Life of the British Working Classes,* Yale U.P. 2001

ROSS, Andrew. *No Respect: Intellectuals and Popular Culture,* Routledge, 1989

SABIN, Roger. *Comics, Comix and Graphic Novels: A History of Comic Art,* Phaidon 1996

SAID, Edward W. *Culture and Empire,* Vintage, London, 1993

SALT, Barry. *Film Style and Technology: history and analysis,* Starword, 1983.

SAMUEL, Raphael & Paul Thompson, eds. *The Myths We Live By,* Routledge 1990

SANJEK, Roger. *Fieldnotes: the making of anthropology,* Cornell U.P. USA 1990

SARGEANT, Jack. *Death-Tripping - The Cinema of Transgression,* Creation Books, England 1995

SARGEANT, Jack. *Naked Lens - Beat Cinema,* Creation Books England 1997

SCOTT, John A. *A Matter of Record: Documentary sources in social research,* Polity Cambridge 1990

SHUSTERMAN, Richard. *Pragmatic Aesthetics: Living Beauty,* Rethinking Art, Blackwell Oxford 1992

SITNEY, Adam P. *Visionary Film, The American Avante Guard 1943 - 1978,* Oxford U.P. 1974 - 79

SOAR, Geoffrey & David Miller, *Interaction and Overlap,* Coracle Press 1994

SPARKE, Penny. *As Long As It's Pink: The sexual politics of taste,* Pandora London, 1995

Squatting: the real story, Bay Leaf Books 1980

STITT, Andre. *Small Time Life,* Black Dog Press, Leicester 2001

STONE, Barbara. *America Goes to the Movies: 100 years of motion picture exhibition,* National Association of Theatre Owners USA 1993

SZCZELKUN, Stefan. *Class Myths and Culture,* Working Press 1990

SZCZELKUN, Stefan. *The Conspiracy of Good Taste: William Morris, Cecil Sharp, Clough Williams-Ellis and the repression of working class culture in the 20* century,* Working Press 1993 /2017

THOMPSON, Dorothy. *Outsiders, Class, Gender and Nation,* Verso 1993

THOMPSON, E.P. *Customs in Common,* Penguin, 1993 (1991)

THOMPSON, E.P. *The Making of the English Working Class,* Penguin 1991 (Orig. Gollancz 1963)

THOMPSON, Paul. *The Voice of the Past: Oral history,* Oxford U.P. 2nd edition, 1988 (1978)

THORNTON, Sarah. *Club Culture: music media and sub cultural capital,* Polity Press 1995

TICH, Mary & Richard Findlater, *Little Tich, Giant of the Music Hall,* Elm Tree Books 1979

TURNER, Richard. *In Your Blood: football culture in the late 1980's and early 1990's,* Working Press 1990

TWITCHELL, James B. *Carnival Culture: The trashing of taste in America,* Columbia

U.P. 1992

TYLER, Parker. *Underground Film: a critical history*, Secker & Warburg 1971 (orig 1969)

URICCHIO, William, and Roberta E. Pearson. *Reframing Culture: The Case of the Vitagraph Quality Films*. Princeton: Princeton University Press. 1993

VAN LEEUWEN, Theo. *Speech, Sound, Music*, Macmillan 1999

VAN LEEUWEN, Theo. & Carey Jewitt. eds. *The Handbook of Visual Analysis*, Sage 2000

VOGEL, Amos. *Film as a Subversive Art*, Random House 1974

WADE, Graham. *Street Video, an account of five video groups*, Blackthorn Press, Leicester 1980

WALKERDINE, Valerie. *Daddy's Girl: Young girls and popular culture*, Macmillan 1997

WALWIN, Jeni. *Low Tide: Writing on artistic collaboration*, Black Dog, Leicester, 1997

WATERS, Chris. *British Socialists and the politics of Popular Culture 1884-1914* Manchester U.P. 1990

WEBBER, R. *Basic Content Analysis*, Sage, Newbury Park, 2nd edition, 1990

WEBBER, Mark. ed. *Shoot Shoot Shoot: The First Decade of the London Film-Makers' Co-operative 1966-76*, LUX 2016

WHITE, Hayden. *Tropics of Discourse: essays in cultural criticis*m, John Hopkins U.P. Baltimore 1985

WHITEHEAD, Fred. *Culture Wars: opposing viewpoin*ts, Greenhaven Press, San Diego, USA, 1994

WILLIAMS, Christopher. *Cinema: the beginnings and the future*, Westminster U.P. 1996

WILLIAMS, Raymond. *Culture and Society: 1780 - 1950*, Pelican 1961-75 orig. 1958

WILLIAMSON, Judith. *Decoding Advertisements: ideology and meaning in advertising*, Marion Boyars 1978

WITTGENSTEIN, Ludwig. *Culture and Value*, Blackwells 1980

WOLF, Eric R. *Europe and the People Without History*, University of California Press Berkeley 1982

WOLLEN, Peter. *Signs and Meaning in the Cinema*, Secker & Warburg/ British Film Institute 1969

WOLLEN, Peter. *Readings and Writings*, Verso 1982

Womens's Work: two years in the life of a women artists group, Women's Work, Brixton, 1986

WORSLEY, Peter. *The Trumpet Shall Sound: A study of 'Cargo' cults in Melanesia*, Mackibbon & Kee, London, 2ᵈ Edition 1968 (1957)

WORSLEY, Peter. *Knowledges: What different peoples make of the world*, Profile Books 1997

YOUNGBLOOD, Gene. *Expanded Cinema*, Dutton, USA, 1970

ZAVARZADEH, Mas'ud. *Pun(k) deconstruction, post-theory and ludic politics*, Maisonneuve Press USA 1994

ZIMMERMAN, Patricia R. *Reel Families: A social history of amateur film*, Indiana U.P. 1995

2. ARTICLES IN JOURNALS, chapters in books, thesii etc

'25 Years from Scratch' (programme) ICA London 20th November 1994

'ALBANY VIDEO Distribution Catalogue', Deptford, London, 1986

ANDERSON, Virginia. 'British Experimental Music: Cornelius Cardew and his contemporaries', MA Thesis August 1983 (now republished www.experimentalmusic.co.uk)

BOURDIEU, Pierre. 'The Purpose of Reflexive Sociology (The Chicago workshop)' in, P. Bourdieu and L.J. Wacquant, eds. *An Invitation to Reflexive Sociology*, Polity 1992

CLAID, Emilyn. 'Yes, No, Maybe: the practice of illusion in dance theatre performance', PhD Thesis, University of Surrey, 1998

CURTIS, Dave. 'A Tale of Two Co-ops', in David E. James, *To Free the Cinema*, Princeton UP 1992

DEACON, David, Alan Brymann and Natalie Fenton, 'Collision or Collusion?: a discussion and case history of the unplanned triangulation of quantitative and qualitative research methods', *The International Journal of Social Research Methodology, Theory and Practice*, (V1 No1 January - March 1998 p47)

DEREN, Maya. 'Amateur Versus Professional', *Film Culture* (v39, Winter 1965 p45)

DERRIDA, Jaques. 'Archive Fever: a Freudian impression', *Diacritics* (Summer 1995)

DUPRE, Francoise. 'Brixton Artists Collective', m/s 6 pp. paper given at London Creative Chaos Conference, Museum of London, October 1997

FULLER, Mathew. 'Now Make a Film! The Exploding Cinema', *The American Book Review*, (V 16 No 5 Feb 1995 p7)

GOMES, Maryanne. 'The Past As Present: the home movie as cinema of record', m/s 1997

HABERMAS, Jurgen. 'Hannah Arendt: On the concept of power' in, *Habermas, Philosophical Political Profiles*, Transl. F.G. Lawrence, Cambridge, MA USA 1985

HALL, Stuart. 'Popular democratic vs authoritarian populism: two ways of 'taking democracy seriously' in, Stuart Hall, ed. *The Hard Road to Renewal*, Verso 1988

HEBDIGE, Dick. 'From Culture to Hegemony' in, S. During, ed. *The Cultural Studies Reader*, Routledge 1993

HOHENDAHL, Peter Uwe. 'Recasting the public sphere (post-war Germany and the depoliticisation of public forms of discourse in modern society)', *October* (No73 Summer 1995 pp 27-54) Cambridge, Mass.

KESTER, Grant H. Discursive Aesthetics: a critical framework for littoral art, m/s 1998

LEGRICE, Malcolm. 'Towards a Temporary Economy', *Screen* (V 20 Nos 3/4 Winter 1979/80)

MAY, Tim. 'Reflexivity in the Age of Reconstructive Social Science', *International Journal of Social Research Methodology* (V 1 No 1 January - March 1998)

MEKAS, Jonas. 'Anti-100 years of cinema manifesto' a large format 8 page artist's magazine published by Agnes B. Paris 1996

PAYNE, Paddy. 'Obituary: Exploding Cinema 1991 – 1994', *Kinokaze*, Report from the Underground, (Issue 3 1995)

PICTON, Tom. 'Two-way mirror (on video)' in, Godfrey Boyle & Peter Harper *eds. Radical Technology*, Wildwood 1976

PORTELLI, Alessandro. 'The Peculiarities of Oral History' in, *History Workshop* (V12 Autumn 1981)

REEKIE, Duncan. 'Boom: the Exploding Cinema ad the London Microcinema Movement'. a chronology 1991 - 2017 www.academia.edu

REEKIE, Duncan. '8 Reasons Why the Exploding Cinema Opposes State Funding for

Film Production or Why Can't Everyone Be Nice', academia.edu 2016

ROUANE, Donal. Kinokaze: Report from the Underground, Issue 1, c1992; Issue 2, c1993; Issue 3, 1995; Issue 4, 1997

RORTY, Richard. 'The Priority of Democracy to Philosophy' in, R. Rorty, *Objectivity, Relativism and Truth,* Cambridge U.P. 1991

SEYMOUR, Benedict. 'The Last Picture Show', *Mute magazine,* (Issue 22, December 2001 pp12/13)

SHUSTERMAN, Richard. 'Of the Scandal of Taste: Social Privilege as Nature in the Aesthetic Theories of Hume and Kant,' *Philosophical Forum,* (V29 1989 211-229).

SHUSTERMAN, Richard. 'Don't Believe the Hype: Animadversions on the Critique of Popular Art,' *Poetics Today* (V14 1993)

SIPE, Dan. 'The future of oral history and moving images' in, Robert Perks & Alastair Thompson, eds. *The Oral History Reader,* Routledge 1997

SKEET, Jason & Mark Pawson. 'Counter Intelligence: Zines, comics, pamphlets, flyers, a catalogue of self-published and autonomous print creations', BM JED WC1N 3XX 1995

SLATER, Howard. 'Post Media Operators', *Break/Flow,* 28.01.97

SLATER, Howard. 'Canon blasting for a living culture', *Resonance magazine* (Vol 8 No 1 London 2000)

SNIPE, Dan. 'The Future of Oral History and Moving Images', *Oral History Review,* (Spring/fall 1991 vol. 19 nos. 1/2 pp75 - 87)

SUTHERLAND, Roger. 'The Death of the Scratch Orchestra'. *Noisegate* (No 8 2001 pp7 - 14)

SZCZELKUN, Stefan.'Sharsted Street Self-Build Housing Co-op', *Variant,* Issue 2 1997

SZCZELKUN, Stefan. Kennington Park: Birthplace of people's democracy, Working Press Pamphlet, Kennington, London, 1998

SZCZELKUN, Stefan. 'Working Press 1987-1997: ten years of an umbrella imprint for working class artists who wished to self-publish', *El Djarida* (No 14, Oslo, Spring 1998)

SZCZELKUN, Stefan. 'The Value of Home Movies', *Oral History Society Journal,* Autumn 2000 (V28 No 2 pp94/98)

SZCZELKUN, Stefan. 'The Scratch Orchestra', *Noisegate* (No 9 2002 p36)

TARRAGO, Paul. 'The Condition of Celebrity: film, audiences and fame'. Goldsmiths College. MRes Thesis. Sept.1996

THOMSETT, Fabian. 'Exploding Cinema', in *Transgressions, a Journal of Urban Exploration,* (No 1 Univ. of Newcastle Summer 1995)

VAN LEEUWEN, Theo. 'Moving English: the visual language of film' in, S. Goochan & D. Graddol. Eds. *Redesigning English: new texts, new identities,* Routledge 1996

WELLMER, A. 'Hannah Arendt on Judgement: the unwritten doctrine of reason' in, L. May and J. Kohn, eds. *Hannah Arendt: twenty years later,* Cambridge, Mass. 1996

WHITE, Hayden. 'The Value of Narraticity in the Representation of the Real' in, W.J.T. Mitchell, ed. *On Narrative,* Chicago U.P. 1981

WILLIAMSON, Judith. 'Meaning and Ideology', in A. Gray & J. McGuigan, eds. *Studying Culture: an introductory reader,* Edward Arnold, London, 1993

WINSLOW, Michelle. 'Polish Migration to Britain: war, exile and mental health', *Oral History Journal* (V27 Spring 1999)

WYNNE, B. 'May the sheep safely graze? A reflexive view of the expert - lay knowledge divide', in S. Lash, B. Szerszynski and B. Wynne, eds. *Risk, Environment and modernity: Towards a new ecology,* Sage 1996

3. VIDEOS, Websites and other media

BAILEY, Fenton & Randy Barbito. Dirs. Videos, Vigilantes and Voyeurism, 60mins, CH4, 19-9-93

www.explodingcinema.org

'A History of Alternative Comedy', (BBC2 6-4-02 R) 90 mins

History in Action: *The Home Front through Home Movies* (video) CH4 Schools, 1998

HOW, Loo. Dir. How to Be a Successful Spectator, How, London, 1994 (Documentary on Exploding Cinema)

MARTIN, Adrian. 'Light My Face: the geology and geography of film canons' in, *Senses of Cinema* Issue 14 June 2001 http://www.filmcritic.com.au/essays/canons.html

SZCZELKUN, Stefan. Exploding Cinema video doc collection: https://youtube.com/search 'Exploding Cinema Archive'

SZCZELKUN, Stefan. Catalogue of Films Shown 1992 - 98 https://archive.org/details/EXPLODINGCINEMACATALOGUEOFFILMS

www.undercurrents.org

www.undergroundfilmjournal.com/underground-film-websites/

ZWIGOFF, Terry. 'Crumb' Robert Crumb documentary, Columbia Tristar 1995

S t e f a n   S z c z e l k u n   2 0 0 2 / 2 0 2 1   (m i n o r   a m e n d m e n t s)

Programme August 1993

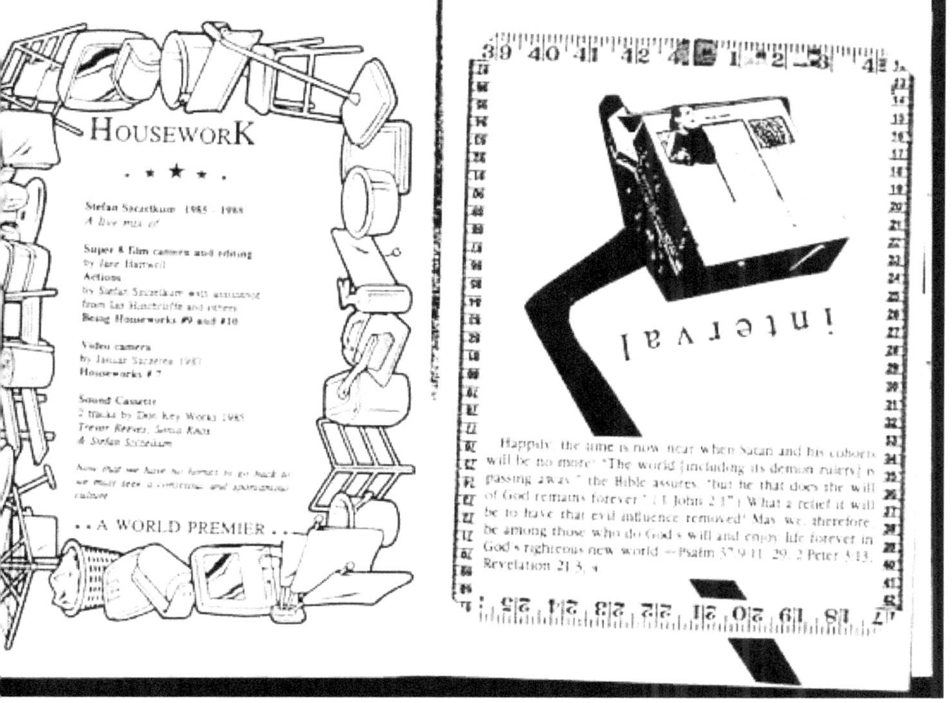

Index of Names

This includes people and places in the body text (not including references which are in the Bibliography). Appendices are not indexed. Text in images and charts not indexed.

The Conspiracy of Good Taste -
William Morris, Cecil Sharp and Clough Williams-Ellis and the repression of working class culture in the C20th This is a new deluxe paperback edition of the 1993 original in which the history of the plotlands is explored in relation to one of the main middle class critics - Clough Williams-Ellis. Cecil Sharp's mediation of working class music is also examined, along with the legacy of William Morris as a model socialist artist.
ISBN 978-1-870736-71-8

There are two further photographic books that survey particular areas of plotlands in full colour.

Chalet Fields of the Gower,
ISBN 978-1-870736-16-9

Plotlands of Shepperton
ISBN 978-1-870736-24-4

SILENCE! - the great silencing of
British working class culture This book continues the themes of The Conspiracy of Good Taste with new research and expanded terms of reference. It is presented in a full colour graphic format. The central argument is that there can be no ending of class oppression without a fully supported working class culture in every sense media.
ISBN 978-1-870736-22-0

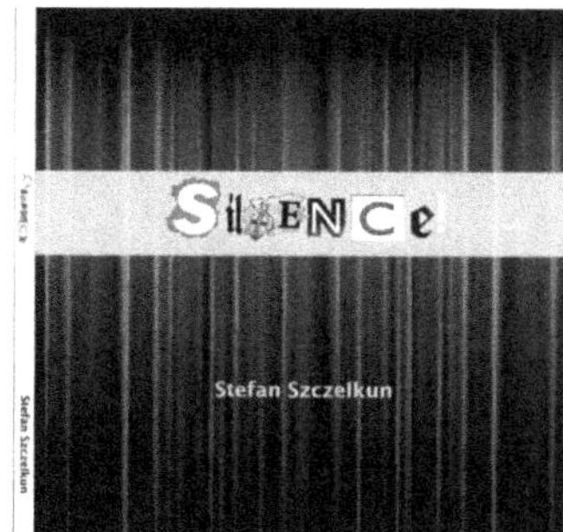

SENSE THINK ACT - a collection of
exercises to describe human ability In this follow up to the Survival Scrapbooks study of basic life supports (1972 - 74) Szczelkun explores elemental human abilities and suggest they could be the basis of rethinking culture, religion, and educational curricula.
ISBN 978-1-870736-12-1

THE EXPLODING CINEMA
AND THE NEW LONDON
UNDERGROUND

BOOM!

EXPLODING

DEEDS NOT WORDS

CINEMA

Coming soon to a bookshop near yo

EDITED BY DUNCAN REEKIE